THE MARKS IN
THE FIELDS

Jean Mabillon. Engraving by Pierre François Giffart
from Thierri Ruinart, *Abregé de la vie de Dom Jean
Mabillon*, 1709.

THE MARKS IN THE FIELDS

Essays on the Uses of Manuscripts

edited by
RODNEY G. DENNIS

with
ELIZABETH FALSEY

THE HOUGHTON LIBRARY

CAMBRIDGE, MASSACHUSETTS

1992

CATALOGUE PRODUCTION: *Thomas Todd Company*

DESIGN AND COVER DRAWING: *Larry Webster*

PHOTOGRAPHY: *Vincent Caira; Rick Stafford, Fogg Art Museum*

COMPOSITION: *Richard Conte*

PRINTING: *Mercantile Printing Company*

BINDING: *Star Bindery Company, Inc.*

Preface

THE QUESTIONS RODNEY DENNIS put to us, as contributors to this catalogue, were brief and to the point. "Here, in my opinion, is an important or interesting manuscript in the Houghton Library collections. What does it tell us? Where has it been? What problems does it pose? What solutions does it suggest?" We were to be brief ourselves, although some of us strayed rather far from our editor's injunction. We were given no choice of *manuscript,* only that of our responses to it; but we were allowed to choose which manuscript opening best illustrated the points we wished to make.

The essays that follow are, with a few interesting exceptions, individual responses, and as such they therefore characterize the different ways in which scholars from sometimes quite different fields interrogate texts that survive for us in manuscript form. The text themselves — and the physical remains of the codex, score, page, or scrap — are enormously varied, and this in itself suggests the remarkable range of our Curator of Manuscripts in the Harvard College Library, who, in the following pages, describes the process by which this current catalogue (and the accompanying exhibition) have been created. The other contributors and I thank Rodney Dennis for his invitation to share the excitement he himself brings to the study of manuscripts; his other colleagues in the Houghton Library and I thank him for his remarkable record of acquiring and cataloguing important and interesting materials — that we shall long take delight in interrogating.

Richard Wendorf
Librarian

December 1991

Contents

III

The History of the Manuscript

IV

The Nature of the Manuscript

Introduction

May no unsharpened stylus plough your field
Or burrow in your board with greedy tooth.

Baudri de Bourgueil,
"To his Writing Tablet"

The linked silhouettes of the man and the
mule moved back and forth like a slow brush
repainting the parched pallor of the winter-
faded land with the wet dark color of loam.

John Updike,
"Harv is Plowing Now"

THIS COLLECTION OF SHORT ESSAYS, a *Geistesspiel* intended to give the Houghton Library as a fiftieth birthday present an exhibition catalogue that would be both lively and useful, is, as of this writing, almost complete. The present task, that of explaining its purpose, its organization, its comprehensiveness or lack of it, its success or the absence of any, seems a little daunting. The essays, or most of them, lie before me, arranged in little thematic heaps; but was the undertaking thematically conceived in the first place, and if not — and it was not — where did the thematic, such as it is, come from?

First of all, the selection of manuscripts was almost completely random. The first forty or so manuscripts that seemed to tell interesting stories were enumerated in an office memorandum with the briefest notes suggesting what was interesting about them. Looking back, I can see that there were, in fact, two tendencies already innate within this initial choice, although I was not conscious of them at the time. One was that early and recent manuscripts were to be used to illustrate common principles. Behind this tendency, one can find a historical, that is, an accidental reason. The Houghton Library, with its "media driven" organizational plan, is a little unusual in combining all manuscripts together in one administrative unit, so that an opportunity was there to do something that might be a little harder to achieve in a library organized according to subject, or epoch. But aside from this accidental reason, there may be a broader thought having to do with the relationship among all handwritten communications seen now in respect to the possibility that the machine-made book might just prove, *sub specie aeternitatis*, a rather short-lived phenomenon. We should not try to develop this here.

The other innate tendency revealed itself in the choice of manuscripts that referred back to themselves, to their structure, their history, their physicality. The items chosen tended to refute the notion that the entire importance of the object resided in the text that it carried. There were questions about inking, about erasures, and about chemistry. There were palimpsests. There were fakes. As I reflected on this, the surfaces of these pages began to seem less flat, and the penetration of ink or graphite into these surfaces became more of a factor. As I reflected in turn upon that, the very old metaphor of the pen as a plough occurred, and reaching for E. R. Curtius, ever ready at hand, and to the section on *Buchsymbolik*, I rediscovered that what I was thinking about, people have always thought about. That the pen is a plough is a commonplace in Classical and Medieval literature. Baudri — whom Curtius found "lovable" and whose celebrated wax tablet, covered with green wax for easy reading almost a millennium before the discovery of "eye-ease green," has more recently attracted the attention of Richard Rouse — Baudri ploughs his green field with a sharp point avoiding the underboard and exemplifying the old saying that a sharp tool is a safe one.

What is being compared to what? A thousand years ago, the stylus, familiar as it was, was not the primary referent: Baudri invoked the even more familiar plough to explain the writing tool. A slightly more complicated use of this comparison, the famous Riddle of Verona, seems to reverse this relationship but, in fact, does not:

> They seemed like oxen,
> Ploughing white fields,
> Holding a white plough,
> Sewing a black seed.

A hand holding a quill pen writing on white vellum with black ink. But although *they*, the fingers, are the starting point, we are dealing with a riddle, and the question is, what are they? So once again, the real point of departure is the familiar plough. We also notice that the support is not wax but parchment, and even though the writing instrument is not actually digging, still it *seems* to be digging.

By now, the ages have succeeded in reversing this relationship. For John Updike in one of his most remarkable stories, the narrator's own life is a subject for archaeology, or digging down, which reveals at last a memory of a man on a hillside ploughing. And the plough? It is like a brush moving back and forth across a page. Ploughing is a known and constant act, but it has acquired a mysteriousness that can be at least partially mitigated by a comparison with the act of writing (or painting), less fundamental perhaps, but by now certainly more mundane. Later in the same story, as if to underline the fact that the physical world provenes, as it were, from the act of writing, the white surf at night, breaking over a black sea, is depicted for us as the moving carriage of a typewriter. In general, however, it appears that the earlier uses of this comparison tend to treat writing as a physical act rather than an act of the imagination.

In common, ploughing and writing move so as to produce parallel impressions; they are hard work; they persist; and they dig into their respective fields, disturbing and changing them. These four traits seem distinct from one another, and I felt, regarding my single, large, still undivided heap of essays, that they might suggest a way of breaking them up into categories, not exhaustive or comprehensive, but ample enough to allow us at least to begin our discussion. Therefore we are going to look at manuscripts in four ways and then we shall see what we have left out.

The first approach, which concerns the actual marks in the field, and the second, which has to do with work, translate rather easily into the two antithetical ways of looking at text: we use manuscripts to establish text and if possible to fix it. We may have varying concepts of what text is, whether the author ever had a fixed and final text, whether some part remained fluid, whether the passage of time may have conspired to produce an altered but still valid version. But on some level we feel that there is a single right version that can be known, and that is probably the first thing we are looking for. This text, however, resulted from a process, and that process holds our interest on quite another level. We see the author at work in his manuscripts as nowhere else, and the way we see this is by observing him making changes. We also see others entering the picture with their own changes, in some cases so extensive as to challenge the author's total ownership of the finished work. Process, then, can shed light on authorship.

The third approach, the persistence of the thing, brings us to questions of provenance, and this not only leads us into stories of theft and romance, which it certainly does, but also tells us something about economics and about readership, two subjects that are particularly hard to deal with and that in these essays are only touched upon here and there and generally by indirection. It is the fourth approach, which involves both the writing instrument and the support or ground, that fastens our attention most specifically on the object itself and leads us to inquire into its nature. This inquiry can be pure and involve simple questions about material and structure. It can view structure aesthetically or relate it to the means of production of the manuscript, to the structure of the text, to the way in which the text was presented to the reader or the listener. It can show how the physical object is necessary to an understanding of the message that is being communicated.

The first of our essays is a brief account of the creation of the discipline of paleography in the seventeenth century and is intended as a sort of prelude. After that the essays reflect this four-fold arrangement with each of the four sections beginning with an instance of special photography used to cast light upon an early manuscript. The first section, "the establishment of text," is restricted to early manuscripts. It need not have been, but it happens by chance that the Houghton Library has three manuscripts of Aristotle's ethical writings that have some textual importance, a surprising fact given the enormous number of manuscripts of those works that have survived. One of these, a Latin translation by Moerbeke, was used long ago by the humanist Pier Vettori to prove the point, highly sophisticated for its time, that certain Latin versions of Greek texts can lead a scholar to readings earlier than those found in the Greek texts at his disposal. Another manuscript, called "the Hoferiana" in Aristotelian circles, a fourteenth-century Italian copy of a French manuscript of Grosseteste's Latin translation, is thoroughly contaminated by readings from an otherwise largely unknown twelfth-century Latin translation for which it is an important witness. The third, a Greek manuscript, was used by Aldus Manutius for his celebrated edition. It seemed best to entrust the discussions of all three of these to Richard Tarrant. They are preceded by Margaret Bent's account of her and our attempt to recover an early polyphonic motet from the back of a vellum pastedown without removing it.

The second section, "The development of text," is broken into two parts, "variants" and "authorship," and preceded by an essay written by a group: a brief unpublished treatise apparently by John Wyclif is a palimpsest, the lower level containing Italian financial records. This manuscript was the semester project of Michael McCormick's Seminar in the Auxiliary Disciplines of Medieval Studies, and each student was responsible for a different aspect of a quite complicated situation. Variants exist in unending variety and so we have forced them into a scheme that may seem rigid and arbitrary but that keeps us in some control: variants that succeed in cancelling a previous idea — Helen Vendler on *To Autumn*, Bernard Böschenstein on Georg Trakl's *Trompeten*; variants that lie hidden beneath the new thought, enriching it — Richard Wendorf on *An Essay on Man*; variants that fail totally to suppress the first version — myself on Henry James's revisions of *The American*; finally, variants that are intended to co-exist on an equal basis with the earlier thought — the treatment of Emily Dickinson by Sharon Cameron became so intermingled with structural issues that it was removed to the last section of the collection.

"Authorship" begins with a discussion by James E. Walsh of the *contestations* on the authorship of *Imitatio Christi* based on a manuscript with early attributions both to Thomas à Kempis and to Gerson. Elizabeth Falsey, having subjected the manuscript of Chatterton's "Songe to Aella" to some scientific analysis, concludes that it is, in fact, a forgery, but not a fake forgery, and tends to reinforce an eighteenth-century authorship of the poem. The Faneuil Hall Resolutions of 5 November 1845 were largely the work of Charles Sumner, working behind the scenes, as discussed by David Donald. Questions of extensive non-authorial revision in Longfellow's *Evangeline* and in Thomas Wolfe's *The Web and the Rock* are considered by Richard Marius and Richard Kennedy. Starting out with the Master of the Harvard Hannibal, Roger Wieck shows how the identities of anonymous medieval illuminators are derived from examples of their work.

The third section, which deals with provenance, begins with two early illuminated manuscripts with erased ownership inscriptions, a *Bible historiale* that had belonged to Charles V whose erased signature François Avril discovered years ago, and a Psalter from St. Riquier. When Paul Meyvaert was asked to discuss an erasure in an early statement of ownership on a flyleaf of this manuscript, he responded by raising the possibility that the statement itself was a forgery and by darkening matters no end before the final clarification achieved by a collaboration with Michel Huglo. In discussing the ownership marks in a manuscript of *De Civitate Dei*, I have tried to touch on the growth and dispersal of several great libraries and say something about price. James Hankins discusses a humanist manuscript written in by Poggio and later owned by Niccolò Niccoli and by Cosimo

4

de'Medici. Mary Hyde Eccles and Donald Reiman give us the romantic histories of the "croquet box" manuscript of *The Life of Johnson* and Claire Clairmont's Shelley notebook, and Walter Grossmann writes of the greatest moment of literary contact between England and Germany, embodied in the manuscript of *Wallenstein* sent by Schiller to England and ultimately used by Coleridge for his translation. Finally, Douglas Bryant, a participant in the events he describes, tells of the almost unbelievable voyages of Trotsky's private archive.

The fourth and last section, "The nature of the object," is the most complicated and indeed problematic. It deals with the physical thing, but the text intrudes and the relationship between the two is fluid to a surprising degree. In introducing this section I have taken a twelfth-century manuscript with a number of curious characteristics of format and binding and tried to show how these resulted from a desire to enlarge the manuscript's contents during a time when books were changing in respect to both aesthetic and technological considerations. The next three essays approach structure in differing ways. Barbara Johnson examines what is perhaps the most mysterious manuscript in the group, Mallarmé's notes and musings on the essential nature of the codex form, *Le "Livre."* Amid difficult questions, the little *cahiers* of which this manuscript consists and the manner in which they have been gathered and folded present a particular problem. A thirteenth-century Parisian manuscript shows in its margins certain marks revealing that it was copied from abbreviated quires or *pecia*. Laura Light explains the role of the medieval stationer functioning under a tremendously increased demand for texts. Sharon Cameron has approached the various problems attaching to the little packets in which Emily Dickinson wrote her poems. Examining variants in the poems, she finds correspondences not only within but between the packets, relates these to readings within individual poems, and suggests that a larger form may be present than has previously been supposed.

What comes next may seem a little random: the object tells one what the text means and how it sounds. Lawrence Buell looks at the inking in a letter from Emerson to his fiancée and makes observations about sincerity. Helen Vendler, remarking that a poem by John Ashbery alludes in great measure to a Spanish comic strip found in the poet's papers, asks what this can mean about the whole process of allusion. William Henry Bond tells how, by reimagining the order of leaves in the manuscript of Smart's *Jubilate Agno*, he brought life and intelligibility to an important poem. Two essays discuss diacritical marks. Christopher Ricks finds ample meanings in a printed poem by Elizabeth Bishop that she marked up for public readings, and these marks suggested to us that we ask David Hughes to talk about the gradual process of "heightening" neumes in an eleventh-century servicebook, the moment in which the mark changes from a gesture into a note.

We become still more random. Jean Bruneau describes two manuscripts of Lamartine, mentioning a tear stain; Roger Stoddard seeks evidence to explain why Max Beerbohm's copy of *The Awkward Age* got battered. We come, at last, to the end of the inquiry: the object as the sole witness to the existence of a text — Warner Berthoff on *Billy Budd*; and the sole witness to an act — Gerald Browne, deciphering a faded pottery shard, tells us how Kalasiris, an illiterate ship owner, paid his taxes on 20 March 131 A.D.

Looking back at this list of manuscripts, I can see one major flaw in the scheme: with one exception it is composed of singletons. A luxurious royal copy of a *Bible historiale* tells us that this was a valued text, and the presence of translations always tells us something; but it is really only in groups that books give us a clue regarding literary taste. Furthermore, it is to archives that one must turn to gain a comprehensive sense of what was discarded as valueless (although the Wyclif manuscript was written on rejected financial records, and two other early manuscripts use out-of-style music as binding elements). *Pecia* manuscripts tell of demand: their absence for certain classes of text suggests, Graham Pollard told us, that in some instances students were not expected to own their texts. Booksellers' marks and collectors' price codes tell about desirability. Still, while the interests of authors, scribes, and manufacturers are present everywhere here, those of the reader are dim and revealed only through indirection, and to bring these out would require an entirely different approach. Another issue not touched on is cost. Once a manuscript enters the trade, price is established, but the actual cost of production is hard to ascertain in a meaningful way. We can multiply these objections.

There is the limited and parochial choice of manuscripts offered. Except for our one ostracon, they are all on vellum or paper, and with three exceptions they are all in roman letters. Where are the Greek uncials and the architectonic letter forms of Georgian and Pali? Where are the manuscripts on leather, on cloth, on papyrus or bark or tortoise shells? The Armenian manuscripts in jewels, the Syriac in silver, African service books in thick leather to protect against arrows, or the great Buddhistic Sutras in carved teak, their dark blue paper folded in the style we call *orihon*? These lie in our stacks as well.

Even in our Western tradition, however, there is no end to what manuscripts can tell us. If, for example, you should become interested in early manuscripts written on vellum and if the structure of the gatherings should seize your attention, as it has mine, with all the importance that then is attached to the hair-sides and flesh-sides of the vellum leaves, this factor accentuated by the Southern way of preparing the skins, which leaves intact, apparently for reasons of beauty, the tiny black patterns of hair follicles in their swirls and linear sallies across the page — if, then, concerned with all this you should depart from the Houghton Library on a brilliant evening and, looking up, see wheeling across the skies a great multitude of small brown birds, it might quite probably occur to you to think at first of the sooty hair-sides of Italian vellum. Then, however, on reflection, you might realize that, like the Milky Way, what you are seeing is just one more of those natural patterns that go on occurring, everywhere and forever astonishing the mind.

In all, thirty-nine persons (including seven students from the Medieval Studies Seminar) have contributed to the essays in this collection. It will be seen that their comments vary considerably in length. The editorial guidelines were evenly distributed: "from 750 to 1,000 words, or more or less, just as you see fit," and one could then observe in the hearts of these gifted and generous scholars how modesty contended with ebullience. It does seem in general as if those writing from abroad tended to cleave more exactly to the stated guidelines, while the closer one got to Cambridge the less tightly reined in were the stallions of expression. I want to give all of these contributors my own warmest thanks and, if I may, the thanks of the Houghton Library, for helping us celebrate our fiftieth birthday in this way. Not one of them hesitated. They all concurred immediately and came through wonderfully. It might be re-emphasized here that the manuscripts were chosen first and that the manuscripts, in turn, determined who should write about them. They determined well.

As for form and style, after the first three or four essays came in, it became clear that consistency could only be achieved by excessive and harmful editorial reworking. I decided, I hope wisely, to let them remain as they were. Neither footnotes nor bibliography were called for, but when they were submitted they were retained with minimal revision.

Beyond the contributors, whom should I thank? Certainly, I should thank Richard Wendorf, Houghton's Librarian, for many things but for one in particular: when I submitted to him the plan for this collection, he, with the greatest possible tact, suggested that it might be interesting if, instead of describing all of the manuscripts myself, I solicited some help from friends, certainly a useful piece of advice. I thank my colleague Vicki Denby, who has mastered many machines and blinks at no software, for working with this text. And I most particularly thank Elizabeth Falsey, Associate Curator of Manuscripts, because I rely so utterly upon her sharp eye and judgment in all matters that I feel strongly tempted to say that, if anything is the matter here, it is really her fault and not mine.

R.G.D.

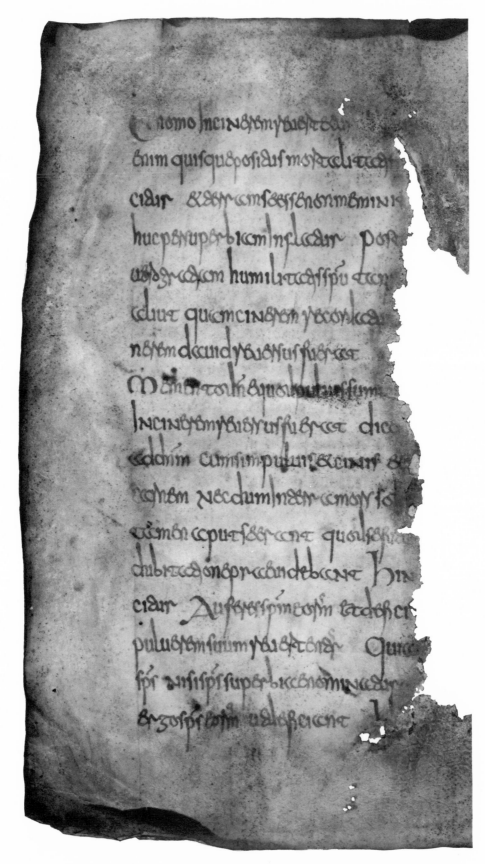

Gregory the Great, *Moralia in Job,* fragment in the script of Luxeuil; France, 8th cent.

1

A Note about Jean Mabillon

ANYONE ENTERING INTO THE FIRST phases of a historical discipline will find that he or she is at a loss until some kind of rudimentary framework has been established upon which the centuries can be hung and arranged. Each has his or her own appropriate scheme. I started out in music, and there was no difficulty in finding my way from the present back to J. S. Bach because of the abundance of familiar incidents. After that I needed orientation points: back to Monteverdi, then to Lassus, to Josquin, to Dufay; then a longish jump to Machaut, a longer one to Leoninus, and finally even to Notker Balbulus, beyond which things got more uncertain. Still, that was a thousand years' framework upon which to arrange other information until one's knowledge became dense enough so that one could seek other ways of organizing it. These ladders into the past were not always available to investigators.

The love of the Humanists for the "lettera antica," the Carolingian minuscule, which they revived and delivered to us as our standard letter form, was intense. They had, often, eleventh-century manuscripts of ancient texts. They spoke of the great antiquity of the writing. They did not often say it was really the writing of antiquity, but one might feel that they thought it was and, in any case, there was no way for them to know that it was not. For Petrarch or for Poggio Bracciolini there were few objective points of orientation. Later, in the 1760's, as we shall see, Thomas Chatterton was circulating poems that he said he had copied from fifteenth-century manuscripts, which had themselves been derived from now lost eleventh-century sources; and even though it was all made up, it is clear that the expectation of travelling back into history step by step, using manuscripts, was in place. The question is: did this expectation result from a gradual and steady accumulation of general knowledge, or did something definite happen having to do with manuscripts?

The hero of this exhibition and of this series of essays, the father of historical geography, as he has been called, is the Benedictine Father Jean Mabillon (1632-1707). One of the greatest benefits ever bestowed by the study of manuscripts came from his work. Dom David Knowles has provided an extremely good discussion of his life in *The Historian and Character*, and most recently Jacques Stiennon has discussed his paleographical contributions in *Paléographie du Moyen Age*. Some issues surrounding his work are particularly interesting, and I would like to touch on one or two of them here, returning to the general approach taken by Mabillon's great successor, the paleographer Ludwig Traube.

The essential background, according to Traube, was the contest, in the seventeenth century, between Jesuits and Benedictines for the power that accrues from scholarship and the last word on matters of historical truth. The power came from manuscripts, and the manuscripts belonged to the Benedictines. The Jesuits took to borrowing manuscripts from the old Benedictine houses and depositing them elsewhere, principally in the Bibliotheca Claramontana at Paris. The Benedictines responded by tightening security and by delivering a good many books to St. Germain des Prés to the care of their elite scholarly community, the Congregation of St. Maur.

Traube is quite definite about this. Earlier scholars are a little more reticent. Léopold Delisle says that there was a story that the Jesuits acquired their reputation as book thieves because they habitually failed to retrieve call slips when they brought back borrowed manuscripts. In respect to the great Jesuit scholar Jacques Sirmond, accused of stealing from the old monastery of Corbie, Delisle says that he himself had inspected Sirmond's library and that it contained only one manuscript with that definite provenance. On the other hand, he does tell Father Martène's story of a visit to the Abbey of Cambron in 1718 when his companion, on seeing a manuscript with the colophon *si quis eum abstulerit, anathema sit*, remarked that there must, by now, be quite a few anathematized Jesuits. The case was finally made by Valentin Rose, who inspected the Claramontana manuscripts that had ended up in Berlin and found that many were from Benedictine houses and that traces of Sirmond's handwriting were everywhere. Presumably, however, the movement of Benedictine books into the Clermont Library had decreased significantly by the second half of the seventeenth century, and there was a standoff.

The Jesuit historian Daniel Papebrock, working in Antwerp on the vast *Acta Sanctorum* named after John Bolland, became, perhaps unwittingly, the radical destabilizer of this situation. The destabilizing element was a fairly modest essay prefaced in 1675 to the second April volume of Saints' lives, which concerned itself with certain very old charters and documents, generally called "diplomas," that Papebrock believed to be forgeries. In fact, as it turned out, at least one of the documents in question was a forgery, but Papebrock, who was not experienced in such matters, proved it by comparing it with documents that were also forged. He then, in a seeming contradiction, concluded that most of the charters claiming to be earlier than the seventh century were wrong, and then — and this was the disruptive moment — he cast a skeptical eye on the entire contents of the cartulary at the Benedictine monastery of St. Denis. That was the slight that could not be endured.

Before discussing the remarkable response to this challenge, I should emphasize that even though an important blow had been dealt to the historical record — one that, because of the extreme skepticism and sensitivity of the times, was quite likely to have force — the issue was initially restricted to charters, land grants, and other documents. Manuscript books had not been mentioned, perhaps because of Papebrock's very limited knowledge of medieval handwriting.

Jean Mabillon, who now entered the scene, had an enormous knowledge of and experience with early writing of all kinds, at least of all of the kinds available in France.

His trips to Germany and Italy came later. He also, apparently, had unusual gifts of character and a presence that was both modest and compelling. His friend and biographer Dom Ruinart reported that when he did travel to Germany, his colleagues there were so taken with him that they pretended to know French, just to get him to say a few words in his mother tongue — "une petite ruse," he called it. We also know that when he was offered a royal pension he turned it down, saying that it was best that God be his only resource. As for his intelligence, it was large and serene, gave ample scope to his extraordinary intuitive powers, and seems on the whole to have been disinterested, although he tended to come down in favor of his country and his order.

In 1681, six years after the appearance of Papebrock's essay, Mabillon's *De Re Diplomatica Libri VI* appeared and, at a stroke, established the discipline of paleography and the possibility of moving step-wise through history on the basis of script. It was, of course, an occasional work, part of a *contestation*, but it was conceived on such a grand scale that the details of the original dispute were left far behind. It is a large, beautiful book, wonderfully printed and engraved. I beg to disagree with Dom Leclercq, who found the allegorical frontispiece "as pretentious as it is mediocre." Certainly the engraved facsimiles of scripts are utterly remarkable, and it is, to a large degree, the plates and Book V, where they are located, that most concern us here. Here Mabillon demonstrates the development of each writing style out of its predecessor, and this is the great achievement. In doing this he also shows the extent to which the scripts of documents and the scripts of books overlap, so that one cannot speak of the inauthenticity of one class without making imputations about the other. More of this later.

The work was an instant success. Papebrock's gracious letter acknowledging his defeat, which Mabillon printed in the *Supplementum* of 1704, has been quoted, as has Mabillon's reply: "I would gladly sacrifice the vainglory of my scholarly repute to have been the author of that one modest letter." The matter was closed. The charters of St. Denis had been defended. Traube is right in stating that from an intellectual standpoint the war had been won after one battle. In fact, however, the war was just beginning and what ensued, the *bella diplomatica* or *les contestations sur la diplomatique*, produced a complex of petty politics and disingenuousness so intermixed with questions of real interest that it has never been fully understood.

The cast of characters was fairly large. On the Benedictine side, which seems the conservative one, aside from Mabillon, were his friend Dom Ruinart and later Pierre Coustant, and in Italy, Archbishop Fontanini, who addressed a pro-Mabillon treatise to the Pope, and the somewhat more shadowy figures Domenico Lazzarini, Antonio Gatti, and Scipio Moranta. Opposing them for the Jesuits, since Papebrock had left the fray, was first and foremost Barthelémy Germon (several major treatises) and Jean Hardouin, an extremely problematic figure. All of these wrote in Latin. Writing in French was a Jesuit, J. P. Lallement, whose extremely clever dialogue, *Histoire des contestations sur la diplomatique*, is of great help in figuring things out. The issues are not all trivial.

Let us peer briefly into this thicket, leaving out the Italians, and look at some issues surrounding one script associated with the Merovingian era. Most of the documents orig-

PRÆFATIO.

ronenſi Epiſcopo in lib. 1 de gloria Martyrum cap. 28. Id monuiſſe hoc loco aliquanti momenti eſt.

VII Secundus liber exhibet Lectionarium Gallicanum, quod in Luxovienſi Benedictinæ Congregationis ſancti Vitoni percelebri monaſterio reperimus. In ipſo hujuſce libri limine nonnulla de Adventu Domini, & de feſtis apud Gallos antiquitus receptis præmittuntur, ſingillatim deinde ſuis locis per totum librum explicanda. Nihil in illo Lectionario non dignum obſervatione : multa ſingularia, præſertim quæ ad Paſſionem Domini & ad Rogationes pertinent. Lectiones ex Scriptura nec multum recedunt à Vulgata noſtra, nec omnino cum illa conveniunt. Varietates inſigniores in fine operis referemus. Lectionarii hujus antiquitas ex feſtis in eo recenſitis, & ex litterarum, quibus exaratus eſt codex, forma intelligitur. Pauca quippe in eo feſta : nullum ſanctæ Genovefæ die natali recentius. Characteres ipſi Merovingicam referunt ſcripturam, quæ ſub prima Regum noſtrorum ſtirpe uſitata erat. Sed ne lectori fucum facere videamur, ſpecimen ſcripturæ, quæ in illo codice ubique æqualis eſt, æri inciſum hîc exhibemus.

Engraving of the script of Luxeuil from Jean Mabillon *De Liturgia Gallicana*, 1685.

inally rejected by Papebrock had been in a script that seems to those not familiar with it to be spiky, eccentric, and illegible. Mabillon termed this writing "Scriptura Francogallica seu Merovingica" and treated it as the early national script of France. He pointedly remarked that this common script is the same as that of "our very old codex of Jerome." In other words, it is used not only in documents but also in manuscripts. In 1683 he travelled into Eastern France and, visiting the monastery of Luxeuil, he encountered an old lectionary in the same script, which he published two years later, taking care to include an engraving depicting the writing. Since then, although the origin of this script is much disputed, it has been called "the script of Luxeuil."

When Germon attacked Mabillon in his first *Disceptatio*, he quickly moved to reject the disputed Merovingian charters, but at the same time he seemed to be aware that he was moving into danger. In the second *Disceptatio*, he expresses horror that any learned person could impute to him the thought that the falseness of documents could extend to old books. Documents are single and therefore easily forged; a text found in many copies in different places cannot be. And yet he clearly found the script of Luxeuil in and of itself anomalous and impossible, and he was certainly aware that Mabillon knew it in books. Reading Germon, it occurs to one briefly that he felt himself being, as it were, pushed to the left by his opponents, who may have wished to place him in a position more and more hostile toward the acceptance of the written records of the past.

The step that he wished to avoid taking, as he must have known, had already been taken by the Jesuit Father Jean Hardouin, who, in a treatise on coins published in 1693, had expressed such doubt about the entire transmission of texts from antiquity that he rejected as spurious everything except Cicero, Pliny the Elder, and certain works of Virgil and Horace. If one takes Montaigne's "Que sais-je?" as a point of departure and proceeds with ever-increasing doubt, one comes finally to the black cynicism of Père Hardouin, a cynicism that in time brought discredit to himself and his associates. As for the *contestations*, Mabillon himself is generally praised for keeping his distance, but in 1705, two years before his death, he wrote a letter to Giusto Fontanini, praising him for his *Vindiciae* and asserted that the contested issues had, in fact, become ones of public concern. In due course, however, the battles were forgotten. Mabillon had not only rescued his charters and established a new discipline, he had also used manuscripts to provide the first detailed and reliable framework for historical research.

Rodney G. Dennis

I

THE ESTABLISHMENT

OF TEXT

Motet fragments pasted on a wood board. Reversed photograph showing some notes on the verso; Italy, ca. 1400.

2

Motets Recovered from a Binding

Barely a dozen manuscript anthologies of polyphonic music from the years around 1400 have survived even partially intact as books, a tiny fraction of those whose existence is documented in inventories, wills, and archives. While we depend mainly on those surviving books for the retrieval of music complete enough to be performed, numerous further lost manuscripts are known to us from just a single leaf or two, rescued from destruction only by later use as pastedowns or flyleaves in other books. In some lucky cases, several leaves from the same manuscript have been assembled from documents in the same archive or from books bound by the same stationer. Examples from around 1400 are the so-called Padua fragments, originating from four distinct manuscripts, recovered from the bindings of volumes in the Biblioteca universitaria, Padua; and the Mancini codex reconstituted from archival bindings in the Archivio di Stato, Lucca, recently augmented from another part of the same archive, and now published in facsimile.[1]

The unit of presentation for polyphonic music is the manuscript opening; singers could see their individual parts, arranged so that all turned the page together. The unit of survival is the individual leaf or bifolium. Deprived of immediate neighbors, such fragments usually fail to yield complete pieces or sections of music, but nevertheless they permit some analysis, as well as inferences about adjacent pieces and about the order and contents of the lost manuscript. Each anthology of polyphonic music was a unique document; fragments cannot be arranged in their original order as readily as when a base or standard text exists, as it usually does for liturgical manuscripts.[2] General patterns may tell us much about how a manuscript was used, about how a repertory was classified: are secular pieces mixed with sacred in the same manuscript? are Glorias grouped together or alternated with Credos as pairs?

Musical styles changed quite rapidly, and repertories underwent rapid renewal and revision. In the centuries before antiquarian, historical, or purely musical interest in old music, outgrown musical manuscripts were exceptionally vulnerable to destruction; unlike paintings, the written text of the composition is the basis for "making" music, not the music itself. New generations have always made or re-made music according to their own taste, whether or not they claim historical authenticity. That is as true for the early music performance movement in our own time as it was for a medieval composer.

We can look at an incomplete painting; but we cannot, without recomposition, perform a piece of music that lacks essential strands or is disabled by gaps, even if the professional can bridge some of those gaps mentally. The reconstruction of repertories for this early period is an apparently unpromising task that has nevertheless scored some major successes in jigsawing pieces together from an assortment of fragmentary copies. Every new fragment counts; the present one contributes important new repertory even though it cannot yet be performed. Medieval notation can also be extremely compact; a piece that takes many pages of large-format modern score will often occupy only a single manuscript opening.

fMS Typ 122, bequeathed in 1984 to the Houghton Library by Philip Hofer, is a French missal of the late fourteenth century from the diocese of Narbonne, written throughout in a bold French Gothic book hand. A seven-leaf gathering of prayers, in a similar hand, interrupts the original foliation between folios 138 and 139. This intercalated gathering may suggest that when the Missal went to Italy it was in an unbound state, which would account for the present binding's distinctly Northern Italian appearance. On folios 1, 142 (Canon), and 145 (Sanctorale), a somewhat later overlay of Italian decoration has been added to the original decoration, which is in the French style and consists of some gold-leaf capitals and marginal ornament. The Italian additions include, on folios 1 and 145, an unidentified coat of arms.[3] The repertories from which the above-mentioned Padua and Lucca manuscripts were compiled seem to have originated in Padua and in Visconti circles in Milan and Pavia. In addition to court and university circles, such as the confluence in Visconti Pavia and Carrarese Padua, the chapters of some cathedrals and the private chapels of bishops and cardinals were among the most significant patrons of music such as that on the present fragment, which is surely of Northern Italian origin.

A parchment bifolium of music is still firmly pasted to the rear wooden board of the binding. It was judged impossible to lift without damage both to the binding and to the fragment. This report must therefore be considered provisional until future techniques give better access to the other side. Some access was, however, possible, thanks to Mr. Dennis, and to Mrs. Marjorie B. Cohn, then Associate Conservator for Works of Art on Paper at the Fogg Art Museum Center for Conservation and Technical Studies, who tested means of making the parchment temporarily more transparent, so that the text on the concealed other side might be photographed in this state of enhanced visibility (as it was, excellently, by Mr. Michael Nedsweski). After various organic solvents had been tried on the parchment, ink, and paints, it was decided to soak the parchment in toluene, on the following grounds: the parchment was unaffected visually by the solvent upon evaporation; toluene evaporates slowly, thus allowing a few minutes more of enhanced visibility; it also seemed less likely than other solvents to have a long-term effect on the parchment's oils.

The visible side of the bifolium appears to be the outside of the fold, and is therefore here designated folios 2ᵛ and 1ʳ, although the two folios were not originally adjacent. Total measurements now average 36 cm wide by 25.7 cm high, each original page having been approximately 21 cm wide. Each side is ruled with nine red five-line staves of about 16.5

cm length, with a rastrum of 16.5 cm gauge.[4] The Italian text hand adopts a more ecclesiastical Gothic form for the designation *Tenor Trinitatem* on f. 1[r], and for *Amen* on 2[v].

Because the bifolium is not from the center of a gathering, it gives no complete musical sections for any of the three pieces written on it; all four pages lack their facing pages. The three items are all, so far as we know, unique:[5]

1) F. 1[r] (exposed, right-hand side) is the final recto of a motet that probably occupied two openings. Its texts seem to deal with the period of threefold papal schism between the councils of Pisa (1409) and Constance (1415); it is not only one of a short list of topical pieces from that period, but is also among two dozen examples of the recently-identified and distinctive genre of the Italian motet.[6] Pietro Filargo, elected as Pope Alexander V at the Council of Pisa, was a patron of composers and was in Pavia in the 1390s. The canon lawyer and cardinal Francesco Zabarella, bishop of Florence from 1410, and patron of the composer Ciconia in Padua, was a principal architect of the resolution of the schism at Constance. The circles in which these men moved is a natural home for sentiments such as those in this text.

2) F. 1[v] (pasted down, right-hand side) contains parts of a presumably Marian motet. The photograph was taken during the few minutes between application and evaporation of the solvent. Clarity is further helped by the blank staves below the motet on the recto. Reading the photograph in reverse, one can see 7¾ staves of a fully texted cantus part, of which the only clearly visible word is "concepisti," and 1¼ staves of a lower part labelled "Tenor," and possibly "Imperatrix."

3) Folios 2[r-v] (left-hand side) contain a fragmentary Credo, probably for three voices, that must have occupied three openings altogether. The concealed recto contains part of the section preceding that on the visible verso.

Margaret Bent

[1]Ed. John Nádas and Agostino Ziino. *Il Codice Mancini* (Lucca, Archivio dei Stato, ms. 184), Lucca, 1990. For an English example, see Margaret Bent, "The Progeny of Old Hall: More Leaves from a Royal English Choirbook," *Gordon Athol Anderson (1929-1981) in Memoriam*, Musicological Studies 49, 2 vols. (Henryville, Ottawa, and Binningen: Institute of Mediaeval Music, 1984), 1: 1-54.

[2]See, for example, Margaret Rickert, *The Reconstructed Carmelite Missal* (London 1952).

[3]The Curator of Manuscripts, Mr. Rodney Dennis, greatly facilitated this work and provided the description of the host manuscript on which this report is based.

[4]The presence of at least some of the following features will usually help to distinguish late-medieval mensural notation from plainchant: staves of five (rather than four) lines; non-liturgical as well as liturgical texts; individual diamond-shaped rhomboid notes as well as square and compound shapes.

[5]It is described, with transcriptions of the visible music, in Margaret Bent, "New Sacred Polyphonic Fragments of the Early Quattrocento," *Studi Musicali* 9 (1980): 171-190, *q.v.* for an analysis of the verbal text by Prof. Michael Connolly of Boston College.

[6]"The Fourteenth-Century Italian Motet," *L'Ars Nova Italiana del Trecento* 6 (Certaldo, forthcoming). Proceedings of international conference at Certaldo, 1984.

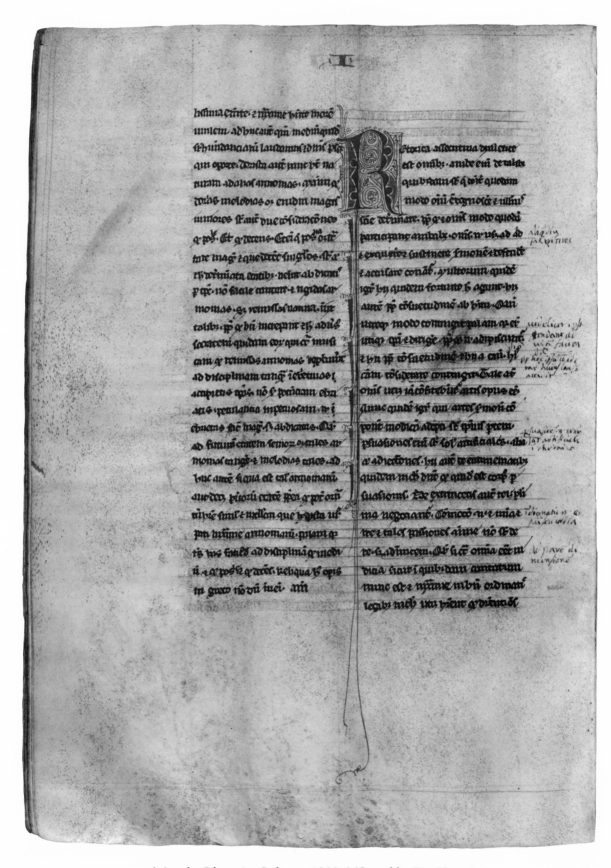

Aristotle, *Rhetorica*; Italy, ca. 1300. MS used by Pier Vettori.

3

An Aristotelian Excursion

Our story revolves around three manuscripts containing ethical works and other treatises of Aristotle, two in Latin translation written around 1300 and the other a fifteenth-century copy of the Greek texts. Though unrelated in their origins and in the paths that brought them to Houghton, their conjunction here discloses a surprisingly rich web of connections, which when traced shows that each has played a key role in the history of Aristotle's text in the Middle Ages and Renaissance.

"In the intellectual history of the Middle Ages one of the most fundamental facts is the persistent and pervasive influence of the writings of Aristotle." So wrote the eminent Harvard medievalist Charles Homer Haskins,[1] and his words find a sort of poetic confirmation in the famous salute of Dante to Aristotle as "the master of them that know" ("il maestro di color che sanno").[2] But for Dante, as for his philosophical guide Thomas Aquinas and indeed almost all of western medieval Europe, Aristotle was a Latin author, encountered at one remove from his original Greek.[3] The process of translation began in the sixth century when Boethius put into Latin the logical works known collectively as the *Organon* and received new impetus in the middle and late twelfth century; by the end of that century "the main Aristotelian treatises were already translated into Latin, either directly from the Greek, or through the medium of Arabic versions, or from both sources."[4] Among the exceptions were the ethical works: until the 1240s only the first three books of the *Nicomachean Ethics* were widely available. The first complete extant Latin translation of the *Ethics* was produced shortly before 1250 by Robert Grosseteste (ca. 1168-1253), bishop of Lincoln, perhaps the first Chancellor of the University of Oxford, and a scholar of astonishing depth and versatility.[5] The following generation saw the closest approach thus far to a complete Latin version of the corpus, the work of the Flemish Dominican William of Moerbeke (ca. 1215-ca. 1286). For some texts (e.g., the *Politics*) William provided the first full Latin translation, while for others, such as the *Rhetoric*, his rendering superseded earlier efforts; he may be responsible for the revision of Grosseteste's translation of the *Nicomachean Ethics* that enjoyed a wide circulation from the late thirteenth century onward.[6]

Our two Latin Aristotles were written shortly after the death of William of Moerbeke near the end of the thirteenth century. MS Lat 39 contains William's translations of the *Politics* and *Rhetoric* and the *Magna Moralia* in the version of Bartolomeo da Messina; the text was carefully corrected soon after being written, with some omitted words and phrases boxed in red by the rubricator. MS Typ 233 contains the *Magna Moralia*, *Nicomachean Ethics*, *Politics*, and the *Oeconomicus*; the script is an expert example of the rounded Italian Gothic known as *littera Bononiensis* and the historiated initials are particularly fine, if not conspicuously Aristotelian in spirit. The manuscript was acquired by Philip Hofer in 1931. MS Lat 39 has a Florentine background: it belonged to the Dominican house of S. Maria Novella, where it was recorded in the 1489 library inventory,[7] and it was purchased in Florence in or around 1819 by Edward Everett, who presented it forthwith to "the College library" — Harvard's first Latin manuscript.[8] Both books illustrate the form in which Aristotle was read in western Europe at the close of the Middle Ages — though, as we shall see, that is far from all they have to tell us.

The eventual circulation of Aristotle's works in Greek was due to the classical interests of Italian humanism. Knowledge of Greek spread slowly among the early generations of humanists, the pace quickening somewhat after 1453 when many Greek scholars entered Italy as refugees following the fall of Constantinople. Still, for much of the fifteenth century Latin translations of Greek authors remained more popular than original Greek texts. The first printed editions of Greek classics began to appear in the mid-1480s.[9] Aristotle's turn came relatively early, in the form of five imposing quarto volumes published between 1495 and 1498 that contained virtually the entire corpus along with some works of his pupil and successor Theophrastus. This set of volumes represented by far the most ambitious publication of a Greek author to that time; it also secured the preeminence in this field of its printer, Aldus Manutius of Venice.[10] Like many early printed editions of Greek texts, the Aldine Aristotle was based mainly on manuscripts of the fourteenth and fifteenth centuries, whose difficult cursive script was reproduced in type with regrettable fidelity. As it happens, one of the manuscripts used can be identified as Houghton's MS Gr 17, which supplied among other texts the copy of the *Nichomachean Ethics* from which Aldus' printers worked (only one quire of the *Ethics* is now left in the manuscript, containing somewhat less than Book 1 of the treatise). A link with the printing house could be surmised from the ink smudges and thumbprints left on several of the pages; the connection with the Aldine edition is clinched by the fact that the page-breaks and page-signatures of the Aldine volume appear in the text and margins of the Houghton manuscript. (A small mystery attends the marking of these page-breaks. On some pages — for example, f. 39ʳ, the first page of the *Ethics* — they correspond precisely with the *mise en page* of the Aldine text, but in most cases there is a discrepancy ranging from a word or two to more than a line of text. It is hard to explain why someone subsequently marking the pages of the printed edition in the manuscript would have been so erratic, nor indeed would there be any point to doing so at all once the text had been printed. It seems most likely that these page-breaks were entered *before* printing as guidelines for the compositor.)

One might think that once Aristotle's works were generally available in Greek the medieval Latin translations would lose most if not all of their interest. There are two main reasons why this is not so. The first is that many of the late medieval translations (including those of Grosseteste and William of Moerbeke) maintained such scrupulous

malijs omib3. teficiens igitur amare. p
inpotentiam. ⁊ accusaticos quis bt tifte
q̄o utiq3 erit amicus no amans. fer au
f̄mone amicicia. n̄o bxe uult.
Amplius utiq3 si fuerit multi. n̄o erit cef
sare tristantem. C Multus enim existen
cib3 mento semp arcauinum quedam
⁊ accidere aliq̄ in fortunium quib3 facti
necessariū tristari. neq3 iterum paucos. ⁊
unum. aut duos. fer conmensuratos
tempore. ⁊ suo moti ⁊ damare. C Post
bxe autem bxe considerandum. omis o;
amico uti. est autem non omi amicicia.
p̄ scruicacio. fer in qua maxime accusare
autem. ⁊ in alijs similiter puta in ea que
patris ⁊ filium non est accusatio talis.
ur dignificant in quib3dam. q̄ ad mo
dum ego te. ⁊ tra time. Si autem non
bxe uexemens accusatio. in equalib3 au
amicis n̄o est equale. est autem que pat
⁊ filium amicicia in inequalez. simili
ter que e mulieris ⁊ uirum. aut fui ⁊ ad
dominum ⁊ domino aut peioris. ⁊ melioz
n̄o bxebunt enim tralia accusaticos. fer
in equalib3 amicis. ⁊ ipa amicicia talis
accusatio. quare scrutandum utiq3 erit
qualit oportet uti amico ⁊ amicicia. q̄ e
in eq̄lib3 amicis.
Explicit lib3 magnoz ethicoz ⁊ p̄is.

Incipit liber ethicoz.

mnis ars. ⁊ co;
omis doctrina.
C Similit aut
⁊ opatio ⁊ elec
tio bonu aliq̄
appetere uidet.
ideoq̄ bene enū
tiat bonum.
qd omia appe
tuntur. differentia aute quedam finum eē
uidetur. C Hij quidē enim sunt actus. hij
autē ⁊ extra hos opus aliq̄.
quoz autē sunt fines quidam ⁊ ea opacice.
In hijs exstit melius actib3 opus. mult⁊
autem opationib3 entib3 ⁊ artib3 ⁊ scientiis
sunt fines. mediante quidem enim sanita.
nauigatiue uero nauigatio. militaris au
uictoria. economice ⁊ diuitie. C Quecūq̄
autem talium sunt sub una aliqua uirtu
tum. queadm sub equestri frenefactiua. ⁊ quē
cūq̄ alie equestrū instrumentoz sunt. bxe
autē ⁊ omis tellica opatio. sub militari. secū
dum eundo utiq̄ modum. ⁊ ralie subaltern.
in omnib3 enim architectonicaz fines ōib3
desirerabiliores sunt hijs que sub ipis se.
bxoz enim gratia illa sequuntur. differunt aut
nichil. actus eos ⁊ê fines opationū. aut p̄
⁊ eos aliud aliquid queadmodum in doctri
nis. sicut utiq̄ finis opationum quem pp
se nolumus. alia uero ipā illam. n̄o omia
pp aliud optamus. Procedent bxe enī in in
finitum ⁊ eē uanum. ⁊ inane desiderium. ⁊
Manifestum aut utiq̄ erit. bxe boū ⁊ ê
optimus. ⁊ ad utrum eius cognitio mag
num bt in uitetum ul in cursum. C Quē
admodum sagittatores signū habentes. ⁊
magis utiq̄ adipiscentur qd oportet. Si au
ten temptandum e ipo suscipe quid id est. et
cui disciplinaz. aut uirtutū sit. Uideat ut̄
principalis e. ⁊ maxime architectonice eē
Talis autem uidet ciuil. Qualis enī ⁊ ê
utiles disciplinaz in ciuitatib3. ⁊ quales u
uniuquēq3. addiscere usq3 quo ipi p̄ ordinat
Uidemus enim darissimas uirtutum. sub
hac eē. ut militare economica. ⁊ rethorica.
ponente autē hac opatiuis ⁊ reliquis opationib3
disciplinaz. amplius autē ⁊ legem ⁊ uiběnt.
quid oportet opari. ⁊ a quib3 abstinere. bui

al accus.
qdam.

uerūt.

ponens.
p̄ bas opi qdam.
p̄.
existit meliam
opomib3 opa.
mlā.
factciue.
uo
qdam uirtute
sie.

itaq3.

p
ponens. actuū.
qdam. teis.
ê as
ipin
desideranī.
ficq̄
qn
Igne.
er.

mur.
figurali.
bi. ar.

uera ⁊ cauil. apprehenden
debitur. e.
bxe.
p̄ciosissimas.
existentes. p̄n
petias.
sponente

Aristotle, *Liber Ethicorum* with marginalia from an earlier translation; Italy, ca. 1300.

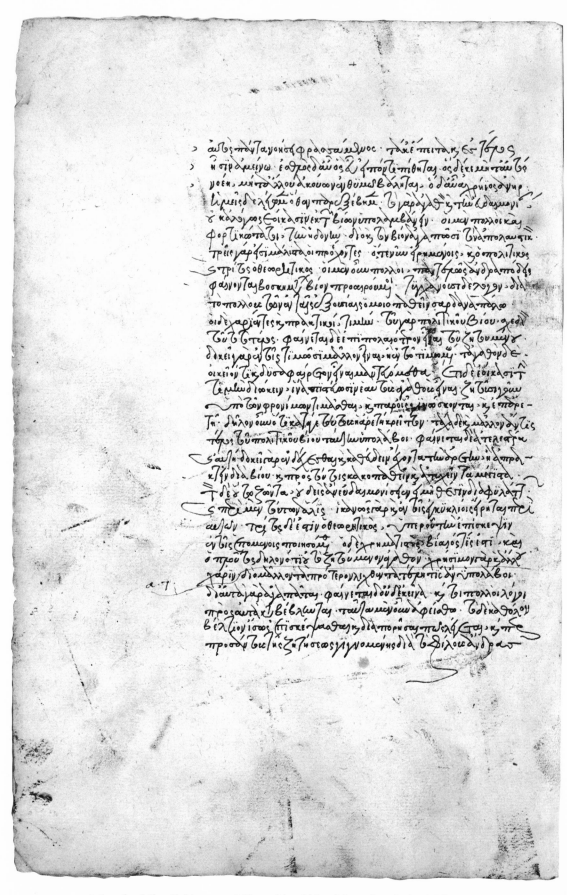

Aristotle, *Liber Ethicorum,* MS used by Aldus Manutius; Italy, 15th cent.

closeness to the Greek text that they can serve as witnesses to the lost Greek manuscripts on which they were based, manuscripts that in many passages preserve a text superior to that found in surviving Greek manuscripts. The first scholar to recognize the value of the medieval Latin Aristotle translations for this purpose was one of the giants of sixteenth-century Greek studies, Pier Vettori of Florence (1499-1585). A less brilliant critic than his great predecessor Angelo Poliziano, Vettori excelled even Poliziano in his ability to see the preservation of classical texts in historical terms; as a recent student of Vettori's work on Aeschylus puts it, he was "one of the few, if not the only one, in his time to realize that the transmitted text of a classical author has had a history in Antiquity and Middle Ages, that this history can be reconstructed, and that this reconstruction can contribute to a better understanding of the transmitted text."[11] Once again a Houghton manuscript functioned as the instrument of progress: a note by Francesco Vettori on the front flyleaf of MS Lat 39 reveals that this is the actual copy of Moerbeke's Latin translation of Aristotle's *Rhetoric* that Pier Vettori used to correct errors in the Greek text.[12] Vettori applied his methodological breakthrough specifically to the *Rhetoric*, but his claim about the textual value of the medieval Latin translations is at least potentially true for the entire corpus, and indeed modern critical editions of many works, among them the *Nicomachean Ethics*, still cite the readings of the *vetus translatio* as having independent importance.

Medieval Latin translations of Aristotle have a second claim on our continuing attention for what they reveal of the reception of Aristotle's thought in the Middle Ages. The remarks of Charles Homer Haskins on Aristotle's medieval influence cited earlier proceed as follows: "always considerable, this influence grew and spread as new groups of the master's works became available to the scholars of western Europe, and it can be measured and defined only as we can ascertain accurately the date, the character, and the diffusion of the different Latin versions of each portion of the Aristotelian *corpus*." This statement could serve as the charter of the *Aristoteles Latinus*, an international project begun more than sixty years ago with the aim of identifying and editing all extant prehumanist Latin translations of Aristotelian texts.[13] One of the most elaborate editions to appear so far is devoted to the *Nicomachean Ethics*, and in it Philip Hofer's manuscript of Grosseteste's translation occupies a place of singular importance. As can be readily seen from the opening folio of the *Ethics* in MS Typ 233 (f. 17ʳ), Grosseteste's version has been carefully collated against another Latin translation and the variants recorded in the margin. In Books I-III of the *Ethics* the translations used for comparison were pre-Grosseteste renderings already known from other sources; for the remaining books, on the other hand, the Hofer manuscript drew on what seems to be yet another pre-Grosseteste translation, whose existence had previously been attested only by fragments of Books VII and VIII found in a Vatican manuscript (Borghese lat. 108) and by citations from those books by Albertus Magnus. Thanks to the Hofer manuscript — whose importance is such that the learned editor for the *Aristoteles Latinus* has dubbed it the *Ethica Hoferiana*[14] — we not only have acquired significantly more fragments of this pre-Grosseteste version, but we also possess a rare specimen of medieval Aristotelian scholarship in action.

For the final stage of our narrative we return to MS Gr 17, the Aldine printer's copy. Few manuscripts that made their way into the workshops of the early printers lived to tell the tale; our Aristotle not only survived its brush with Aldus, but later found itself taken up by some very distinguished company indeed. At several places it bears inscriptions in the hand of Johannes Cono (or Cuno, originally Kuhn?, ca. 1463-1513), a German Dominican who studied in Italy in the early years of the sixteenth century and then returned to his native Nuremberg; one of his manuscript entries (on f. 173ʳ) reveals that he had our book with him there in 1507. Though a plan in which he was involved to move the Aldine press to Germany came to nothing, Cono still played an important part in transplanting the classical humanism of Italy to southern Germany and Switzerland; his last years were spent in Basel, where he devoted himself to teaching Greek and editing patristic texts. At his death the bulk of his library, our manuscript apparently included, passed to a far more illustrious humanist, the Alsatian Beatus Rhenanus (1485-1547), who in turn seems to have given it to his young protégé Mathias Schürer of Strasbourg (ca. 1470-ca. 1520): on the verso of an otherwise blank page at the front are the words "Beatus Rhenanus Mathiae Schurerio Suo s. d. p." (B. R. sends warmest greetings to his friend M. S.), a formula that usually introduces a letter but that here perhaps records the gift of the manuscript. Schürer helped make Strasbourg a vital center for the diffusion of classical learning, publishing more than a hundred editions of Greek and Latin authors — not including Aristotle, unfortunately — between 1508 and 1520.[15] It is not often that a single book (and a rather unprepossessing one at that) encapsulates so much intellectual history: in our manuscript's wanderings, late and early, we can both trace the propagation of Italian humanism across the Alps and also mark a crucial step in the reception of Aristotle's original text, as it ceases to be the possession only of a rare polymath like Grosseteste or a professional scholar like Vettori and begins to enter the mainstream of western intellectual life.[16]

Our Aristotelian excursion has dwelt most of all on the ethical treatises, and so it is appropriate that it should end with a moral. In view of the manifold generosity that has brought these manuscripts — and all the others in this exhibition — to Houghton, the following words from the *Nicomachean Ethics* may offer a fitting epilogue to our story: "acts of virtue are noble, and are performed for the sake of their nobility; the liberal person therefore will give for the nobility of giving."[17]

R. J. Tarrant

[1] *Studies in the History of Mediaeval Science* (Cambridge, Mass.: Harvard University Press, 1924), p. 223, cited by Callus (below, n.4).

[2] *Inferno* 4.131.

[3] On knowledge of Greek in Europe between the end of Antiquity and the Renaissance see Walter Berschin, *Greek Letters and the Latin Middle Ages: from Jerome to Nicholas of Cusa*, trans. Jerold C. Frakes (Washington, D.C.: Catholic University of America Press, 1988). A short survey of the medieval Aristotle translations is given by L. Minio-Paluello, "L'Aristoteles Latinus," *Studi medievali* ser. 1 (1960), 304-27 (reprinted in *Opuscula: the Latin Aristotle* (Amsterdam: Hakkert, 1972), pp. 459-482.

[4] D.A. Callus, "Introduction of Aristotelian Learning to Oxford," *Proceedings of the British Academy* 29 (1944), 3.

[5] For Grosseteste's life see A. M. Emden, *A Biographical Register of the University of Oxford to A.D. 1500* vol. 2 (Oxford: Clarendon Press, 1958), pp. 830-833; on his scholarly work D. A. Callus, "Robert Grosseteste as Scholar," in D. A. Callus, ed., *Robert Grosseteste: Scholar and Bishop* (Oxford: Clarendon Press, 1955), pp. 1-69 (62-64 on his translation of the *Ethics*). Grosseteste's knowledge of Greek and his deployment of that knowledge are well discussed by A.C. Dionisotti, "On the Greek Studies of Robert Grosseteste," in A.C. Dionisotti, Anthony Grafton, and Jill Kray, eds., *The Uses of Greek and Latin: Historical Essays* (London: Warburg Institute, 1988), pp. 19-39.

[6] On William's translations in general see B. Schneider, *Die mittelalterlichen griechisch-lateinischen Übersetzungen der Aristotelischen Rhetorik* (Berlin: De Gruyter, 1971 [*Peripatoi* 2]), pp. 5-9. His connection with the revision of Grosseteste's *Ethics* is considered — and a sober *non liquet* rendered — by R. A. Gauthier in his edition of the *Nicomachean Ethics* in *Aristoteles Latinus* (Leiden-Brussels: Brill-Desclée De Brouwer, 1974) vol. 1 pp. ccxxxix-xlv.

[7] The manuscript is item 321 in the inventory as published by S. Orlandi, *La Biblioteca de S. Maria Novella in Firenze dal sec. XIV al sec. XIX* (Florence: Il Rosario, 1952), p. 42. Following the Aristotelian works the inventory lists "propositiones Procli," but, apart from its appearance in a list of contents on the flyleaf verso, no trace of this text appears in the manuscript at present.

[8] Everett described his acquisition of the manuscript in a postscript to "An account of some Greek Manuscripts, procured at Constantinople in 1819, and now belonging to the Library of the University at Cambridge," *Memoirs of the American Academy of Arts and Sciences* 4.2 (1821), 409-415. Edward Everett (1794-1865) was at the time Eliot Professor of Greek Literature at Harvard, a position to which he was appointed at age 21 with only a B.A. degree; he obtained his doctorate at Göttingen while occupying the Eliot chair. It is no surprise that a *curriculum vitae* thus begun continued in an uncommon way: leaving behind classical pursuits Everett served as member of the House of Representatives (1825-1835), Governor of Massachusetts (1836-1839), Minister Plenipotentiary to Great Britain (1841-1845), President of Harvard (1846-1849), Secretary of State (1852-1853), and U.S. Senator from Massachusetts (1853-1854). He is probably best remembered as the principal speaker at the consecration of the cemetery at Gettysburg on 19 November 1863, an occasion on which President Lincoln also pronounced some brief dedicatory remarks.

As a collector of Greek manuscripts the young Everett was a man of his time: while excusing the outrage of Greeks ("who feel for the literary degradation of their native country") at the removal of these books from convents and schools, he stoutly maintained that "it cannot of course be doubted that the cause of literature at large authorizes the European traveller to avail himself of the ignorance and insensibility of the Greek priests and monks, and to induce them to sell those manuscripts which can only become generally useful, by being taken from their present places of deposit, and brought to regions, where they will be collated and made known to the world" (409). The forthrightness of this statement is all the more striking in that Everett had not bought the manuscripts in question from an ecclesiastical foundation, but from "the family of a Greek prince in decay" (410).

[9] For a list of the *editiones principes* of Greek authors see J. E. Sandys, *A History of Classical Scholarship* vol. 2 (Cambridge: Cambridge University Press, 1908), pp. 104-105.

[10] On Aldus' activities see in brief L. D. Reynolds and N. G. Wilson, *Scribes and Scholars*, 3rd edition (Oxford: Clarendon Press, 1991), pp. 154-8, 278-9 (with further bibliography).

[11]J. A. Gruys, *The Early Printed Editions (1518-1664) of Aeschylus* (Nieukoop: B. De Graaf, 1981), pp. 88-9. On Vettori as a scholar see in general Anthony Grafton, *Joseph Scaliger: A Study in the History of Classical Scholarship I. Textual Criticism and Exegesis* (Oxford: Clarendon Press, 1983), pp. 52-70, 248-57; for his work on Aristotle's *Rhetoric* cf. Schneider (above, p. 2 n.2) pp. 73-76.

[12]"Hic est liber ille veteris tralationis non nullorum librorum Aristotelis cuius saepe mentionem fecit Petrus Victorius; praecipue autem in epistula ad studiosos artis dicendi, in commentarios suos [sic] in tres libros Aristotelis de arte dicendi, affirmat huius auxilio se usum fuisse in corrigendis libris illis temporum ac librariorum iniuria deformatis. Cum enim haec tralatio multis antea saeculis confecta fuerit, quo tempore libri Aristotelis integriores emendatioresque erant, auctorque ipsius, quicumque ille fuerit, negotium cum multa fide administraverit, ac ne verborum quidem ordinem variaverit, inde se cognovisse Victorius narrat quam scripturam in suo exemplari ille habuerit . . . ."

[13]A brief account of the project is given by Minio-Paluello (above, p. 1 n.3).

[14]René-Antoine Gauthier, ed., *Ethica Nicomachea (Aristoteles Latinus* XXVI 1-3), 5 vols. (Leiden-Brussels: Brill-Desclée De Brouwer), especially vol. 1 pp. cxv-xxxiii and vol. 2 pp. 97-124.

[15]On Cono, Beatus Rhenanus, and Schürer see the respective entries in Peter G. Bietenholz and Thomas B. Deutscher, eds. *Contemporaries of Erasmus: A Biographical Register of the Renaissance and Reformation* (3 vols. Toronto: University of Toronto Press, 1985).

[16]Even in this century our manuscript has attracted the notice of leading scholars: a set of notes on its contents tipped into the opening fly-leaves appears to be the work of Giovanni Mercati (1866-1957), the learned Prefect of the Vatican Library from 1919 to 1930 who was named Cardinal by Pius XI in 1936.

[17]*Nic. Eth.* 4.1.12 (Loeb translation).

II

THE DEVELOPMENT OF TEXT

John Wyclif, *Summula Summularum,* ultraviolet photograph of a palimpsest; Italy, 1291
and ca. 1400.

4

A New Work By John Wyclif?

This palimpsest, which has received very little attention in the scholarly world to date, is a brief treatise on the elements of logic, superimposed on a group of thirteenth-century Italian notarial documents. If, as it claims to be, the work is by the English theologian John Wyclif (1335?/1338?-1383), it shows that Wyclif was interested in the education of children as well as in the finer points of the scholastic discipline of logic, which was among the most popular subjects of study at Oxford during his lifetime. It also illumines and expands what we know of this very competent diplomat and highly controversial thinker of the later Middle Ages and demonstrates the speed with which British logic penetrated the curricula of the schools of Northern Italy.[1]

I. The Manuscript

1. (Upper script) Iohannes Wyclif(?), *Summula summularum.* s.xiv^ex^/xv^in^

a. f. 1^r^, ll. 1-16. (Prologue) *inc.* Sum<m>ularum et tractatuum lo<g>icalium tanta est multitudo, tanta varietas et obscuritas tanta . . . *des.* Et sic resecatis superfluis et obscuris atque magis difficilibus, subtilibus clericulis reservatis, solum clariores regulas puerulis proponam quam breviter potero in hac summula sum<m>ularum.

b. f. 1^r^, l. 17 — f.8^v^, l. 42 (Text) *inc.* Terminus est in logica large loquendo quicquid in grammatica dicitur dictio. Sed magis proprie solum nomen rectum vel obliquum (vel id quod potest reddere suppositum verbo) dicitur terminus. . . . *des.* (mutilated) verbi gratia, quia bene sequitur hoc currit . . .

The text is incomplete and has not previously been edited.

The MS consists of one quire of eight parchment folios (29 x 20.5 cm <22 x 12.5cm>). Hair side faces hair and flesh faces flesh, but flesh is on the outside. Foliation (1-8) in a modern hand in pencil appears in the lower right corner of each recto page. The text is written in long lines with between 38 (in 8^r^) and 45 (on 1^r^) lines per page. There are master prickings (round, 0.25 cm from the edge of the pages), but no line prickings. Ruling is in lead, with two vertical lines on either side of the text and one horizontal line across the top and bottom of each page; there are no individual line rulings. A catchword — *ergo aliter* — occurs at the bottom right of 8^v^.

The MS is in a single hand throughout, a neat, consistent Gothic cursive (Lieftinck type "C") of the late fourteenth/early fifteenth century, probably Italian. Standard scholastic abbreviations are used. The same hand makes corrections by crossing out the error and adding the new text above the line. Marginal notations throughout are also in the same hand. Brown ink is used; initials are in red. There are three diagrams (two on 2^r and one on 2^v), in red and brown ink, in a mix of Gothic cursive and bastarda.

The quire is bound by two strips of parchment drawn through holes in the gutter of the manuscript — 3 and 5 cm from the top and 6 and 8 cm from the bottom — with the ends twisted together. *Secundo folio: univoce.* Three still unidentified marks are written in modern hands in pencil on the manuscript: "C 559" on f. 8^v; "EN" on f. 1^r; "55 GC\$" on f. 8^v. The MS was acquired by the Houghton Library in January 1974 from Bernard Quaritch Ltd., London.

2. (Lower script) Notarial documents. ca. 1291

Ultraviolet light reveals earlier writing on both sides of four large folios (29 x 41 cm, written space varies), which have been turned into four bifolia to receive the upper script. UV also reveals line rulings, possibly in dry-point, 0.5 cm apart where visible. Various Italian notarial hands of the thirteenth century have copied numerous texts that are very inconsistent (in terms of both size and layout) and highly abbreviated. The correspondence of notches in the edges of the MS when the folios are oriented so that all the lower script runs in the same direction suggests that the four folios of lower script originally came from the same source. The notches probably evidence a previous binding, implying that this original work was in codex form. The writing of the two outermost folios (as they are bound today) runs in the opposite direction from the two innermost, meaning that the orientation of the sheets of the codex from which these leaves were originally taken has been altered.

Although erasures and the upper script have obscured the lower texts, they are clearly notarial in character: the protocols of the documents in the lower script approximate those of edited notarial documents.[2] These may be pages from a register. Several elements are clearly consistent with notarial practice in contemporary registers: the inconsistent hand and layout noted above; the presence of sections of text that have been crossed out with bold, diagonal freehand strokes; notes (usually delineated by a sweeping pen stroke) in the left-hand margin at the beginning of each new section of text; and a date in Roman numerals at the top center of one of the pages.[3] Occasional proper names are identifiable in the text, but the exact tenor of the documents has not been determined. The dating and localization of the lower script are quite certain from the protocols. This example is from the outer margin of f. 6^v: "In Dei nomine amen. Anno incarnatione ei<us>dem millesimo ducentesimo nonagesimo primo . . . Actum Flor(entiae)."[4]

The text copied in the upper script is identified by a rubric to the text: "Incipit sumula sumularum magistri Johannis Wycliff." This introductory treatise on logic contained a prologue and, according to the table of contents, six chapters, five of which survive here in whole or in part. The most recent catalogue of Wyclif's works does not contain this MS, although the author of that volume has since noted its existence.[5] Bod-

32

leian Library MS Lat. Misc. e. 79 fols. 44ᵛ-45ᵛ has been proposed as the end of this incomplete text,[6] but this seems unlikely. The Oxford MS is concerned with *insolubiles*;[7] none of the six chapters identified in the prologue of the Houghton MS deals with this topic (although another work by Wyclif — the *Summa insolubilium* — does). The Houghton MS resembles more closely Wyclif's *De logica* (see below).

The upper script reinforces the textual evidence from the lower script on the MS's Italian origin. Among the characteristically Italian elements in the upper hand are a distinctive double-crescent "s"; vertical lines through capitals; a waved titulus for "r"/"er"/ "re" — a survival from Italian notarial script; the uncrossed "et" symbol extending below the line; and Italian spellings, both doubling of consonants and the persistence of "tio" for "cio." At one point the scribe also uses the common abbreviation for the Italian title *Ser* within a Latin word: *s(er)vata* (f. 1ᵛ, l. 14). The neatness of the hand suggests a professional scribe, but the fact that the text is a palimpsest — very rare in this period — would indicate that the commissioner of the MS lacked either the means or the desire to have the text copied onto better parchment. The MS bears none of the distinguishing marks of the *pecia* system, which was prevalent among European universities in the later Middle Ages.[8] The wear on the outer folios, however, suggests that this quire circulated independently for a considerable amount of time.

II. The Problem

Given the origin and date of the manuscript itself, is this "*summa* of little *summas*" really a new work of John Wyclif? From a philological standpoint, the *Summula summularum* bears a marked resemblance to Wyclif's well-known treatise *De logica*.[9] Although the works diverge in several places, a comparison of three corresponding segments of the two texts reveals remarkable similarity of content and style (see Appendix). Entire passages often follow one another word for word, although the more elementary nature of the *Summula* is evident from its approach to the material. Definitions of terms are often expanded, as in the explanation of "signification" (f. 1ᵛ, ll. 12-14). Sometimes, difficult concepts are glossed over, or simply left out; didactic and theological examples are not used to illustrate the discussion. Since the two texts are almost parallel, it is tempting to assume that one derives from the other. The *De logica* was probably written c. 1360 and is in fact reckoned to be the earliest known work of Wyclif.[10] If this is correct,[11] the MS could be exactly what it says it is in the prologue, a simplified *summa* on logic for children. The author would have based the *Summula* on the *De logica* but, as the prologue has promised, excised information that could be considered superfluous or obscure and discussed the material in a somewhat more concise manner.

But can we conclude that Wyclif himself performed the redaction? Though not impossible, it seems unlikely that anyone else would have chosen to summarize Wyclif's treatise on logic in this way, or that both treatises derive from a third (lost?) work. While the *De logica* is identifiable as an Oxford treatise, it is very different from the standard logical texts used at Oxford in the late fourteenth century, such as the writings of Ockham.[12] This may have been because Wyclif was in constant disagreement with other Oxford logicians, many of whom were Franciscans of the Ockhamite school.

In further defense of Wyclif's authorship of the shorter treatise, there is evidence to suggest that he employed a *summula summularum* format on at least one other occasion. Shortly before his death, Wyclif abbreviated his theological works in the *Trialogue*.[13] Might he not have written a "little *summa*" on logic as well?

III. Conclusion

Finally, the historian may inquire how an Oxford logical treatise came to be copied by an Italian on discarded Italian documents only a few decades after its apparent date of composition. In fact, scholars have noted that the bulk of Wyclif's works are known from manuscripts produced in his native England — or in Southern Germany and Bohemia, where his controversial doctrines found a warm reception.[14] There were, however, a few copies of his works made in Italy,[15] and Wyclif's *summula* might have helped to satisfy the craving for British logical works that raged at the new university of Florence in the late fourteenth century.[16] We conclude, therefore, that the MS text was redacted from the *De logica* of John Wyclif sometime during the last decades of the fourteenth century and that it quickly found an audience among the avid students of logic and philosophy in the Florentine schools.

The Seminar in the Auxiliary Disciplines of Medieval Studies, Department of History, Harvard University

Richard C. Adler   *Philip Daileader*   *Carol Symes*
Rafael Burgos-Mirabal   *Adam J. Kosto*   *Professor Michael McCormick*
Alan Cooper   *Thomas Spence*

Bibliography on Houghton Library fMS Lat 338

Catalogue of Manuscripts in the Houghton Library, Harvard University, 8 vols. (Alexandria, 1987), viii, 428; Jeremy Catto, "Some English Manuscripts of Wyclif's Latin Works," in Anne Hudson and Michael Wilks, eds., *From Ockham to Wyclif*, Studies in Church History, Subsidia 5 (Oxford, 1987), 353-9 at 354 and n. 5; Anne Hudson, "Wyclif, John," in *Dictionary of the Middle Ages*, 13 vols. (New York, 1982-9), xii, 706-11 at 707; Anne Hudson, Review of Paul Vincent Spade and Gordon Anthony Williams, eds., *Johannis Wyclif Summa Insolubilium*, in *Review of English Studies* 39 (1988), 160; Williel R. Thomson, "Manuscripta Wyclifiana desiderata: The Potential Contribution of Missing Latin Texts to Our Image of Wyclif's Life and Works," *From Ockham to Wyclif*, 343-51 at 344 n. 4.

The seminar compared the two texts as follows:

Houghton, fMS Lat 338	Johannes Wyclif, *De logica*[17]
f. 1ʳ, ll. 18-44	c. 1ᵃ [De categorema/1]
f. 1ʳ, l. 45 — f. 1ᵛ, l. 25	c. 1ᵇ [De categorema/2]
f. 3ʳ, l. 29 — f. 3ᵛ, l. 15	c. 4 [De conversionibus]

The two texts follow one another closely. Several parallel passages can be found in the first *distinctio* of the Houghton MS, as follows:

Houghton, fMS Lat 338	Johannes Wyclif, *De logica*
f. 1ʳ, l.18	p. 2, ll. 2-5
f. 1ʳ, ll. 18-25	p. 3, l. 33 — p. 4, l. 4
f. 1ᵛ, ll. 20-23	p. 6, l. 30 — p. 7, l. 1
f. 1ᵛ, ll. 23-25	p. 7, ll. 1-3

In certain cases, the words and word order correspond almost exactly. Examples of this correspondence appear below. Note the abridgement of certain portions of the text of *De Logica* in the MS text, as well as the occasional expansion or simplification of the definition of a given term:

Houghton, fMS Lat 338 (f. 1ʳ, ll. 33-35)	Johannes Wyclif, *De logica* (p. 4, ll. 33-38)
Terminus uniuocus est qui propter eandem rationem significat res diuersas, sicut iste terminus *animal* significat omne animal sub ista ratione *substantia animata sensibilis.*	Terminus univocus est qui per eandem nominis racionem significat res diversas; sicut iste terminus, *homo,* significat omnem hominem sub ista racione que est *animal racionale.* Et iste terminus, *animal,* significat omne animal sub ista racione qua est *substancia animata sensibilis . . .*

(f. 1ʳ, ll. 35-37)
Terminus denominatus est qui imponitur alicui ab arte, uel habitu, uel officio, uel potentia siue proprietate aliqua, et habet consimile principium et dissimilem finem illi termino a quo dicitur, ut a *grammatica grammaticus*, et a *fortitudine fortis*.

(p. 5, ll. 5-10)
Terminus denominatus est, qui imponitur alicui aliene rei ab arte vel ab habitu, vel ab officio, vel a potencia sive a proprietate alia, et habet consimile principium et dissimilem finem ab illo termino a quo dicitur; ut a *grammatica* dicitur *grammaticus*, tanquam ab arte, et a *fortitudine* dicitur *fortis* . . .

(f. 1ᵛ, ll. 6-8)
Termini distrahentes sunt ut *mortuum, consummatum, corruptum*. Et termini ampliatiui sunt qui suam significationem extendunt universaliter ad futura uel preterita uel possibilia et aliquando impossibilia, ut isti termini: *oppinabile* [*sic*], *intelligibile, possibile*; similiter verba intelliget: *potest, significat, appetit*.

(p. 6, ll. 2-7)
Termini distrahentes sunt isti termini: *mortuum, corruptum, falsum*, etc. Termini ampliativi sunt qui secundum suam significacionem extendunt universaliter ad futura vel ad praeteritia vel ad possibilia vel aliquando ad impossibilia; ut isti termini, *fuit, erit, opinabile, impossibile, intelligibile, significabile, potest, significat*, etc.

(f. 1ᵛ, ll. 8-11)
Termini modales sunt isti: *possibile, impossibile, contingens, necessarium*; et eorum adverbia *possibiliter, impossibiliter, contingenter, necessario*, et quilibet terminus qui modificat significationem alicuius orationis, sicut: *contingit hominem currere*, vel *contingenter homo currit*.

(p. 6, ll. 8-12)
Termini modales sunt isti: *possibile, impossibile, necessarium, contingens* et eorum adverbia; ut *possibiliter, impossibiliter, necessario, contingenter*, et quilibet terminus qui modificat significacionem alicuius oracionis, sicut hic: *contingit hominem currere*, vel *contingenter homo currit*.

Notes

[1]The description and analysis of this manuscript was the final project of the Auxiliary Disciplines Seminar for the Spring term, 1991: Richard C. Adler, Rafael Burgos-Mirabal, Alan Cooper, Philip Daileader, Adam J. Kosto, Thomas Spence, and Carol Symes; with the advice of Professor Michael McCormick. The division of labor was as follows: Adler and Cooper studied the notarial documents, Daileader analyzed the codicology, and Kosto examined the paleography; Burgos-Mirabal, Spence, and Symes edited and compared textual soundings with John Wyclif's *De logica*. Kosto and Symes redacted each student's individual report into this discussion.

[2]See, for example, Elio Conte, ed., *I notai Fiorentini dell'età di Dante* (Florence, 1978), *passim*. Jeremy Catto ("Some English Manuscripts of Wyclif's Latin Works," in Anne Hudson and Michael Wilks, eds., *From Ockham to Wyclif*, Studies in Church History, Subsidia 5 (Oxford, 1987), 354) suggests "court documents."

[3]On registers see, e.g, Diane Owen Hughes, "Towards Family Ethnography: Notarial Records and Family History in the Middle Ages," *Historical Methods Newsletter* 7 (1974), 61-71. V. Federici, *La scrittura delle cancellerie italiane dal sec. XII al XVII*, 2 vols. (Rome, 1934; repr. Turin, 1964), plate LI (a page from a twelfth-century Genovese register) bears striking similarities to the lower script.

[4]The month of February is indicated on both sides of the innermost bifolium, which would make the date of the documents February 1292 by modern reckoning: the Florentine calendar began on the Feast of the Annunciation.

[5]Williel R. Thomson, *The Latin Writings of John Wycliff: An Annotated Catalog*, Subsidia Medievalia 14 (Toronto, 1983); "Manuscripta Wyclifiana Desiderata: The Potential Contribution of Missing Latin Texts to Our Image of Wyclif's Life and Works," *From Ockham to Wyclif*, 344 n.4.

[6]Catto, 354 n.5; Anne Hudson, Review of Paul Vincent Spade and Gordon Anthony Williams, eds., *Johannis Wyclif Summa Insolubilium*, in *Review of English Studies* 39 (1988), 160.

[7]Hudson, Review, 160; L. M. de Rijk, "Logica Oxoniensis," *Medioevo* 3 (1977), 153-4.

[8]Jean Destrez, *La Pecia dans les manuscrits universitaires du xiiie et du xive siècle* (Paris, 1935).

[9]Michael Henry Dziewicki, ed., *Johannis Wyclif Tractatus de logica* (London, 1893).

[10]Thomson, *The Latin Writings*, 4.

[11]Although several scholars believe that the *De logica* may have been revised and expanded by Wyclif as late as 1383; see Norman Kretzmann, "Continua, Indivisibles, and Change," in Anthony Kenny, ed., *Wyclif in His Times* (Oxford, 1986), 41 n.35.

[12]de Rijk, 159.

[13]Anthony Kenny (*Wyclif* [Oxford, 1985], 97) notes that "the proportions of the work are less distorted than is usual in Wyclif's later works."

[14]See, for instance, Katherine Walsh, "Wyclif's Legacy in Central Europe in the Late Fourteenth and Early Fifteenth Centuries," *From Ockham to Wyclif*, 397-417.

[15]Catto, 354. Catto, however, assumes that the Houghton manuscript must have been made by an Italian studying at Oxford.

[16]E. Garin, "La cultura fiorentina nella seconda metà del Trecento e i 'barbari Britanni' " in *L'età nuova: ricerche d'istoria della cultura dal XII al XVI secolo* (Naples, 1969), 144-166. We wish to thank Professor James Hankins for bringing this reference to our attention.

[17]Ed. Dziewicki.

Season of Mist and mellow fruitfulness,
Close bosom friend of the maturing sun;
Conspiring with him how to load and bless
The Vines with fruit that round the thatch eves run
    To bend with apples the moss'd Cottage trees
    And fill all fruits with ripeness to the core
        To swell the gourd, and plump the hazle shells
With a white kernel; to set budding more
    And still more, later flowers for the bees,
Until they think warm days will never cease
        For Summer has o'er brimm'd their clammy cells —

Who hath not seen thee? for thy stores?
    Sometimes whoever seeks abroad may find
Thee sitting careless on a granary floor
Thy hair soft lifted by the winnowing wind
    While bright the sun slants through the barn;
    on on a half reap'd furrow sound asleep
    Or sound asleep in a half reaped field

    Dosed with red poppies; while thy reaping hook
Spares from some slumberous minute while warm slumbers creep
        Or on a half reap'd furrow sound asleep
    Dos'd with the fume of poppies, while thy hook
    Spares the next swath, and all its twined flowers
    Spares for some slumbrous minutes the next swath;

    And sometimes like a gleaner thou dost keep
        Steady thy laden head across the brook;
        Or by a Cyder-press with patient look
    Thou watchest the last oozing hours by hours

5

Reading Keats in Manuscript

Areader comes to the manuscript of a poem knowing the poem itself by heart. What can the manuscript tell her that she doesn't already know?

I learned the answer to that question early, in the almost indecent amount of time that I spent, in my sixteenth year, among the Dylan Thomas manuscripts (on microfilm-loan to me at the Boston Public Library from the Lockwood Library in Buffalo). The thirty or forty versions of *Fern Hill* or *The Ballad of the Long-Legged Bait* taught me something about how poems were made. They yielded up secrets not to be found in the printed poem, obscure links to other poems, primitive versions of accomplished lines, repeated mannerisms repeatedly censored. And even when the manuscript matched the printed version, the mere work of puzzling out handwriting made my eye notice aspects of the poem that the more regular appearance of print had smoothed over.

"What can the manuscript of *To Autumn* tell me?" I wondered when I first read it in transcription (later I was to see it on display in the Keats Room). For a long time, I hadn't even known there was a manuscript of the single supreme lyric that I prized, then as now, higher than any other. The survival of the manuscript seemed miraculous (and was, in effect, almost that; Keats's brother George, in Kentucky, gave it to a young woman from New Orleans who had brought him flowers from Keats's grave in Italy; she brought it to Boston with her when she married, and later presented it to her granddaughter, who gave it to Amy Lowell, from whom it passed to the Harvard College Library).

I have seen different things in the manuscript over time, since one sees according to the questions one asks. I want to mention some of them here, by way of illustration of the use of manuscripts, especially such a rich one as this first draft. Unlike some first drafts (those of Yeats, for instance) it gives us, more or less, the poem we already know: a poem in three stanzas, addressed to the allegorical figure of Autumn (a figure drawn from the myth of Demeter, and endowed with her attributes, poppies and a reaping hook). The first stanza, beginning with the mists of dawn, celebrates the cooperation of the warmth of the masculine sun and the moisture of the maternal earth to bring about swelling autumn fruitfulness; and it shows the earliest harvest, that of the bees from the flowers. The second, a noontide stanza, sketches the figure of Autumn in repose during the corn-harvest activities of threshing, reaping, and gleaning, and the apple-harvest activity of pressing the apples to extract their juice for cider. The third, an evening stanza, presents the earth after all the harvests are over, and makes us hear the chorus of the creatures singing above the stubble plains, made rosy by sunset. The first stanza is in close focus, the second in middle focus, and the third expands outward in space to the horizons and the skies. The poem is written in eleven-line stanzas; the first four lines, rhyming *abab*, make a "Shakespearean" quatrain (Keats had been reading Shakespeare's sonnets); the last seven lines make up an expanded "sestet" (as from a Petrarchan sonnet), rhyming *cde cdde* in stanzas two and three, and *cded cce* in stanza one. I will return to the anomaly of stanza one.

The very appearance of the ode on the handwritten page is different from that of the printed version. In the manuscript, the poem seeps rightward, with the closing "sestet" indented further than the opening quatrain; the poem, in this draining slope, enacts the wanings and last oozings that it confronts, mourns, and celebrates. We notice, here, what we probably missed on the printed page: the anomaly of rhyme in stanza one. Lines 5-8 of stanza one (rhyming *trees: core: shells: more*) "look like" another quatrain, matching more or less, only with alternate rhyme, the quatrain of lines 1-4. Lines 9-10 compose a couplet (*bees: cease*); and it is not until we come to the last line, with its rhyme-word *cells*, that we see that what we have is not Q-1, Q-2, C, ? but rather Q-1 plus expanded "sestet." After stanza one, the poem "decides" not to give the appearance of being written in Shakespearean quatrains and couplets, and in the next two stanzas, no "false quatrain" obscures our sense that the initial quatrain in each stanza is clearly separate in form from the following "sestet." Keats used a hybrid ten-line ode stanza (a Shakespearean quatrain followed by some version of a Petrarchan sestet) in the *Ode on a Grecian Urn* and the *Ode on Melancholy*, wanting to get away from the "pouncing" couplet of the Shakespearean sonnet form. In *To Autumn*, he changes this form by making his "sestet" seven lines long, the "extra" line marking his reluctance to see Autumn end. The "extra" tenth line acts out, in the first two stanzas, its own message — the bees believe in their own self-deceiving prolongation of a summer mood; the watcher at the cider-press keeps a death-bed vigil (long after it is necessary) over the last oozings of the apple-pressing. Only in the last stanza is the "extra" line neutral and even cheerful, adding yet another sound, the redbreast's whistle, to the evening chorus.

Keats's many misspellings are in part surely the result of haste, as his mind races too fast for his pen. But some misspellings are suggestive. The sun is *naturring* (for *maturing*): *orr* (for *or*) has been proleptically contaminated by the upcoming *furrow*; *red* becomes (by contamination from *reap*) *read*; and (by the same process) *thou dost* becomes *thost dost*. By associative contamination, *slumbers* become (from *slump*) *slumpers*, and *wailful* becomes *waiful* (the gnats are waifs). In the most interesting of all, *aloft* is transcribed as *afots*, by contamination, I'd guess, both from *afoot* (remembering the gleaner keeping her head steady across a brook) and by the nearby *soft*. The rhyme *c-reep* arises from *reap-ing*, but is discarded.

And that brings us to the rhymes. The first stanza is so free of corrections that one suspects Keats had already composed it mentally while on his walk to St. Cross:

How beautiful the season is now — How fine the air. A temperate sharpness about it. Really, without joking, chaste weather — Dian skies — I never lik'd stubble fields so much as now — Aye better than the chilly green of the spring. Somehow a stubble plain looks warm — in the same way that some pictures look warm — this struck me so much in my Sunday's walk that I composed upon it.

It was the second stanza that gave Keats trouble on many counts, one of which was rhyme. The first line originally ended with the word *many*, and we can imagine Keats thinking forward to a possible rhyme for it in line 3: *henny? penny? fenny? Jenny?* Hardly. And so he changes it, influenced by the many *-ore* rhymes he had probably run through in composing stanza 1 with its *core* and *more*. He writes *oft amid thy stores*, cancels the plural, and follows it with the wonderful picture of Autumn *sitting careless on a granary floor*. He then begins his sestet with two very promising lines, but the same problem arises: what rhymes with *barn*? *Yarn? darn? tarn?* No, too improbable for a rustic pastoral. And what rhymes with *field*? The possibilities are more numerous, but they too are lexically unsuited to agriculture: *keeled, pealed (peeled), wield, steeled, healed, sealed,* and so on. A few moments later Keats is in trouble again when he ends a line with *swath* (*cloth? froth? moth? broth?*). Again he changes the rhyme. And so the three opening lines of the "sestet" are rewritten with the easier rhymes *asleep* and *hook* and *flowers*, generating the further end-words [*creep*] *keep, brook, look,* and *hours*. Without the (allegorically necessary) reaper's hook, we might not have had the brook, or the third-stanza river it pours into, which marks one boundary of the farm, concentrically described around its focal cottage.

The third stanza shows only one line-long revision: *While a gold cloud gilds the soft-dying day* is changed to *While barrèd clouds bloom the soft-dying day*. The revision tells us that Keats recognized that he was here lifting an effect from Chatterton ("with his *gold* hand *gilding* the fall*ing* leaf") who had borrowed it from Shakespeare ("Kissing with *golden* face the meadows green, / *Gilding* pale streams with heavenly alchemy"). Probably Keats realized, too, that the "artificiality" and "courtliness" of gilding was not what he wanted in a poem about nature and agriculture. The *gold/gilding* went, and were replaced by the more vegetative *bloom*, which drew in its wake the alliterating *barrèd*.

Even minute revisions can reveal a whole atmosphere. The first and third stanzas are full of the specificity of the definite article: the sun, the vines, the thatch eaves, the gourd, the hazel shells, the bees; the stubble plains, the river sallows, the gnats, the redbreast, and so on. But in the second stanza, Keats wants to write in general terms, and the articles change to the indefinite: a granary floor, a half-reaped furrow, a brook, a cider press. We can see that at first Keats was tempted to continue the specificity of stanza 1 in stanza 2, as he began "While bright *the* sun slants through *the* husky barn." And he kept that specificity quite a long time, in fact, writing further down "across *the* brook." The fact that he consciously de-specified the brook into "a brook" and deleted the sun and the barn tells us he was aware of wanting to make the second stanza general rather than specific. The only specifying *the's* that remain are given from the harvester's own perspective, not the speaker's; she feels her hair lifted by *the* wind, she is drowsed with *the* fume of poppies, and she briefly spares *the* swath that lies next in her reaping.

The generalities — "Who hath *not* seen thee?" (everyone has, in fact) and "*Whoever* seeks abroad may find / Thee" — determine that the sights summoned up in this stanza are available to anyone walking through autumn fields, and are not rare, but familiar. The verbs of the stanza are in the habitual present, introduced by "often" or "sometimes." Keats's very care in correcting this stanza into generality — any granary floor, any half-reaped furrow, any brook, any cider-press — means that we are expected to recognize, in the first stanza, the specificity-to-the-speaker of the central cottage with its thatched eaves, its vines, its apple-orchard, its vegetable-garden, its hazelnut tree, and its beehives. Keats once referred to himself as a "spiritual cottager."

In the last stanza, the implied "now" of stanza 1 (palpable in its humming present participles and infinitives of purpose) becomes a voiced *now*, bringing us into the instant and specific moment of the lyric speaker: "And *now* with treble soft / The redbreast whistles." We know not only the speaker's "now" but also his "here": he is standing where he can see the sunset clouds touching the stubble plains with a rosy hue, and where he can hear the choir of gnats *among* the willows at the river; *from* the hill above him he hears the sheep, *from* the hedges the crickets, *from* a garden-croft the redbreast, and (as he lifts his eyes) *in* the skies the swallows. This stationing of a particular speaker in a particular place at a particular instant is far from the generalized "Whoever" of stanza 2. The central panel of Keats's triptych offers us, as if by overflow from the perceptions of the speaker, the general experience of Autumn available to any one of us. That central panel is flanked on either side by a panel of personal and individual response.

Keats's last revision, in the last line of the poem, bears looking at. He first wrote *gathering* swallows, changed it to *gather'd* swallows, and then (apparently having changed his mind) let it appear in print as *gathering* swallows. We might hazard a guess about his motives. *Gathering* participates in the run of -*ing* words (nouns, verbs, and participles) so important to the poem: *maturing, conspiring, budding, sitting, winnowing,* [*reaping*], *oozings, Spring, dying,* [*touching*], *sinking, sing.* (Keats was thinking *sing* so intensely that he wrote *Sping* for *Spring*, and saw the -*wing* in *winno-wing* so clearly that he wrote *wing* first for *wind*.) On the other hand, *gather'd* could also participate in a significant run of words, the past participles in -*ed* or -'*d* of the poem: *moss'd, o'er-brimm'd, lifted, reap'd, drows'd, twinèd, barrèd.* The word *gathered* implies agency (gathered sheaves have been brought together by reapers, but no one has, in this sense, "gathered" the swallows). Keats deletes God from his poem when he restores *gathering*, and attributes to the swallows their own voluntary clustering at dusk.

My next observation on the use of looking at manuscripts has nothing to do with what one gains from thinking about revisions, important and revealing as these are. Rather, I want to add that it wasn't until I saw *To Autumn* word by word (as one does in manuscript work) rather than line by line, or stanza by stanza, or sentence by sentence, that I realized the great amount of lexical redundancy in the poem. Keats repeats the phonemes -*ed* (-'*d*) and -*ing* astonishingly often, as we have seen. But, as he composes, he also repeats whole words: *fruitfulness/fruit/fruits; sun/*[*sun*]*; still/still; creep/reap; flowers/flowers; days/day; sometimes/sometimes; oft/soft-/soft-/soft; wind/wind; songs/ sing; -dying/dies.* This is a very large amount of lexical repetition for a 33-line poem, and like the "extra" tenth line, contributes formally to the sense of plenitude the poem exists to convey. However, one can read the poem in print, receive the effect, and yet not see its means. "What she sang," says Stevens about his singer in Key West, "was uttered word by word." It is the word-by-word reading prompted by a manuscript that raises repetition to saliency.

My final point has to do with the cancellation in stanza 2 of the wonderful line *While bright the sun slants through the husky barn*. The word *bright* functions both as adverb ("brightly") and as adjective ("the bright sun"); and the sun's presence in the barn filled with the motes of chaff connects both to its maturing presence in stanza 1 and to its presence making the stubble plains rosy in stanza 3. Why then would Keats cancel the presence of the sun in stanza 2? The difficulties of rhyme posed by *barn* could easily have been avoided by writing something like *While bright the sun slants through the husky air / Withindoors*. Why would Keats give up this brilliant image of the sunbeam made visible by floating grain-husks, which would connect the sun of noon to the sun of misty morning and the sun of rosy evening?

Such a question leads us to look more closely at the appearances of the sun or its effects throughout the poem. We then notice that the sun is occluded in stanza 1 by mists, as he is in stanza 3 by clouds. And, now that Keats has made his revision, the sun is altogether invisible in stanza 2. The sun — though doing his work (contributing the paternal warmth that makes his partner the maternal earth generate fruit, guaranteeing the *store* of the noontide harvester, and conferring even on the denuded stubble fields the evening *bloom* reminiscent of spring) is in this poem not directly accessible to the speaker.

It is probably only by knowing Keats's lifelong attempts to write of Apollo (the Sun-God who is also the god of medicine, Keats's first profession, and poetry, his vocation) that we can approach an answer to the question of the occluded and even cancelled sun. Keats had decided at this point to de-Miltonize himself, and to de-classicize his poems: "English must be kept up." This means writing about Demeter the Harvester and Apollo the Sun-God without giving them their mythological names (as he had in his earlier work, where Apollo makes many appearances). In sober modern English reality, we cannot see the Sun-God; and so here we are allowed only to intuit his presence behind mists and clouds, morning and evening; and at noon, where we might most expect radiant theophany, we see him not at all.

To secularize his poem thus was for Keats a radical departure. "The beautiful mythology of Greece" (as he had called it in writing about his long poem *Endymion*) had been his creed, replacing the Christianity in which he had been baptized and which he had rejected. The secular spirit of the ode *To Autumn*, in which Apollo is invisible and the goddess Demeter has been replaced by a human harvest-figure everywhere visible to everyone, reflects Keats's sacrifice, for the sake of truth, of one of his warmest and most deeply-felt resources, explicit classical myth. Because the manuscript of *To Autumn* exists, we can read the cancelled *While bright the sun slants through the husky barn,* and understand more deeply how, for Keats, "Truth is best music," even if it means a farewell to a visible Apollo.

Helen Vendler

Trompeten

von GEORG TRAKL

Unter verschnittenen Weiden, wo ~~weisse~~ Kinder spielen
Und Blätter treiben, tönen Trompeten. Kirchhofsschauer.
Fahnen von Scharlach stürzen durch des Ahorns Trauer,
Reiter entlang an Roggenfeldern, leeren Mühlen.

Oder Hirten singen nachts und Hirsche treten
In den Kreis ihrer Feuer, des Hains uralte Trauer,
Tanzende heben sich von einer schwarzen Mauer;
Fahnen von Scharlach, Lachen, Wahnsinn, Trompeten.

12

Georg Trakl, *Trompeten,* periodical print used as printers' copy for *Gedichte,* 1913.

6

A Variant in Trakl's Trompeten

DURING THE FIRST WEEKS OF NOVEMBER 1912 Georg Trakl sent to his friend Erhard Buschbeck in Vienna the first version of his poem *Trompeten*. It contains several verses quite different from the final text:

> Unter verschnittenen Weiden, wo *weisse* Kinder spielen
> Und Blätter treiben, tönen Trompeten; *Verfall und Trauer.*
> *Scharlachfarben, Marschtakt stürzt durch Staub und Stahlschauer,*
> *Durch ein* Roggenfeld, *entlang an* leeren Mühlen.
> Oder Hirten singen nachts und Hirsche treten
> In den Kreis ihrer Feuer, des Hains uralte Trauer.
> Tanzende heben sich von einer schwarzen Mauer;
> *Scharlachfarben*, Lachen, Wahnsinn, Trompeten.

Trakl wanted Buschbeck to insert this poem in the third number of a periodical called *Der Ruf*, which was to come out in that month, collecting writings related to the war. He asked him to put his poem at the end of the number to be sure it would not be in bad company. Later on he asked Buschbeck to correct the end of the second verse into "Kirchhofstrauer," to change completely the third verse into "Fahnen von Scharlach stürzen durch des Ahorns Trauer," and to modify the fourth verse: "Reiter entlang an Roggenfeldern, leeren Mühlen." Finally he mentioned a second stanza (which means that he had meanwhile divided the poem in two equal parts) and wanted the last verse to run as follows:

> Fahnen von Scharlach, Lachen, Wahnsinn, Trompeten.

About this verse he wrote later: "The last verse is a criticism of the delirium that drowns itself."

The printed page we have here is from the periodical *Der Ruf*. It has two corrections in Trakl's hand: instead of "weisse Kinder" he writes "schmutzige Kinder"; and he adds "*Ein* Kirchhofsschauer." In the final version, in *Gedichte* (Leipzig: Kurt Wolff 1913, Der jüngste Tag 7/8, p. 39), the first verse changes again: "wo *braune* Kinder spielen."

The first version was written at the end of September 1912 at Innsbruck. In the first version the war theme is represented directly with "Marschtakt" and "Staub und Stahlschauer," less directly with "Scharlachfarben" instead of "Fahnen von Scharlach" and with the omission of "Reiter." The addition of "Ahorn" stresses the color red, and with "Kirchhofsschauer" the anticipation of death enters the poem.

On the whole it constitutes a mixture of war themes and of motives particularly characteristic of Trakl, like Weiden, Kinder, Kirchhof, Trauer, Hain, schwarze Mauer, Lachen, Wahnsinn. The fragmentation of the world — leaves, sounds, showers, flags, laughter — invokes a situation of violent disturbance. But simultaneously a solemn, even a holy atmosphere surrounds the scene. An arcadian night — "Hirten," "Hain" — confers an archaic tone upon it.

The only uncertainty in the final elaboration process is the color of the children under the willows. First they are *white*, later *dirty*, at the end *brown*. The change visible on our page is the only word soon to be abandoned again. "Schmutzig" occurs very rarely in Trakl's poems and is usually related to a world inherited from Rimbaud (for instance, for the dirty water of laundry!). It doesn't fit into this poem. The solution "brown" instead of "white" passed through the transitional "dirty." "Brown" is well accorded to the autumnal trees and to the cemetery in this season. It was important for Trakl to concentrate not on the children, but on the war elements (trumpets, flags) and on the final delirium in a Dionysiac apocalypse. The coincidence of dances and of a black wall indicates the double presence of ecstasy and death. And both break into the quiet sphere of an archaic pastoral scenery.

Trakl is an artist who combines in an original way elements belonging to quite opposed themes. His text ends with isolated evocations, a final dissolution in concentrated and intense debris. The language, kin to that of Rimbaud and Hölderlin, creates density through destruction. This process owes much to the use of colors. They signify death (white, black) or decadence (dirty, brown) in an always fluctuating and hesitating manner. Our page is a pertinent example of this strange particularity, which struck Paul Celan, as his copy of Trakl's poems testifies. (He underlined the four last words of our poem!)

This poem appears immediately next to "Psalm," a great poem that follows Rimbaud's method of adding verses by the use of an anaphoric "or." There we have also war, dances, delirium, and a paradise lost. This great poem was written in the same weeks as *Trompeten*. In both cases Trakl used a new rhythmical system, free verse. It is quite possible that the changes we observe on our page (*schmutzig*; *ein* Kirchhofsschauer) are also related to this innovation.

Bernard Böschenstein

7

Alexander Pope, An Essay on Man, Epistles I-III

In examining familiar things we come to such
unfamiliar conclusions that our very language
is twisted and bent even as it guides us.
Writing "under erasure" is the mark of this
contortion.

Gayatri Spivak

I F, AS VALERY SUGGESTED, "a poem is never finished, it is only abandoned," then authorial manuscripts — even more than their printed counterparts — should provide us with the materials for a poetics of abandonment. Such a poetics would be based, of course, on a principle of imperfection, on the knowledge that even the greatest poems are willfully (or reluctantly) abandoned by their authors to the public, passed as fresh currency in the literary marketplace before they could be even more finely wrought. And of revision, polishing, and embellishment there is no end, unless author and text alike are to become rotten with perfection.

No one in English has written poems more finely nor drawn such incessant attention to the niceties of his craft than the enigmatic figure who translated the roughshod Homer for his eighteenth-century audience:

> Be *Homer*'s Works your *Study*, and *Delight*,
> Read them by Day, and meditate by Night,
> Thence form your Judgment, thence your Maxims bring,
> And trace the Muses *upward* to their *Spring*.

And yet Pope, of all people, discloses an unusual ambivalence in his strategies of textual abandonment. Take, for example, the opening epistle of *An Essay on Man*, which Pope delivered to the public in late February of 1733. Rarely has a poem of such disarming ambition been published in such a tentative way. Pope "Address'd" the poem "to a FRIEND," but did not name him. He stipulated that this was merely "PART I," thus signaling that more text (and more expense) would follow. He not only published the

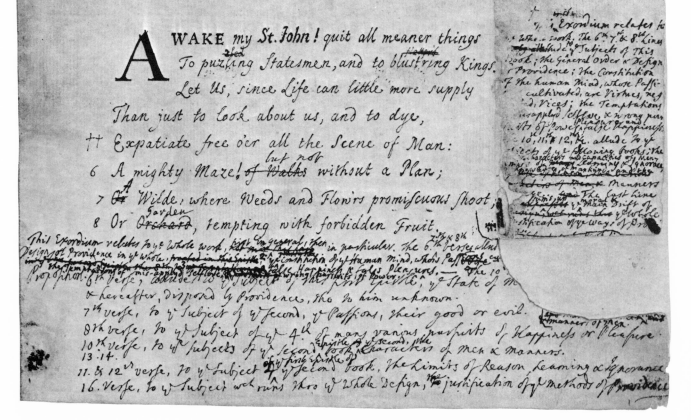

ETHIC EPISTLES.

THE

FIRST BOOK,

TO

Henry St. John Lord B.

AWAKE my St. John! quit all meaner things
To puzzling Statesmen, and to blust'ring Kings.
Let Us, since Life can little more supply
Than just to look about us, and to dye,
†† Expatiate free o'er all the Scene of Man:
6 A mighty Maze! of Walks without a Plan;
7 A Wilde, where Weeds and Flow'rs promiscuous shoot;
8 Or Orchard, tempting with forbidden Fruit.

Alexander Pope, *An Essay on Man,* autograph.

epistle anonymously, but went out of his way to convince his readers that he was not the poem's author: "*As he* imitates *no Man, so he would be thought to vye with no Man in these Epistles, particularly with the noted Author of* TWO *lately published*" (the "Epistle to Bathurst" and "The First Satire of the Second Book of Horace," both of which bore Pope's name). It was also his practice to purchase several copies of his newly published poems so that he could mark them up for later editions. It should therefore not surprise us that only three months later he would issue the text again, "Corrected by the AUTHOR," only to supersede it the following year when the four epistles were published in a corrected, collected edition that still failed to proclaim Pope's authorship but did include the formal dedication to Bolingbroke.

It might therefore be prudent to say that Pope did not abandon his poems so much as *launch* them: delivering them to the public without, at least at first, benefit of authorial protection; carefully gauging their progress in the coffeehouses and the press; correcting, revising, and amplifying them as epistle followed epistle; and then collecting them in a standard edition that itself would take different forms (folio, quarto, octavo) and eventually be superseded by later collections, with the text continuing to be fine-tuned even for the so-called "death-bed edition" compiled by Warburton. Important substantive changes were introduced at several stages in the chain of textual transmission, but no detail was too small to be neglected. Pope tinkered assiduously with punctuation, capitalization (including small caps), the spacing as well as the precise sequence of verse paragraphs, the ornaments, initial letters, and introductory material, the frontispiece, and especially the play between roman and italic, preferring a consciously simple, unadorned, roman style for the collected editions, but providing helpful italics for the readers of his popular editions. A poem by Pope, in other words, may have been easily — if carefully and cunningly — abandoned into print, but it finally escaped the authorial imprint of its progenitor only with the poet's death.

Pope's manuscripts tell an even more complicated tale. Two holographs of *An Essay on Man* have survived; both were at one time in the possession of Jonathan Richardson the Younger, to whom Pope presented all of his papers "for the pains I [Richardson] took in collating the whole with the printed editions, at his request, on my having proposed to him the 'making an edition of his works in the manner of Boileau's.'" The earlier of the two manuscripts, now at the Pierpont Morgan Library, actually contains all four of the completed poem's epistles, whereas the Houghton manuscript, which may date from the summer of 1731, contains only the first three. It is generally agreed that the Houghton manuscript began as a fair copy of the Morgan manuscript before the fourth epistle was begun (we know that Pope often produced such fair copies for his friends, only to begin treating them as alternative working copies soon afterwards). On the first page of text in the Houghton manuscript (illustrated here), we encounter, for instance, not only a full title and dedication — both lacking in Morgan — but also an example of Pope's formal, "print" hand actually imitating the letters and rules of a typeset edition. This marvelously fine, spidery hand fills both manuscripts. Pope's informal hand (much rougher, larger, and angular) is rarely to be found, although both holographs include numerous revisions and additions that betray some of the heat of composition, particularly in the marginal commentaries on the poem.

Generally speaking, the Morgan manuscript is more heavily reworked than Houghton's, especially the fourth epistle, which Maynard Mack describes as "the roughest of all Pope's surviving working papers"; but many of the more extensive (and permanent) revisions occur in Houghton, and some — not surprisingly — occur in both. The text of the first edition (1733a) follows neither manuscript exactly, nor would we expect it to; the uncertainty of both holographs suggests that there must have been yet another working copy that reconciled these two and, beyond that, perhaps a fair copy for the printer as well. This is certainly borne out by the rest of Richardson's commentary: "As for his *Essay on Man*, . . . I was witness to the whole conduct of it in writing, and actually have his original MSS. for it from the first scratches of the four books, to the several finished copies (of his own neat and elegant writing these last)." What is certain, however, is Pope's reluctance to abandon earlier, rougher, less visually pleasing drafts, even after the poem had been launched into print. (Nor, for that matter, did he completely abandon the textual variants themselves after the printed poem had appeared: the 1736 collected edition of his works included variants in the manner of a classical text!) Two examples from the opening of the poem pose some of the complications. Consider, in the first place, the poet's invocation of his friend Bolingbroke:

> *Morgan*: Awake my Memmius, leave all meaner things
> *Houghton*: Awake my St. John! quit all meaner things
> *1733a*: AWAKE! my LÆLIUS, leave all meaner Things
> *1733b*: AWAKE! my LÆLIUS, leave all meaner Things
> *1734*: AWAKE! my ST. JOHN! leave all meaner things

Here we can see Pope moving initially from the classical and anonymous Memmius of the Morgan manuscript to the honest and familiar St. John of the Houghton copy, which also substitutes "quit" for "leave." Neither change, it should be noted, emerges at the expense of a deletion; both were fresh (but mature) thoughts *before* Pope wrote out what appears, at first, to have been a fair copy. By the time the first epistle was published (1733a), Pope had decided to return to "leave" and to choose a more formal name for Bolingbroke — but not the Memmius of the Morgan manuscript. The second edition that followed a few months later (1733b) included no changes in the opening line, but a year later, having now dedicated the four-epistle poem to Bolingbroke, Pope reverted to the St. John of the Houghton manuscript and stayed with it until he died.

The sixth, seventh, and eighth lines disclose a textual transmission that is almost as convoluted — and much more famous — as Pope invites us to join him in examining the "*Scene of Man*":

> *Morgan*:
> A mighty *Maze!* of *Walks* without a Plan;
> Or *Wilde*, where Weeds and Flowrs promiscuous shoot;
> Or *Orchard*, tempting with forbidden Fruit.

Houghton:

> A Mighty Maze! but not without a Plan;
> A Wilde, where Weeds and Flow'rs promiscuous shoot;
> Or Garden, tempting with forbidden Fruit.

1733a:

> A mighty Maze! of walks without a Plan;
> Or Wild, where weeds and flow'rs promiscuous shoot;
> Or Garden, tempting with forbidden fruit.

1733b:

> A mighty Maze! but not without a Plan;
> A Wild, where weeds and flowers promiscuous shoot,
> Or Garden, tempting with forbidden fruit.

In this collation we see that all three variants which emerge in the Houghton manuscript are interlineations that suppress a cancelled original, and this naturally suggests that they were afterthoughts made following the publication of the first edition, which follows the Morgan text. But this is not true of Pope's transition from an "*Orchard*" to a "Garden" within the Houghton manuscript, for "Garden" was printed in the *first* edition. The ink, the hand, and the method of insertion are identical here to the examples in the previous two lines, even though it is logical to conclude that those changes were made at a slightly later date.

Uncertainties and ambiguities such as these are the stock-in-trade of both the Morgan and the Houghton manuscripts, and it is unlikely whether the precise relationship of the two holographs to each other — and to the early printings — will ever be completely gauged without recourse to even more manuscript material. If we are faced with an embarrassment of riches, it is only because the generation and makeover of Pope's works are so unrelentingly complicated that we continually aspire to possess *all* of the poetical documents that the author presented to the younger Richardson. Even working within these inevitable restraints, however, scholars have been able to put the two surviving manuscripts to remarkably good use. Mack has demonstrated how the progress from Morgan to Houghton to the first edition discloses the development of a more serious decorum in the poem that can be glimpsed in its increased gravity and abstraction. "But the right decorum did not reveal itself to the poet in a flash," Mack cautiously warns: "it was painfully won." Miriam Leranbaum has carefully examined the manuscripts in her effort to chart the relationship between *An Essay on Man* and the ambitious but never completed *Opus Magnum* of which it was to form the first part. And David Foxon, who has scrutinized both the manuscripts and the early printings of this and other poems by Pope with an unusual eye for the telling detail, has been able to suggest just how closely the poet worked for (and with) his printers, and how carefully he prepared his texts with both their immediate *and* their later editions in mind. For a comparable example of such extraordinary forethought one would have to turn to Hogarth's practice of executing his paintings in reverse so that the inverted engravings later taken from them would possess the image the artist originally had in mind and ultimately wished to disseminate.

But the problems and ambiguities persist, and justifiably so in a philosophical poem that marked a new turning in the author's career. Critical fervor has been most heated, moreover, whenever it has focused on the revision in the sixth line that instructed Pope's readers to envision "the *Scene of Man*" not as a mighty maze "of *Walks* without a Plan," which was the reading in the Morgan manuscript and the first printing (1733a), but rather as a mighty maze that is "not without a Plan," the interlinear reading in the Houghton copy and in the second (and all subsequent) editions. But how significant, precisely, is the difference between these two variants? Most criticism has in fact tended to explain any distinction away. In his *Life of Pope*, Samuel Johnson — who was no great admirer of this particular poem — bluntly concluded that the poet made this change because, "if there were no plan, it was in vain to describe or to trace the maze." A. D. Nuttall is in agreement: "It is sometimes thought that this change shows how far Pope's mind was from serious theology, since he could switch in a moment from a planless (Godless) universe to a God-directed one. But the earlier version need only imply that we do not possess the plan of the maze."

The young William Empson struck a similar note, arguing that the two lines "are very nearly the same; a *maze* is conceived as something that at once has and has not got a *plan*" in the sense that "it was designed with a *plan* to start with, but the *plan* has since been lost, or at any rate is not being shown to you." This is a level-headed conclusion, especially considering that it derives from a citation of the poem ("A mighty maze, and all without a plan") that neither the Morgan nor the Houghton manuscript can support! And it has essentially been corroborated by Mack, who points out that there is both intricacy and plan in either reading: the first emphasizes the fact that man does not have a chart (or drawing, or sketch) of the maze; the second stresses the fact that there is order in the maze ("plan" here signifying a scheme of arrangement), even though man can obtain only glimmerings of its nature. Mack had recourse to the OED to support his distinctions, but the language he invoked had already been broached by Pope in the "Design" to the collected edition of 1734:

> *What is now published, is only to be considered*
> *as a* general Map *of* MAN, *marking out no more*
> *than the* Greater Parts, *their* Extent, *their*
> Limits, *and their* Connection, *but leaving the*
> *Particular to be more fully delineated in the*
> Charts *which are to follow,*

by which Pope meant the moral epistles and presumably the unfinished poems that were to complete his *Opus Magnum*.

Each of these explanations is reasonable, and yet none tells us why Pope made such a change, nor what the revision does to the larger poetical passage in which it occurs. Let us begin, then, with the maze itself.

A maze is, above all else, a profoundly paradoxical structure. It is manmade, artful, and (because it partakes of natural elements) artificial. A maze makes nature appear to be orderly, but in fact provides more difficulty and mischance than we normally find in nature itself. On the one hand, it tames nature, cultivating — or at least embellishing — the landscape; on the other hand, it intentionally bewilders those who would attempt to penetrate its mysteries. It places natural and human, tame and wild elements in a deliberate tension. By bewildering us, moreover, it figuratively (and paradoxically) places us once again in the wild. As Pope put it in the *Essay on Criticism,*

> Some are bewilder'd in the Maze of Schools,
> And some made *Coxcombs* Nature meant but *Fools.*

Mazes can most easily be analyzed from above (and thus we are asked to "Expatiate free, o'er *all* the *Scene of Man*"), but can only be experienced from below. The maze is, in short, a remarkably rich metaphor that figures the complexity Pope attributed to the human condition.

By specifying that this is a mighty maze "of *Walks* without a Plan," Pope is simply expanding upon the central contradiction that is compressed in the figure of the maze itself. The very fact that there are "*Walks*" signals the presence of design and agency; the italics and capitalization within the Morgan manuscript, moreover, visually reinforce the importance and formality of Pope's expanded metaphor. The maze tempts us to enter, but we have not been provided with a plan (a map, a chart) that will show us how to proceed; and we therefore lack both direction and a sense of security.

The richness of the figure, however, is complicated by Pope's desire that we see the maze in two ways at once. Like so much eighteenth-century verse, *An Essay on Man* is a prospect poem, and our difficulty lies in establishing a perspective or point of view. The invitation Pope extends to us to move freely "o'er" the scene of man prepares us to view the maze from above, whereas the transition to its walks and to the missing plan of its design firmly returns us to our normal, terrestrial perspective (as do the metaphorical "*Wilde*" and "*Orchard*" or "*Garden*" that follow). It is difficult to invoke the language of the senses to describe metaphysical matters but, as Pope discovered in the course of writing his most abstract and philosophical poem, it is the only language we have. In the margins of the manuscripts (and often in the explanations that were appended to the printed texts), Pope could strive toward an even plainer idiom. As the note beneath the exordium on the first page of the Houghton manuscript states, "ye State of Man [is] disposed by Providence, tho to him [to man] unknown." Or as the muscular lines of the first epistle's conclusion protest (perhaps too loudly),

> All Nature is but Art, unknown to thee;
> All Chance, Direction which thou canst not see;
> All Discord, Harmony not understood;
> All partial Evil, universal Good. [1734]

Each of these terms and each of these paradoxes is closely associated with the figure of the maze — even though they are separated from one another by almost 300 lines of verse — but the tension between nature and art is the most telling, for it values art above nature and equates what is artful with what is divine.

The eventual shift in the Houghton manuscript and in later printings of the poem to "A mighty Maze! but not without a Plan" marks more than a mere refinement of Pope's original reading. In the original line, the second half extends and explains the first; in the revised line, however, the second half is set in opposition rather than apposition to the first ("but not without") in a gesture of reassurance. The revision replaces both the logic of the maze and the structure of the poetical argument. If we understand what a maze is, then why do we need to be told there is a design? The only question is whether we will be able to reach the center of the labyrinth, or — to quote from the argument of the poem added in 1734 — view the "NATURE and STATE of MAN, with respect to the UNIVERSE." As Nuttall remarked, "the earlier version need only imply that we do not possess the plan of the maze," and I would argue that it is clearly the weakness of mere implication alone that troubled Pope as he moved in the second half of the line to an explicit statement concerning providential agency. I think it is entirely likely that, in the months following the initial publication of the first epistle, Pope discovered that his readers needed to be given specific directions so that the poem itself did not become an ambiguous and bewildering maze.

What, then, are we to make of the "*Wilde*" of the seventh line and the "*Orchard*" or "*Garden*" of the eighth? Both lines offer us fresh ways of visualizing, through the language of sense, the "mixed" condition that is the "*Scene of Man.*" In the wild, "Weeds and Flowrs promiscuous shoot": here the setting is entirely natural and uncultivated, but the second half of the line necessarily privileges the flowers that are worth cultivating, and underscores the illicit mixing of the two. ("Passions are cultivated or neglected," as Pope's marginal gloss on this line in the Houghton manuscript points out.) The figure of the orchard returns us to the artful nature of the maze, tempting us to enter its exotic domain. The revision in the Houghton manuscript to "Garden" reinforces the Miltonic allusion and domesticates the natural figure even more than a maze does. Here we find an entirely cultivated nature that is *open* to view, even if what it offers is both unfamiliar and forbidden to us. The "*Wilde*" and "Garden" do not modify the maze; they offer us alternative ways of thinking about the scene of man. But together they contain the elements of the maze — a bewildering garden that tempts the beholder to enter — and like the maze they combine the natural and the artful, what is wild and what is cultivated (weeds and flowers, forbidden fruit).

The revisions in the Houghton manuscript should therefore be seen as part of a careful process of domestication (and reassurance) in the opening lines of the poem. They reinforce the reader's sense of human agency and providential order. Pope's need to tinker with his original text, moreover, betrays his difficulty in writing philosophical verse by naturalizing religion (or, at the very least, it betrays his concern for the progress of his readers). Do these surviving variants also provide a record of the poet working through his own argument? Were the marginal plans and commentaries and exordia meant to help *him* as well as us? Was he as struck as we are by his disclaimer in the "Design" that "*There are not many certain Truths in this World*"? Possessing no answers to these questions, we may join Mack in finding what in his "own experience has proved true of poetical manuscripts generally, no matter whose — that they cast little light on the questions of greatest interest."

Poetical manuscripts do, however, inevitably change the way we read the poems they become. Our view of an entire manuscript, or of the transition between one and another, or of the larger chain of textual transmission once the poem has been printed provides us with an extended view of the poet's creative process: a perspective above as well as within the maze. By showing us the alternatives, these manuscripts visually remind us that, no matter how polished and finely wrought the poetical icon may become, texts actually evolve as decisions are slowly and sometimes haltingly made. Textual variants, moreover, enable us to argue with a writer in his or her own terms. What may have been abandoned in printed editions — even in critical editions as elaborate as the Twickenham Pope — remain as pentimenti in the manuscript. It is language *sous ratûre*: not precisely in the Derridean sense, for textual variants are eventually *displaced* rather than simply crossed through or placed "under erasure." But it is nonetheless language that has been claimed, decided against because of its inadequacy, but never entirely abandoned to obscurity so long as these manuscripts survive and scholars continue to be sucked into their vortex.

Readers of manuscripts are no longer innocent readers. Variants inevitably condition our response to a poem or to a particular passage. The phrase "of *Walks* without a Plan" would surely seem less ominous — might, indeed, appear to be perfectly logical — if it had no successor. The line "A Mighty Maze! but not without a Plan" would certainly read differently today if we did not know what had preceded it. And the very fact that I can argue with Pope is based on the evidence we have that Pope argued with himself. My own view is that the revision in the sixth line, while it may have been necessary for Pope's readers, both dissipates the power of the paradox that is figured by the maze and disrupts the strategy by which each introductory metaphor in these three lines is extended (rather than modified) in the words that follow. For Pope (no less than for Derrida) our very language is twisted and bent even as it guides us. But the more important point is that, whether or not the variant here improves or maims the text, the change itself (which speaks so emphatically) actually reflects the tentativeness of the poem. Balance, antithesis, and linguistic tension are crucial throughout the poem. Surely the emendation here is too final, too affirmative, too lapidary for an opening stanza: its self-assurance has not yet been earned.

Perhaps only the language of paradox and contradiction is appropriate to a description of human nature: not just in these few lines but in the many etched passages that follow, and particularly, of course, in the beginning of the second epistle with its rich Shakespearean echoes:

> Plac'd on this Isthmus of a middle state,
> A Being darkly wise, and rudely great;
> With too much Knowledge for the Sceptic side,
> With too much weakness for a Stoic's pride,
> He hangs between; in doubt to act, or rest,
> In doubt to deem himself a God, or Beast,

In doubt his mind or body to prefer,
Born but to die, and reas'ning but to err;
Alike in ignorance, his Reason such,
Whether he thinks too little, or too much.
Chaos of Thought and Passion, all confus'd;
Still by himself abus'd, or dis-abus'd;
Created half to rise, and half to fall;
Great Lord of all things, yet a Prey to all;
Sole Judge of Truth, in endless Error hurl'd,
The Glory, Jest, and Riddle of the world! [1734]

Perhaps we can only augment the paradoxical vision of the *Essay* by turning to Burke —
to *our* Burke, Kenneth — for a definition of man that specifically takes account of the
double-edged nature of the language we wield:

> Man is the symbol-using (symbol-making, symbol-
> misusing) animal, inventor of the negative (or
> moralized by the negative), separated from his
> natural condition by instruments of his own
> making, goaded by the spirit of hierarchy (or
> moved by the sense of order), and rotten with
> perfection.

Richard Wendorf

Burke, Kenneth. *Language as Symbolic Action.* Berkeley: Univ. of California Press, 1966.

Butt, John. "Pope's Poetical Manuscripts." *Proceedings of the British Academy* 40 (1954): 23-39.

Derrida, Jacques. *Of Grammatology.* Trans. Gayatri Chakravorty Spivak. Baltimore: The Johns Hopkins Univ. Press, 1974.

Empson, William. *Seven Types of Ambiguity.* London: Chatto and Windus, 1930.

Foxon, David. *Pope and the Early Eighteenth-Century Book Trade.* Rev. and ed. James McLaverty. The Lyell Lectures, Oxford, 1975-1976. Oxford: Clarendon Press, 1991.

Johnson, Samuel. *Lives of the English Poets.* Ed. George Birkbeck Hill. 3 vols. Oxford: Clarendon Press, 1905.

Leranbaum, Miriam. *Alexander Pope's 'Opus Magnum' 1729-1744.* Oxford: Clarendon Press, 1977.

Mack, Maynard. " 'The Last and Greatest Art': Pope's Poetical Manuscripts." In *Collected in Himself: Essays Critical, Biographical, and Bibliographical on Pope and Some of His Contemporaries.* Newark: Univ. of Delaware Press; London and Toronto: Associated University Presses, 1982, pp. 322-347.

——————, ed. *The Last and Greatest Art: Some Unpublished Poetical Manuscripts of Alexander Pope.* Newark: Univ. of Delaware Press; London and Toronto: Associated University Presses, 1984.

Morris, David B. *Alexander Pope: The Genius of Sense.* Cambridge, Mass.: Harvard Univ. Press, 1984.

Nuttall, A. D. *Pope's "Essay on Man."* London: Allen and Unwin, 1984.

Pope, Alexander. *An Essay on Man.* Ed. Maynard Mack. Vol. 3, Pt. 1 of the Twickenham Edn. of *The Poems of Alexander Pope.* New Haven: Yale Univ. Press; London: Methuen, 1950.

——————. *An Essay on Man: Reproductions of the Manuscripts in the Pierpont Morgan Library and the Houghton Library with the Printed Text of the Original Edition.* Introd. Maynard Mack. Oxford: Roxburghe Club, 1962.

Sherburn, George. "Pope at Work." In *Essays on the Eighteenth Century Presented to David Nichol Smith in honour of his seventieth birthday.* Oxford: Clarendon Press, 1945, pp. 49-64.

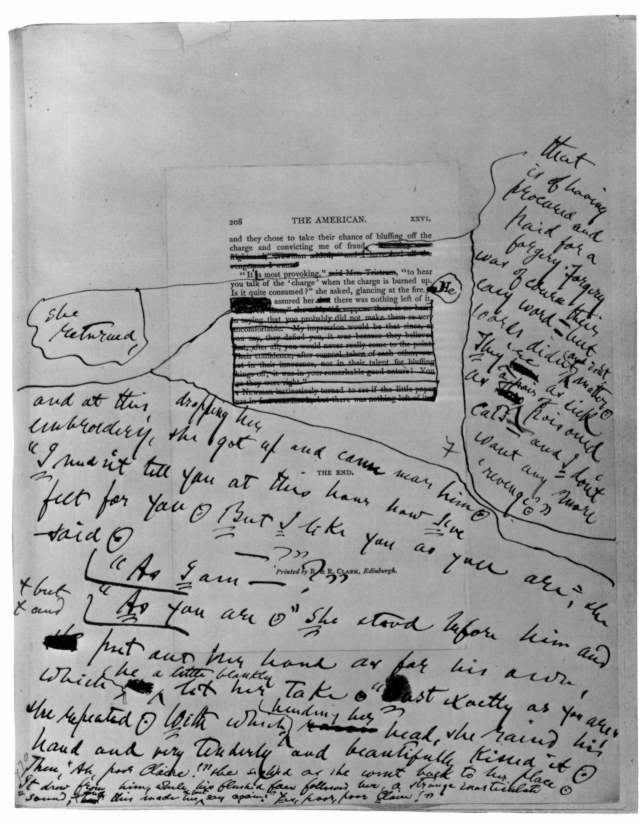

Henry James, *The American,* edition of 1883 pasted-up and revised for the
"New York Edition."

8

The Two Versions of Henry James's The American

WE MAY NOT BE ABLE TO ASCERTAIN, even approximately, when the modern notion of an "oeuvre" appeared or where it came from. The musical arena is likely, because after Beethoven, everyone's career seemed to fall into three periods that were then apt to assume a certain shape. Composers became persuaded that, even at the very end, every last note could shed a new light on everything that had come before and, in fact, change its original meaning. Stravinsky thought this. One possible procedure was the actual modification of early works in response to later discoveries. Whatever the background may have been, the force of Henry James's desire to leave behind a unified and intelligible work still astonishes us, and no object more exemplifies this force than the relic of *The American*, rewritten from beginning to end, with the young James and the Master confronting each other on every page. From this confrontation emerges a question about how much revision is actually possible once a work is finished. Experience can produce remarkable strategies, but youth is resilient.

First the object itself: *The American* had been published in 1877. In preparing to rewrite, James took apart two (or more) copies of the two-volume edition published in 1883 in London by Macmillan as volumes 6 and 7 of the Collective Edition (Edel and Laurence, *Bibliography*, no. A20). Each page of printed text was pasted more or less centrally onto the recto of a cream-colored sheet of paper measuring 257 by 205 mm., leaving wide margins all round. This procedure resulted in as many leaves as the book had pages. The revising that ensued (Edel has called *The American* "The most rewritten of all the novels") was prodigious. When the alterations required by a passage were too great to be accommodated within the margins of the mounting sheets, James discarded the printed page in question and substituted typescript or, towards the end, autograph revisions on sheets of paper measuring 253 by 193 mm. In one case he expanded the text by seven pages.

These sheets went in batches to James's agent, James B. Pinker, during 1906, and they formed the basis for typescripts, which were in turn revised and used for the setting of proofs that, undoubtedly, contained further revisions. These stages have been established in Hershel Parker's "Literary Log, 1905-1907." Unfortunately the typescripts and proofs have not survived, and there is considerable discrepancy between the text of our sheets and the version of the New York Edition. James gave our sheets to Pinker, who had them bound. His son, Eric Pinker, returned them to Henry James, 3rd, who presented them to Harvard in 1928 with the provision (since lifted) that they might be reproduced only by "one holding a Harvard Faculty appointment with the rank of not less than Assistant Professor." The whole manuscript, if we may call it such, was produced in facsimile by the Scolar Press in 1976.

A great deal of critical effort has been spent in comparing the early and late versions of this work. Both versions are still read and this is likely to continue. Parker has remarked that "modern editors or introducers of *The American* have chosen, time after time, against James's revisions, even while most literary critics have justified these revisions." Much of the criticism of the revisions has tended to attach to a certain blurring of the character of Christopher Newman, a loss of simplicity and crispness (perhaps the elder James found him vulgar after all), and a similar blurring of the plot itself, a plot not without romantic flaws. Certainly the early version has greater tempo. The later version arrests one from time to time with passages that are beautiful. A particular problem is the ending.

Claire, as we remember, has joined a Carmelite order and is in permanent seclusion. Newman, having thrown into the fire the document that would have brought down his enemies, is reminded by Mrs. Tristram that they doubtless had anticipated his good action. "Newman instinctively turned to see if the little paper was in fact consumed, but there was nothing left of it." So ends the first version. The heavily rewritten later version denies Newman his moment of questioning. He has acted with intentionality, but the women have the last word. Mrs. Tristram comforts him and kisses his hand. "Then, 'Ah, poor Claire' she sighed as she went back to her place. It drew from him, while his flushed face followed her, a strange inarticulate sound, and this made her say, again: 'Yes, a thousand times — poor, poor, Claire!' "

To hear at this point that our nun is "poor Claire" or rather a "Poor Clare," comes as something of a shock. Is this a new idea? Is that why her name was Claire in the first place? I am not sure. Looking through the early version, one sees that light was Claire's great quality: she had "eyes that were both brilliant and mild"; "Claire looked at him again with the same soft brightness"; "She gave him her hand with a smile that seemed in itself an illumination"; Mrs. Tristram exclaims "She is a saint and a persecution is all that she needs to bring out her saintliness and make her perfect." This is not unlike Thomas of Celano's description of "the lady Clare, shining in name, more shining in life, most shining in conversation." Turning to the feast of St. Clara in the Roman Breviary we find at Vespers a hymn with the following strophe:

> Novum sidum emicuit.
> Candor lucis apparuit.
> Nam lux quam lucem influit.
> *Claram clarere* voluit.

And it seems likely that the allusion was really there all along. But why was it suppressed and why now so starkly revealed? Most people, after all, knew what a Poor Clare was. At this point the ending of *The Ambassadors*, the parallel late novel, written two years before these revisions, occurs to one. Strether and *his* friend are stalled briefly in a situation of considerable bleakness until she manages to sigh and "sighed it at last, all comically, all tragically away," and this then allows Strether his final, wonderful "There we are." Seen in this light, the "Claire" pun, for it is like a pun, seems from Mrs. Tristram a wry benediction, and one that neither the early nor the late Christopher Newman was likely to have understood.

Rodney G. Dennis

Thomas à Kempis, *Imitatio Christi,* MS with two contemporary attributions; Buxheim,
late 15th cent.

9

Attributions in a Manuscript of Imitatio Christi

THE DISPUTE OVER THE AUTHORSHIP of the *Imitatio Christi* is an ancient one, dating back almost to the time when the work first appeared in the early fifteenth century. Manuscripts of the work vary in attributing it to Thomas à Kempis, Jean Charlier de Gerson, Chancellor of the University of Paris, a certain Johannes Gersen, supposed to have been Benedictine abbot of Vercelli, St. Bernard of Clairvaux, and Walter Hilton, while many manuscripts avoid the question by omitting any attribution at all. By far the greater number, however, are divided among Thomas à Kempis, Gersen, and Gerson; but it is well to remember that in this matter of attribution there was no such thing as copyright or scholarly determination of authorship in the fifteenth century, so the fact that a manuscript attributes a work to a particular author does not always mean much. One has only to consider the mass of pseudepigrapha associated with the names of such authors as St. Bonaventura, Albertus Magnus, or Thomas Aquinas to see examples of that. Thomas à Kempis was a Canon Regular of the Augustinian order, while Gersen was supposed to have been a Benedictine. It was therefore inevitable that the authorship controversy should develop into a dispute between the two monastic orders, each anxious to uphold the cause of its own candidate. The Benedictines, unfortunately, based their claim on the rather flimsy ground of the name Gersen being distinct from that of Gerson and not simply a variation of it, for Gerson, of course, had no Benedictine connection.

In 1640 Cardinal Richelieu, planning to print a deluxe edition of the *Imitatio* at the Imprimerie Royale in Paris and wanting to be sure under whose name he should issue it, ordered the question of its authorship to be referred to an impartial court of savants. In their deliberations they consulted Charles Labbé, a learned Parisian lawyer, who stated his conviction that the author was neither à Kempis nor Gersen but Gerson. There seems to have been a reluctance to disoblige the Benedictines, however, and Labbé's opinion, perhaps shared by others, was quashed. The court declared its inability to make a definite decision, and the Cardinal's edition was issued anonymously. Both Augustinians and Benedictines continued to press their cases until Gabriel Naudé, librarian of Cardinal Mazarin, accused the Benedictine Constantine Cajetan of having tampered with the manuscript on which the Benedictines chiefly based their claim for the authorship of Johannes Gersen. The matter was referred to the French Parlement for settlement, with the result that that court forbade the printing of the *Imitatio* under Gersen's name and authorized its being issued under that of Thomas à Kempis. The Benedictines, in desperation, hunted high and low through the libraries of Europe for a manuscript that could be authentically dated in the fourteenth century and thus make impossible the authorship of à Kempis: to no avail. Early in the eighteenth century Eusebius Amort, a Canon Regular of Pollingen, published his *Scutum Kempense*, which presented the case for à Kempis so succinctly and forcefully that contrary arguments were silenced for a long period. Eventually, however, the dispute came to life again when a manuscript, reputed to have come from Italy and to have been written in the fourteenth century, was discovered by a bookseller in Paris, along with a fourteenth-century *Diarium* making mention of the same manuscript under the year 1349. Critical examination of both, however, proved that the manuscript dated from the fifteenth century and that the *Diarium* was a forgery. So ended the myth of "Johannes Gersen," who never existed. Johannes Gerson, however, still has his defenders; but the number of fifteenth-century manuscripts ascribing the *Imitatio* to Thomas à Kempis, the witness of contemporary writers, and studies of stylistic differences between Gerson's writings and the *Imitatio* all add up to a preponderance of opinion favoring à Kempis's authorship.

Our own MS Lat 246 states in its colophon "Compilator huius opusculi fuit quidam frater Thomas nomine ordinis canonicorum regularium Sancti Augustini Montis Sanctae Agnetis Traiectensis. Anno Domini 1471." Immediately underneath this, however, another and not much later hand has written, "Secundum alios intitulantur isti quattuor libri videlicet Magistri Johannis Gerson Cancellarij Parisiensis De contemptu mundi." The manuscript comes from the Carthusian monastery at Buxheim in Bavaria, near Memmingen, diocese of Augsburg, secularized in the early nineteenth century. The library, which had passed into the ownership of the Graf von Waldbott-Bassenheim, was sold at auction in September 1883, lot no. 2651 being the present MS Lat 246. The manuscript was apparently bought by Eadmond Waterton, either directly or through an agent, for the *Imitatio* collection he was forming. Waterton's own collection of several manuscripts and 1170 printed editions was auctioned by Sotheby's on 18 January 1895 and was bought *en bloc* by the London dealer Henry Sotheran, who gave the British Museum first choice of any of the printed works it did not already have. The rest, along with the manuscripts, were sold to Walter Arthur Copinger, who in 1908 printed his *Hand List of What is Believed to be the Largest Collection in the World of Editions of "The Imitation" of Thomas à Kempis*. His collection was acquired by the Harvard College Library in 1921 as the gift of James Byrne, '77. MS Lat 246, Codex Buxheimensis, has been recorded as lost until comparatively recently, probably because no one studying manuscripts of the *Imitatio* could trace what had become of it after the Buxheim auction.

Some authorities have assumed a connection between MS Lat 246 and the *editio princeps* of the *Imitatio*, which was printed by Günther Zainer at Augsburg, perhaps in but certainly not after 1472. A partial collation of the manuscript against the printed text of the *Imitatio* as well as of the *Summa de articulis fidei et ecclesiae sacramentis* of Thomas Aquinas, which is also contained in this manuscript and which was also printed by Zainer at the same time as the *Imitatio*, makes it seem unlikely that MS Lat 246 served as Zainer's copy text. There are no inky fingerprints or compositor's markings in the manuscript and, even more tellingly, there are too many variations between manuscript and printed text for any close connection to be maintained.

James E. Walsh

Thomas Chatterton, *Songe to Aella,* autograph of a forgery of a 15th cent. MS.

10

Thomas Chatterton, 1752-1770.
[Three poems]:
To Johne Lydgate and Songe toe Ella
[by Thomas Rowley, fl. 15th c.];
Johne Ladgate's Answer [by John Lydgate, c. 1370-c. 1451].
A.MS. in the hand of Thomas Rowley;
Bristol, October 1768. 1s.(1p.)
With A.MS.s. (by Rowley) drawings of inscriptions
and prose description, verso.

THE CRITICAL QUESTIONS TURN ON A MATTER OF PUNCTUATION, as do the moral, psychological, paleographical, and historical questions. "Original." The quotation marks appear in every discussion of Thomas Chatterton's Rowley parchments. The object on display, the manuscript of a Pindaric ode invoking a ninth-century Bristol hero's care for the present (fifteenth-century) and future city, together with two poems explaining how a fifteenth-century monk/antiquary/poet came to write the ode, is the "original." The parchments embody Chatterton's own past, his version of England's, particularly Bristol's past, his version of his city's past poet's poem about that poet's city's past. There are no drafts. There are "transcripts," after which came the "originals."

Chatterton was fifteen in October 1768, with the sensibilities of a Byron or a Keats, in the occupation of a Bartleby. He was being advised by two local grownups — William Barrett, a physician and historian of Bristol in need of "material," and George Catcott, a pewterer and antiquary. These two sometimes seem well-meaning, credulous, themselves deceived, and sometimes seem about as naive, in relation to Chatterton and Rowley, as the Duke and the Dauphin hitching a ride on the raft with Huck and Jim. For their enthusiasm we must be grateful, since it may have occasioned and certainly preserved the poems. Chatterton was the posthumous son of a writing master, had learned to read from a black-letter Bible, and had before that learned the alphabet from "an old Folio musick book of father's," possibly a French manuscript on vellum in which, according to his mother (who gave sewing lessons and used as book covers and thread papers the old parchments her husband had been given by the wardens of St. Mary Redcliff Church), he had "fallen in love with the illuminated capitals." Looking through a microscope at the exhibit now on display, my Fogg Museum colleague Craigen Bowen remarked that he was a young "hacker" in his bold, desperate, lawless, and playful approach to historiography, to the new enthusiasm for the past. (Walpole, it seems to me, understood this at the time and was kind.) Later, having abandoned Rowley and the raft that was Bristol, he lit out for the territory, but Grub Street was not kind. He had no one with whom he'd openly shared the whole game (as, for example, the young Brontës had one another). One wonders what the understanding was between him and Barrett and Catcott at the time he set out for London.

It seems appropriate to let the story tell itself in fragments, because the problems of credulity or skepticism continue. This manuscript and the "Yellowe Rolle," the other "original" Rowley document now in the Houghton Library, were lost for over one hundred years. Word of their continued existence surfaced first in an 8 June 1889 letter from C. G. Crump of the Public Record Office to *The Athenaeum*. Fifteen years later, on 21 December 1914, they were shown by Sir Ernest Clarke to members of the Bibliographical Society of London (together with the wrapper that had contained them and autograph letters from Bishop Percy mentioning them). Collotype facsimiles and, with the help of Herbert Milne of the British Museum, transcripts were published with Clarke's talk in the Society's *Transactions* (vol. 13, 1916), and they were thereafter available to alter subsequent readings and printed versions of the texts. They were identified by Clarke as the property of William Rose Smith (whose property they remained when E. H. W. Meyerstein consulted them in the 1920s for his great biography, from which, and from Clarke, I derive most of this account). Smith had inherited them through the third wife (born Elizabeth Smith) of Archdeacon Robert Nares, to whom they were given, presumably sometime after 1822, by Frances Chambers, the widow of Justice Robert Chambers, among whose papers she had "at different times lately" found them and at whose funeral Nares had been present in 1803. Chambers, on his way through Bath and London to take up his judgeship in the East Indies in 1773, three years after the death of the poet, was to have returned them, after showing them to Thomas Tyrwhitt, Chatterton's first editor, from Thomas Percy to Lord Dacre, who had sent them to Percy for his opinion on their age. Percy, then Chaplain to the Duke of Northumberland, had examined them and shown them to Thomas Butler, the Duke's agent; they questioned Rowley's authenticity but Percy had written to Dacre that the poems ought to be printed as samples of Chatterton's genius. Lord Dacre in 1772 had borrowed them, over Catcott's objections, from William Barrett, to whom they had been given, through Catcott, by Thomas Chatterton in October 1768, the first originals — and the *Songe* manuscript one of only four originals of poems — produced by the poet when Barrett wanted to see the source of Chatterton's transcripts. The documents in the possession of William Rose Smith at the time of Meyerstein's biography in 1930 made their way, as "The Property of Miss N. M. Smith," to the Sotheby's sale of 29 October 1968, where they were purchased (for £2,750) through Winifred Meyers by Arthur A. Houghton, Jr. and presented to this library. There are gaps in this account; we believe that what we have *are* the original originals.

Before this original surfaced, the texts of the three poems had been based on that printed in Tyrwhitt's 1777 edition, which was based on a Catcott transcript, now in the

Bristol Public Library, made from a thin copy book in Chatterton's hand (now vanished), informed by Barrett's transcript of this parchment and a Chatterton transcript made for Barrett. Tyrwhitt had also seen one of two transcripts made by Dr. Joseph Fry from a Chatterton transcript, and Fry, who had also seen the original, had been the first to comment on the writing out of the *Songe* as though it were prose. Donald S. Taylor and Benjamin B. Hoover's splendid 1971 edition bases the texts of the poems on Chatterton's transcripts (and, for *Answer*, on Barrett's) in a miscellany now at the British Library (part of the Robert Glynn bequest, ultimately from Barrett). They collate it with our manuscript (which they find "largely illegible" because of deliberate antiquing and later deciphering techniques — Chatterton, if he did it at all, may not have been the only one to hold the parchments over a candle, and Barrett is said to have washed them with galls in order to read them) and the Clarke transcript, with Tyrwhitt, and with the Catcott and, for *Songe*, Fry transcripts now in Bristol.

The present contents of fMS Eng 1279 form a set; they authenticate one another as Chatterton's Rowley texts and documents do. There are the two supposed fifteenth-century parchments in Thomas Rowley's hand, the one with the three poems including Rowley's fifteenth-century gloss/footnote (often omitted in printed editions) identifying Ella as "Lorde of the Castel of Brystowe [ynne daies] of yore." Here the *Songe* is itself set into a context: it is preceded by Rowley's poem on the "boutynge matche" that occasioned it, a kind of quytting or rhyming joust with John Lydgate: "Ladgate" in the transcripts and Taylor is here corrected to Lydgate in the first poem since Barrett has convinced Chatterton he had misread in his original the name of the real poet who was Rowley's friend and, by the evidence of *John Ladgate's Answer*, a much inferior poet. *Ladgate's Answer*, here transcribed by Rowley after *Songe*, connects Rowley with Chaucer and with Turgot, the eleventh-century historian who is Rowley's source for tales of the imaginary Ella. There is the document named, in Rowley's hand, "Yellowe Rolle" (opening with two direct quotations enclosed in quotation marks) addressed by Rowley to his patron William Canynge (another historical figure), establishing Rowley's credentials as an antiquary, and listing "My Volume of Verses wyth letters toe and from John Lydgate" in an account of Cannynge's library in "England's Glorye revyved." Then there is the paper from Frances Chambers, complete with watermark and seal, and there are two letters to Chambers from Percy, asking that the documents be returned and referring to — historical figures all, we know from other evidence — Johnson and Boswell and Sir Joshua Reynolds.

The verso of *Songe* is still not in print, even in Taylor, but this exhibition makes an occasion for a photograph in which the words may be more legible. Legibility of both sides of the manuscript is enhanced considerably by ultraviolet light. Through a microscope the surface of the parchment is seen to be covered with black, gritty, granular, sooty stuff, which might have been rubbed or washed on or might have come from holding it over a flame. Infrared light does not show any carbon-based media in either the ruling lines or the text. The ruling lines are done in the same wet ink as the words, probably iron gall, a fact confirmed by examination under a microscope, where the inks look the same, and under ultraviolet light, where the ruling lines and the writing are enhanced to the same degree. Ultraviolet light does not reveal any evidence of prior text on the page, though it doesn't preclude the possibility that the parchment is older than the eighteenth century and might in fact have come from that cache in the church. There seems to be a fingerprint, in a drip of apparently the same ink as the lines and words. In the drawings on the verso the surface looks incised as though with a metal pen. On the text side, the ink has flaked off where the sheet has been folded.

Dating problems raised by the antiqued words and spelling have long been available for discussion through the transcripts, but there is much to observe from the manuscript. Most peculiarly, there are two lines of text between every two ruling lines. The contextual poems, Rowley to Lydgate and Lydgate to Rowley, are written as metric lines but the *Songe* itself is written as prose, from one margin right to the other, perhaps like a charter, making it, the centerpiece, the hardest to read of the three poems. One tends to read it with a printed version as a crib, so that the eye overlooks points of punctuation nowhere transcribed or printed. (The word "bolde" in the middle of the transcript's third line is not in the original, where it would have been the last word in the first line of the prosed poem.) There is that footnote. What did he think he was doing? Clarke and Milne read the hero's name on this manuscript as "Ælla," and Taylor reads it as "Ella": perhaps the superscript mark over the capital E in *Songe*'s title is Chatterton's attempt to imitate the subscript mark under a capital A which in the fifteenth century sometimes indicated the dipthong Æ. The handwriting looks more like a court hand than a book hand or letter hand, and perhaps more like a fourteenth-century than a fifteenth-century hand, but it is round and strange, irregular, the size of letters differing from one line to the next. It doesn't, finally, resemble any court hand with which I've compared it; a colleague says it looks more like Pali.

Parchment, pen, and certain court hands for models would have been available in John Lambert's law office, and there were all those charters from the church (most of them now in the Bristol Public Library). One wants to know what the documents looked like that Chatterton saw every day in those long seven or eight A.M. to nine P.M. days at Lambert's when he was underoccupied at the task of copying legal precedents for only two hours a day. He is said to have spent the days reading or copying on old parchments, and his sister said he took their father's parchments to the office. He appears, in the biography, showing at different times two young acquaintances how to "antiquate" parchment, with a candle, or, at a "breeches maker's," where apparently both ochre and parchment were readily available, by rubbing it in first with ochre, then on the ground, finally crumpling it. Whatever the techniques and models, it is the peculiarity of the original itself, material evidence produced to prove the case for early composition of the texts, that raises all sorts of doubts about the supposed authorship of the poems.

How does looking at the original affect the reading of the poem? Punctuation and a few words change, but the chief effect is to prepare the reader's mind. First, in several ways, there is an increased sense of the dramatic. Certainly, the three poems belong together as a single piece: they are a conversation, an epistolary novel or a play with three characters, only two of whom speak. The poems, including the ode, become what Rowley says they are, performances: Rowley, relaxed, to his friend; Rowley, ecstatic, heroic, to Ella; Lydgate, humble and appreciative, to Rowley. A problem has existed for Chatterton's poems: legend and the biography and the controversy have made them hard to read; the reader's mind won't let go of the chest in the room over the porch in St. Mary Redcliff, which was empty when Catcott showed it to Johnson and Boswell in 1776. Looking at the parchment, where it is difficult even to see the words and almost impossible simply to read them, the biographical distraction disappears. In the look of the page, the prosing of the *Songe*, the "Wasteland"-like footnote, the contact with Rowley's handwriting, there is a kind of shock that prepares for the mood of the ode. Given the world in which Chatterton was operating, in which the word "original" was about to undergo a great change, the parchment balances print as the proper form for *Songe to Ella*. The manuscript gives the reader something of what must have been Chatterton's exhilaration in the literal, in the conjunction of the verbal and the physical: things with words on them, the words on the things about the things, or about other words on other things. All of it at hand, nothing is lost, and everything connects: Ella, Turgot, Chaucer, Lydgate, Rowley, Chatterton, Barrett, Percy . . . .. Turn from the "original" to the words of the poem:

> O thou, or what remaynes of thee,
> Ella, the darlynge of Futuritie,
> lett thys mie songe / as thie Courage be,
> As everlastynge to posterytie.

Elizabeth Falsey

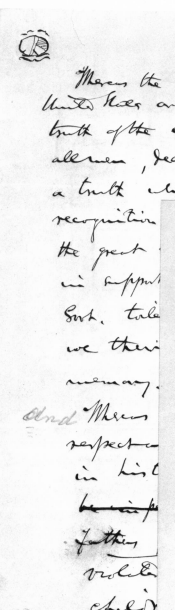

BOSTON, NOVEMBER 5, 1845.

SIR:

At a meeting of citizens of Massachusetts, without distinction of party, held last evening in FANEUIL HALL, BOSTON, the following Preamble and Resolutions were adopted by a unanimous vote, namely:

Whereas, the Government and Independence of the United States are founded on the adamantine truth of the equal rights and brotherhood of all men, declared on the 4th of July, 1776; a truth which receives new and constant recognition in the progress of time, which is the great lesson from our country to the world, in support of which the founders of our Government toiled and bled, and on account of which we their children bless their memory;

And whereas, it is essential to our self-respect as a nation, and to our fame in history, that this truth, declared by our fathers, should not be impeached or violated by any fresh act of their children;

And whereas, the scheme for the annexation of the slave state of Texas, begun in stealth and fraud, and carried on mainly with the view of confirming slavery and extending its bounds, in violation of the fundamental principle of our institutions, *is not consummated*, and may yet be arrested by the zealous and hearty coöperation of all who sincerely love the institutions of their country and the liberty of mankind;

And whereas, this scheme, if successfully perpetrated, involves the whole country, the free as well as the slave owners, in one, and threatens to involve them in the other, of the two greatest crimes a nation can commit, slavery and unjust war; slavery of the most revolting character, and war to sustain slavery;

And whereas, the state constitution of Texas, which is soon to be submitted to Congress for its adoption or rejection, expressly prohibits the Legislature, except under conditions rendering the exception practically void, from passing laws for the emancipation of slaves, and from abolishing the slave trade between Texas and the United States, thereby entirely reversing the natural and just tendency of our institutions towards freedom;

And whereas, the slaveholders seek the consummation of the scheme of annexation for the purpose of increasing the market for human flesh, and of extending and perpetuating the unrighteous institution of slavery;

And whereas, the slaveholders seek also, by the consummation of this scheme, and by creating within the limits of Texas new slave states, to control the political power of the majority of freemen represented in the Congress of the Union;

Therefore, *be it resolved*, in the name of God, of Christ, and of Humanity, that we, belonging to all political parties, and reserving all other reasons of objection, unite in protesting against the admission of Texas into this Union as a slave state.

Resolved, That the people of Massachusetts will continue to resist, to the last, the consummation of this wicked scheme, which will cover the country with disgrace, and make us responsible for crimes of gigantic magnitude.

Resolved, That we have the fullest confidence that the Senators and Representatives of Massachusetts, in Congress, will never consent to the admission of Texas as a slave state, but will resist to the utmost this fatal measure, in every stage of its progress, by their voices and votes.

And furthermore, whereas the Congress of the United States, by assuming the right of connecting this country with a foreign state, have already involved the people of the free states in a great expense for the protection, by force of arms, both by sea and land, of the usurped territory; and whereas, a still greater expenditure may hereafter be incurred to maintain by violence what is held by wrong;

Resolved, That we hereby protest against the policy of enlisting the strength of a free people to sustain, by physical force, a measure threatening to be consummated for the criminal purpose of perpetuating a system of slavery, at war with the fundamental principle of our institutions.

Resolved, That the Honorable John G. Palfrey, of Cambridge, Honorable Stephen C. Phillips, of Salem, and Honorable Charles F. Adams, of Boston, be a Committee to present copies of these Resolutions to the Senators and Representatives from Massachusetts, and also to send them to every Senator and Representative in Congress from the free states.

We perform the duty assigned to us, by forwarding to your address a copy of the Resolutions, and have the honor to be,

Very respectfully,

Your obedient servants,

John G. Palfrey
S. C. Phillips
C. Fra. Adams

} COMMITTEE.

Charles Sumner, autograph draft of the Faneuil Hall resolutions of 5 November 1845, with printed copy.

11

On the Faneuil Hall Resolutions of 5 November, 1845

Tʜɪs ᴄɪʀᴄᴜʟᴀʀ, from the collections of the Houghton Library,[1] illustrates how careful a historian has to be even when using unquestionably genuine sources. The preamble and resolutions adopted by the anti-Texas meeting in Faneuil Hall on 5 November, 1845, were not drafted by John G. Palfrey, who reported them to the assembly, nor by any of the other members of the committee who signed them. They purported to be a clear statement of principle on the question of the annexation of Texas, but were in fact a skillful compromise among the views of several factions that opposed acquisition of that territory. And they claimed to represent the virtually unanimous views of the outraged Commonwealth at a time when the Massachusetts consensus against admitting Texas to the Union had largely eroded. Only a close examination of the document itself and a study of the handwritten drafts on which it was based — all, fortunately, preserved in the Houghton Library — can provide a correct understanding of a complicated and confused situation.

These resolutions were not entirely in error in claiming to represent the wishes of the citizens of Massachusetts concerning the impending annexation of Texas to the United States. Except for Democratic loyalists, pledged to support expansionism, virtually all New Englanders were opposed to the annexation. Some feared it would tip the sectional balance of power in the national government, precariously maintained since the Missouri Compromise, in favor of the South. Others worried that it would involve the United States in a war with Mexico. But most New Englanders, who were fundamentally anti-slavery, objected to admitting Texas because it was a new slave state — a slave state of vast extent, which might be subdivided into additional slave states — that would strengthen the South's "peculiar institution." Abolitionists, of course, objected to any extension of slavery, as did the members of the minuscule Liberty party. More important, the Whig party, the dominant political group in Massachusetts, also opposed annexation. Even Daniel Webster, whose presidential aspirations made him keep an eye constantly on the South, was against bringing into the Union "a new vastly extensive, slaveholding country," and the ultra-conservative Rufus Choate trembled "for the consequences, of annexing an acre of new territory, for the mere purpose of diffusing this great evil, this great curse, over a wider surface of American earth."[2] In 1844 both Massachusetts Senators voted to defeat a treaty of annexation, earnestly supported by President John Tyler, and the Massachusetts General Court in January 1845 resolved that the Commonwealth would "never by any act or deed give her consent to the further extension of slavery to any portion of the world."[3]

Yet by November Massachusetts opposition to Texas annexation had begun to wane. When the Democrat James K. Polk, pledged to expansion, defeated Henry Clay in the presidential elections of 1844, many practical men regretfully concluded that the question was decided. If they had any doubts, the precipitous action of President Tyler, who did not wait for the inauguration of his successor but pushed through the annexation of Texas by joint resolution of the two houses of Congress, seemed to settle the matter. Though Congress had still to approve the constitution of the new state of Texas, most saw no point in further resistance. Factious opposition would only serve to split the Whig party and to alienate Southern congressmen at just the time when incoming President Polk was planning a downward revision of the tariff seriously injurious to New England manufacturing. More important in the minds of some Massachusetts Whigs than even the manufacture of cotton was the manufacture of a Whig presidential candidate for 1848, as both Webster and Abbott Lawrence aspired to the White House. Whig elder statesmen like Nathan Appleton and Robert C. Winthrop agreed that the Texas issue should be dropped, because it was not "good policy to waste our efforts on the impossible."[4]

But these voices of caution were slow to reach the younger leaders of the anti-Texas coalition, who were generally disaffected toward party politics and were on the whole more idealistic than their seniors. Charles Francis Adams, the son and grandson of Presidents of the United States, Stephen C. Phillips, a wealthy Salem merchant with political ambition, John G. Palfrey, formerly professor of theology at Harvard and currently Secretary of State to the Commonwealth, and Henry Wilson, the Natick cobbler turned politician, were the early leaders of these "Young Whigs."[5] (They would later proudly assume the name "Conscience Whigs.") They were presently joined by Charles Sumner, whose Harvard education and European travels made him one of the most conspicuous, as well as one of the most learned, figures in Boston society.

Persisting in their opposition to Texas, these Young Whigs were necessarily driven into a loose alliance with the abolitionists and the Liberty party men. Up to this point the abolitionists, especially those who were followers of William Lloyd Garrison, had eschewed involvement in political organizations and, in turn, had been generally scorned by the leaders of both the regular parties. But now the most practical of the Young Whigs, Henry Wilson, began putting out feelers toward the abolitionists, and soon Young Whigs and abolitionists were planning how best to resist the continued encroachments of the Slave Power. Once identified with this abolitionist-sponsored movement, Adams, Palfrey, Sumner, and Wilson found it necessary to become increasingly active in it, lest it be taken over by the Garrisonians, who hoped to divert public interest from the annexation of Texas to their own program for the immediate abolition of slavery.

The Faneuil Hall meeting of 5 November, the culmination of this brief alliance, was choreographed to give an appearance of unity among these mutually distrustful but temporarily cooperating groups.[6] All agreed that Charles Francis Adams, because of his great family name, should preside. To make sure that matters went smoothly, a committee was named to draft resolutions in advance. After Samuel E. Sewall, of the Liberty party, produced some resolutions that struck the Whigs as intemperate, Adams gave Sumner the assignment of composing a protest that would at once satisfy the abolitionists who wanted to end all slavery immediately and not alienate those Whigs who were simply opposed to expansion. The manuscript draft shows how adroitly Sumner appealed to both groups. With its talk of "crimes of gigantic magnitude," the "market for human flesh," and a war with Mexico that "would be wicked beyond all comparison with any war in history," his draft echoed the rhetorical extravagance of abolitionist propaganda, but his resolutions urged no action beyond the strictly constitutional rights of petition and protest.

There has been some disagreement among historians about the authorship of the preamble and resolutions adopted at the Faneuil Hall meeting. Since Palfrey presented the resolutions to the meeting, he was the ostensible author, but one scholar thinks the style and tone clearly betrayed the hand of Adams.[7] The manuscript itself, however, clearly proves that they were primarily Sumner's work, with a few changes suggested by others. It is not clear who made the decision to drop Sumner's last two resolutions, which claimed that the annexation of Texas would "reduce a portion of our own free-citizens to slavery" and announced that a war with Mexico would "let loose the contagion of Hell." But the manuscript shows that Palfrey made some relatively minor, verbal revisions in Sumner's draft and added a final resolution naming a committee to present the views of the meeting to the Congressmen from all the free states. Adams, whose much neater handwriting appears on the final page of the manuscript, appended a concluding resolution, somewhat less vehement in tone than those proposed by Sumner.

At the meeting itself, where Adams presided, the speakers were carefully paired, with Sumner, Palfrey, and George S. Hillard representing the Young Whig faction and Wendell Phillips, Henry B. Stanton, and William Henry Channing the abolitionist group. How their remarks were received is difficult to ascertain, for newspaper reports reflected the editors' biases. Garrison's *Liberator* praised this "grand rally of the freedmen of the North" and even commended the extremely unpropitious weather — "the rain pouring down violently, the thunder roaring, and the lightning blazing vividly at intervals" — as "emblematic of the present moral and political aspects of the country." On the other hand, the Democratic *Boston Daily Times* found it appropriate "that such a foul project should have foul weather as an accompaniment. The night was dark, and so were the designs contemplated."[8]

In the end, little came directly from the anti-Texas meeting. In December Adams and John Greenleaf Whittier presented the resolutions, with accompanying petitions bearing thirty thousand signatures, to Congress, where they were ignored as Texas was admitted to statehood. Returning to Massachusetts, Adams and Palfrey grew anxious over Whig defections from the cause after Abbott Lawrence and Nathan Appleton bluntly announced that the Texas question was now settled. At the same time they worried that their abolitionist allies were "growing very wild." Deciding that it would "be wise to dissolve the committee as soon as it may be decent," they disbanded the anti-Texas committee on 30 December 1845.[9]

Perhaps the most important result of the anti-Texas movement was the emergence of Charles Sumner as a political leader. Hitherto known for his erudition, his cosmopolitan acquaintance, his interest in humanitarian reform movements, Sumner exhibited considerable political skill in the Young Whig movement, where he proved more effective, both as a draftsman and as a mediator, than any of his colleagues. His address to the Faneuil Hall meeting, his first political speech, made a lasting impression. With his injunction that "the supreme requirements of religion, morals, and humanity" were superior to "the controlling political influence," he reminded his audience what Massachusetts was supposed to stand for. Begging his listeners to countenance no measure that would extend or perpetuate slavery, he urged: "Let us wash our hands of this great guilt. God forbid that the votes and voices of Northern freemen should help to bind anew the fetters of the slave! God forbid that the lash of the slave-dealer should descend by any sanction from New England! God forbid that the blood which spurts from the lacerated, quivering flesh of the slave should soil the hem of the white garments of Massachusetts!"[10] Massachusetts had found a new voice.

David Herbert Donald

---

[1]John Gorham Palfrey MSS., bMS Am 1704.13 (130)

[2]Thomas H. O'Connor, *Lords of the Loom: The Cotton Whigs and the Coming of the Civil War* (New York: Charles Scribner's Sons, 1968), pp. 61, 59.

[3]David Herbert Donald, *Charles Sumner and the Coming of the Civil War* (New York: Alfred A. Knopf, Inc., 1960), p. 136.

[4]Kinley J. Brauer, *Cotton Versus Conscience: Massachusetts Whig Politics and Southwestern Expansion, 1843-1848* (Lexington: University of Kentucky Press, c. 1967), p. 152.

[5]For excellent biographies see Martin B. Duberman, *Charles Francis Adams, 1807-1886* (Boston: Houghton Mifflin Company, c. 1960); Frank Otto Gatell, *John Gorman Palfrey and the New England Conscience* (Cambridge: Harvard University Press, 1963); and Ernest McKay, *Henry Wilson: Practical Radical* (Port Washington, N.Y.: Kennikat Press, c. 1971).

[6]Brauer, *Cotton Versus Conscience*, Chapter VII, offers the fullest account of the Faneuil Hall meeting and its preliminaries.

[7]Ibid., pp. 145-146. Sumner correctly stated that "The Resolutions adopted at the meeting were drawn by Mr. Sumner, although introduced by another [i.e., Palfrey]" (*The Works of Charles Sumner* [Boston: Lee and Shepard, 1875], 1:149). He helped confuse matters, however, by printing in his *Works* not his original draft of the resolutions but the final version, which dropped two of his own resolutions and included paragraphs written by Palfrey and Adams (Ibid., 150-151).

[8]Sumner, *Works*, 1:149.

[9]Duberman, *Adams*, pp. 107-109.

[10]Sumner, *Works*, 1:156-157.

12

Non-Authorial Revisions in the Page-proofs for Evangeline

Evangeline WAS THE EPIC POEM THAT MADE Henry Wadsworth Longfellow famous at home and abroad. Within three months of its publication in the spring of 1847, it had passed through six American editions, and it was soon to be translated into German and other European languages where it met with similar enthusiasm.

It is a lugubrious tale of the removal of the French citizens from Acadia when Britain took over Nova Scotia and Prince Edward Island in 1755. Longfellow provides an idyll of Acadian village life, including the betrothal of his heroine Evangeline with Gabriel, the sudden intrusion of British warships, and the helter-skelter exile of the French-speaking Acadians to Louisiana. The lovers are separated, and Longfellow sends Evangeline on a quest for her lost Gabriel that takes her all over the United States and its western territories until, as a sister of mercy, she finds him in an almshouse, dying of yellow fever in Philadelphia.

Lugubrious and absurdly romantic though the poem was, its stunning success confirmed Longfellow in the literary career he had longed to pursue since his student days at Bowdoin College. It opened the doorway of blessed freedom from his onerous duties of teaching at Harvard College — duties he dolefully described in a letter to his friend Cornelius Conway Felton as "grind, grind, grind." He resigned his professorship seven years after publishing *Evangeline* and, in time, became a living national monument.

The Houghton Library possesses an unusually full record of Longfellow's composition of the poem. Among the items is an incomplete draft in pencil, set down on large folded sheets of rough paper and triumphally marked at the end, "Half-past Nine at Night Feb 26, 1847." This draft lacks the prologue and part of the first section and some other parts of the poem. It is folded to make unstitched folios.

A manuscript bound up in half-green leather contains an entire draft of *Evangeline* and several lesser works on fine gray paper. It is written in ink, and on the last page of the poem is inscribed, "Finished February 27, 1847" — which happened to be Longfellow's fortieth birthday. The date and the completion of the manuscript would seem momentous, but in a letter to his sister, Anne Longfellow Pierce, written the next day, Longfellow does not mention the poem. He does ask her if she remembered his birthday.

The relation of the two manuscripts is problematic. Apparently Longfellow set out to write the poem in ink in the bound version. The date "April 27" inscribed in pencil on

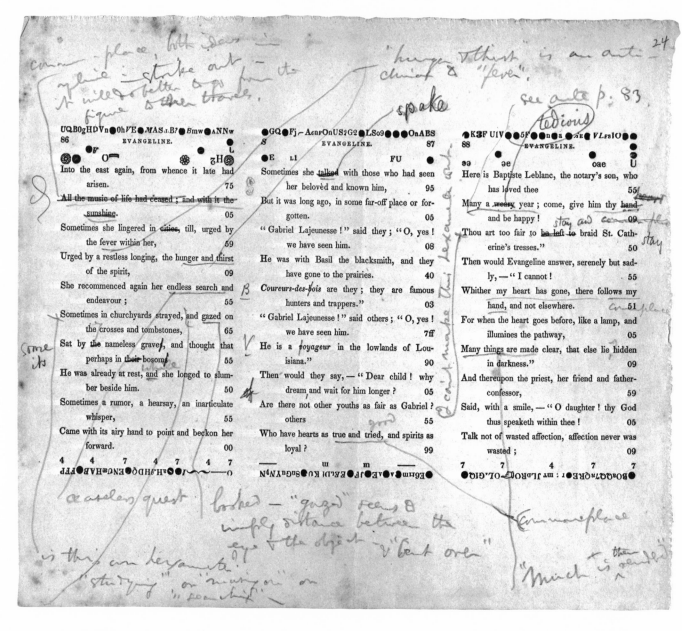

EVANGELINE.
86

Into the east again, from whence it late had
arisen. 75
All the music of life had ceased; and with it the
sunshine. 05
Sometimes she lingered in cities, till, urged by
the fever within her, 59
Urged by a restless longing, the hunger and thirst
of the spirit, 09
She recommenced again her endless search and
endeavour; 55
Sometimes in churchyards strayed, and gazed on
the crosses and tombstones, 65
Sat by the nameless graves, and thought that
perhaps in their bosoms 55
He was already at rest, and she longed to slum-
ber beside him. 50
Sometimes a rumor, a hearsay, an inarticulate
whisper, 55
Came with its airy hand to point and beckon her
forward. 00

EVANGELINE.
87

Sometimes she talked with those who had seen
her belovèd and known him, 95
But it was long ago, in some far-off place or forgotten. 05
"Gabriel Lajeunesse!" said they; "O, yes!
we have seen him. 08
He was with Basil the blacksmith, and they
have gone to the prairies. 40
Coureurs-des-bois are they; they are famous
hunters and trappers." 03
"Gabriel Lajeunesse!" said others; "O, yes!
we have seen him. 7ff
He is a voyageur in the lowlands of Louisiana." 90
Then would they say, — "Dear child! why
dream and wait for him longer? 05
Are there not other youths as fair as Gabriel?
others 55
Who have hearts as true and tried, and spirits as
loyal? 99

EVANGELINE.
88

Here is Baptiste Leblanc, the notary's son, who
has loved thee 55
Many a weary year; come, give him thy hand,
and be happy! 09
Thou art too fair to be left to braid St. Catherine's tresses." 50
Then would Evangeline answer, serenely but sad-
ly, — "I cannot! 55
Whither my heart has gone, there follows my
hand, and not elsewhere. 51
For when the heart goes before, like a lamp, and
illumines the pathway, 05
Many things are made clear, that else lie hidden
in darkness." 09
And thereupon the priest, her friend and father-
confessor, 59
Said, with a smile, — "O daughter! thy God
thus speaketh within thee! 05
Talk not of wasted affection, affection never was
wasted; 09

Henry Wadsworth Longfellow, page-proofs for *Evangeline* with annotations by Charles Sumner and others.

page 91 of this volume suggests that he began in the early spring of 1846. But tiny notations on the pencilled draft begin November 14, 1846, and in Longfellow's hand at the end of Part One is marked "November 25, 1846 Nine at Night." "Part Second" is noted as "Began Dec. 10. 1846."

We may surmise that Longfellow began writing in ink, but almost immediately began striking out words and lines and replacing them with others. Like most writers, he had special trouble with his beginning. He probably worked for several days or even weeks on the poem and then put the manuscript up. In the fall he seems to have started again, writing out a draft in pencil. It appears that after trying out a few lines or even a few pages in pencil, he transferred them in ink to the other version. The pencilled draft has remarkably few corrections. The bound draft, clearly dependent on the pencilled version, seems to indicate a certain authorial anxiety when the poet came to set down his words in a more permanent form. Like the Mississippi down which his heroine journeyed, the course of the inked draft is at times smooth and serene with pages showing little hesitation and few corrections. But then it may become a mess of sharp lines drawn through words, other words inserted and in turn scratched out, and yet other words incised in ever diminishing size in their place.

A fair copy, now missing, apparently stood between the inked manuscript and the first of three sets of printed proofs now in Houghton, for there are a number of variants between the notebook version and the proofs. Longfellow might have stood over his printer, making changes as his work was set in type. We know that some sixteenth-century authors mistrusted their printers enough to do just that. But such seems not to have been nineteenth-century practice; book printers at least had become much more skilled, and the author's presence was not necessary to ensure quality. It is noteworthy that few casual typographical errors exist in these proofs.

Longfellow's revisions continued through the three successive sets of galley proofs. In addition, he called on friends for help — a practice he was to continue throughout his writing life. Three of them have left their track across the surviving proof sets.

Two were intimates: Charles Sumner (1811-1874) and the already mentioned Cornelius Conway Felton (1807-1862). Sumner was in 1847 a lecturer at the Harvard Law School — a task he found unfulfilling and tedious. He was already known throughout Massachusetts as a spellbinding orator, and in 1848 the state legislature would send him to the United States Senate. There he would become one of the most powerful and vehement voices raised against slavery and slave-holders. In 1856 Representative Preston Brooks of South Carolina would beat him senseless with a walking stick while Sumner sat working at his desk late one evening. Sumner had denounced one of Brooks's relatives, Senator Andrew P. Butler of South Carolina, in a speech on the floor of the Senate. Brooks's attack was part cause and part symbol of the increasing bitterness of sectional conflict that would shortly plummet into civil war.

Longfellow's other close friend was Felton, Eliot Professor of Greek Literature at Harvard. In letters Longfellow addressed him affectionately as "Feltonius." Felton would become president of Harvard in 1860, but his death in 1862 gave him little time to make a reputation in that capacity. One of Longfellow's biographers calls Felton "stout and jovial," an ideal foil, one might say, for Longfellow's persistent melancholy. Together, Longfellow, Felton, Sumner, and their friends Henry R. Cleveland and George Hillard called themselves "the Five of Clubs" and met frequently, dining with one another and dropping in for visits.

The third reader of the proofs was Charles Folsom (1794-1872), a friend at greater remove. Longfellow did not frequently correspond with him. Folsom was in 1847 the librarian of the Boston Athenaeum, having served earlier as librarian at Harvard College and being active throughout his life in the work of the Harvard University Press.

Folsom was an indefatigable collector of trivia who took obvious delight in showing off his knowledge of obscure facts. Various Boston writers of the period thanked him for commenting on their proofs, so he seems to have functioned as an unpaid freelance editor. He was by far the most extensive commentator on the proofs, and his is the only hand that appears on all three sets. Longfellow also accepted more of his suggestions than he did those of the others. The reason may have been simply that Folsom's counsels were so much more numerous than those of Felton and Sumner. In the end Longfellow rejected many more suggestions than he accepted. He annotated the proof sheets himself, of course, and sometimes he rejected even his own advice. Some changes made in his hand on the final proof sheets were not made in the finished edition of the poem. (The nature of the corrections on the third set supposes a missing fair copy that Longfellow made up for the printing of the final version.)

Two kinds of comments adorn these proofs — those about accuracy and those about style, including many recommendations as to how to hold to the hexameters in which Longfellow composed the poem. In addition Folsom used a red pencil to make all sorts of marks concerning punctuation and spacing on the first proof set, emendations Longfellow routinely accepted.

Folsom inclined towards pedantry — not a bad quality in an editor. Many of his precise comments on rural matters come across as ironic, given Longfellow's propensity in *Evangeline* and other poems to making himself the bard of the bucolic. It seems obvious that he did not know country life very well.

For example, in I.1 Longfellow had observed that Young Evangeline in Acadia "bore to the reapers the nut brown / Home-brewed ale, with cheeks as bright as the poppy, whose blossom / Blushed in the corn by her side." Folsom observed, "You know that the poppy is *only* a garden plant, not only not being indigenous, but having hardly got into fields at all except a little of late in Westchester Co." Folsom announces with what may be a touch of wit that he is "very learned" in this matter, having looked over some proof sheets from a book about plants in the northern states. Longfellow dutifully weeded the errant poppy out of his poem.

The poet had also set mistletoe to curling around an Acadian sycamore. Folsom objected. He had, he said, seen mistletoe growing only in the southern states and doubted that it would grow as far north as Acadia. Longfellow pulled down the mistletoe and replaced it with woodbine. Under Folsom's prodding Longfellow also moved the Acadian

Indian Summer — which he calls the Summer of All-Saints — from October to September.

When he has the autumn wind "rattle the bars of the gate," Folsom tells him that country people call a gate only those bars fixed in a frame so that they cannot rattle. Longfellow replaced the gate with "wooden bars." Such was also the fate of "tinkling bells" in the saddles of horses, shaken, said the poet, "as a hollyhock shaketh its blossoms."

Folsom reproved him: "But the blossoms of hollyhock are *sessile* on the stalk, and will not shake, any more than the jewels on a royal mace." Longfellow replaced the bells with "tassels of crimson," and made them nod "in bright array, like hollyhocks heavy with blossoms."

Longfellow accepted other emendations of a similar kind, but he more often ignored Folsom, doubtless finding the librarian's literalism too much for a poet to bear. Folsom doubted that English soldiers had "brazen drums" in the eighteenth century, but Longfellow allowed the brass to pound. Folsom said that he had never heard of a river called the Nebraska, and indeed there is none. The criticism was fair enough since Longfellow had seen only the city of Philadelphia of all the places he describes with such adjectival gusto in the poem. (He seems to have taken most of his inspiration from a traveling diorama of the Mississippi that visited Boston about the time he was inspired to write *Evangeline*.) He probably meant the Platte, but the poet allowed "the Nebraska" to flow on in his imagination and in his poem. Probably the word "Platte" would have seemed flat in comparison.

Folsom objected strenuously to Longfellow's use of the word "buffaloes." The American animal, said Folsom, is the *bison*. "They are each grand in his own way," he said, "but so wholly unlike to the eye of the naturalist & the poetical observer of nature." Longfellow ignored him and left his "loud bellowing herds of buffaloes" to roam across his poem as they chose. In a similar fashion Longfellow rejected one of Felton's rare suggestions: "*Titan* being one name for the *sun*, it is not wise to compare the *moon* with Titan a giant." But the poet's impression of the Titanic moon remained serenely afloat in the skies of the finished poem. At I.4 Folsom remarks, "Your use of 'casement' is questionable. It means window *frame* rather. Why not say 'window'?" And Longfellow does. But he rejects Folsom's suggestion that the peasants of Acadia may not have had glass at all in their windows.

The other kind of commentary in these proofs is mostly about style — either the meter of the lines or Longfellow's choice of words. All three commentators made some observations of this sort. Sumner seemed especially eager to point out what he regarded as the infelicities (or worse) of Longfellow's rhetoric. The poet was much less inclined to accept this sort of criticism. Although he was still teaching himself how to be a poet, he seems to have had a firm idea of what he was doing and usually held stubbornly to his course.

But even here he sometimes did listen. Sumner's comments are often harsh. "Commonplace. Both ideas in the line," writes Sumner of this sentence: "All the music of life had ceased: and with it the sunshine."

"Strike out," Sumner commands, and Longfellow obeys. Sumner makes the same stern judgement on the line "Many a weary year," which Longfellow used twice in II.1. In the second use, the poet replaces "weary" with "tedious."

But much more often than not Longfellow ignored suggestions about style. In II.1 Longfellow has his heroine lingering in towns "till, urged by the fever within her, / Urged by a restless longing, the hunger and thirst of the Spirit," she went on. Sumner, ever the orator with the formal training in rhetorical balance and the general rhetorical rule that progressions should move from the weaker to the stronger, commented, " 'hunger and thirst' is an anti-climax to 'fever.' " Longfellow ignored him.

Near the end of II.1, the innocent phrase "Here and there" aroused Sumner's ire. Said he, "this is obnoxious to Addison's criticism on a phrase or two in Paradise Lost as being below the tone of the poem. This is a beautiful passage. It should be made perfect." At the very end of II.1 a few lines later, Sumner commented on the line, "Happy, at length, if he find the spot where it reaches an outlet." He substituted "place" for "spot" and underlining "reaches an outlet," he declared, "Make this better." The whole passage was good enough for Longfellow to leave untouched, and so it remains, contending we may suppose with the grumbling ghost of Addison's criticism of those few lines in Milton.

Now and then the restless shades of New England Puritanism stalk through Sumner's notes. In describing the mosses "trailing in mid-air" from the live oak trees of the lower Mississippi, Longfellow says that they "waved like banners that hang on the walls of ancient cathedrals." Stormed Sumner, "I detest the idea of 'banners in ancient cathedrals.' They shouldn't be there." But in the final texts, the banners wave on. The use of the word "brain" as the seat of Evangeline's sweet fantasies Sumner found "more phrenological than poetical," but Longfellow left it. And at the line "Tired with their midnight toil," Sumner found "tired" to be "trivial" and suggested "spent" in its place. Longfellow ignored him — as he ignored other suggestions of this sort. Sumner invariably suggested the more "poetic" word over the lesser. The modern reader, perusing a poem freighted with flamboyantly artificial language, can only be thankful that Longfellow resisted advice to add further ladings of the same.

Sometimes the meanings of Sumner's criticisms elude us just as they must have eluded Longfellow. In II.I Longfellow speaks of Evangeline as a "poor soul," wandering in search of her lover. Sumner calls "poor soul" "Commonplace" and declares, "Woman is simple and better, besides it exalts the sex." What could Sumner have meant? Whatever the meaning, Longfellow found no reason to comply with his friend's opinions.

The Sumner of these curt and speciously authoritative comments is remarkably of a piece with the later Sumner of the Senate and post-Civil War politics when his confidence in his own righteousness isolated him from political friends and foes alike. Equally evident is Longfellow's fundamental sweetness, so often remarked upon by contemporaries, which kept him writing affectionate letters to Sumner after receiving these slashing criticisms. Longfellow may have been more irritated than he shows. Sumner's remarks are concentrated near the beginning of Part II of the poem in the third proof set. We may conjecture that Longfellow divided the proofs and circulated the parts among his friends, intending to have them comment successively. When he received Sumner's comments on the part allotted to him, the poet may have decided not to pass on any more.

Longfellow himself made some changes in his text. Stylistically speaking, we cannot say whether his changes improved the poem. Its mannered style with its pseudo-archaic language and its monotonous pattern of artificially inverted sentences and its near-fatal infection by adjectives combine to make it a chore to read today. The saccharine virtues of Evangeline herself do not help.

Even so we can admire Longfellow's devotion to getting things right, or at least to not getting them very wrong. In his early drafts he developed a description of one of those elaborate clocks that came to be part of nineteenth-century lore, the "grandfather's clock" of song and story complete with the hourly appearance of the cuckoo — which, in fact, was more Germanic than American or French. Describing Evangeline looking at the great clock, he writes:

> She had beheld the moon, as it rose o'er the dial
>   beheld the
> Stately ships as they sailed, and the lighthouse
>   that stood by the harbour,
> And through the painted glass in the panel the
>   pendulum swinging.
> And when the clock struck the hour, with accents hoarse and
>   ancestral,
> Watched the mysterious door that swung on
>   invisible hinges,
> Till as it opened, a bird came forth and sang,
>   and then vanished
> Suddenly in at the portal, that closed with a
>   clatter behind it. [I.2]

This little description is a window into writerly delight, a vision of an object that for a moment captures Longfellow's imagination as he has it seize the young Evangeline's. But in the first proof set, we find this commentary in the poet's strong hand: "Question: Could an Acadian farmer have had a clock of this kind? Answer: —" On reflection, he filled in the blank with a "no," and pencilled the lines out.

Whatever help his friends gave him, the poem is in all its essentials Longfellow's own. No suggestion surviving in these incomplete proofs shows any inclination to change the meaning or question the philosophy of the whole. Indeed what is remarkable about the collection of manuscripts and proofs is how few changes were made between the inked draft in the bound notebook and the final version of the poem. Compared to, say, the surviving proofs of Longfellow's somewhat older contemporary Balzac, these represent an artist whose inspiration seems relatively uncluttered by cosmic dissatisfaction.

Evangeline resounds with an unmistakable ring of melancholia, filled with nostalgia for a simple and innocent world that has given way to an urban culture removed from nature and devoid of the family and communal loyalties extolled in the poem. One might say that all the things that make Evangeline who she is are those supposed by Longfellow and his friends and his myriad readers as being most at risk in the changing world around them.

Evangeline was published in the year that the Mexican War added vast territories to the United States. If indeed Longfellow began his poem in the spring of 1846, as the annotation "April 27" in the inked draft suggests, its genesis was contemporary with the rising tensions between the United States and Mexico and with the first fighting on April 25.

Longfellow had already written poems against slavery, and in his circles the Mexican War was a conspiracy of the slave power to extend its domain to the Pacific Ocean. The overwhelming victory of the United States could provoke no joy among such people. The sturdy rural world of yeoman farmers here idealized by Longfellow and elsewhere by John Greenleaf Whittier and others seemed about to be swallowed up by the rural economics of an aggressive and expanding slave-holding society.

How strong were Longfellow's abolitionist sentiments? An intriguing clue lies in one change in the text of *Evangeline* that Longfellow made on his own, apparently without prodding from his friends. After the expulsion from Acadia, Basil the Blacksmith, Gabriel's father in the poem, finds prosperity in Louisiana, and Longfellow notes the marvel of Basil's friends at "all his domains and his slaves." It was, of course, common at this time to measure the wealth of a farmer in Louisiana by the number of slaves he possessed, and Longfellow found nothing wrong with this habit until he had his third proof set before him. Then something stirred in his mind, and he crossed out "slaves" with a dark stroke of his pencil and replaced it with "herds." Whatever his own thoughts, it would not have been politically correct in Cambridge during those feverish times to leave the impression that a good man might in good conscience own slaves.

Yet the melancholy persists, and it is deeper than mere nostalgia for vanished simplicity. In his scene setting at the start of his poem, Longfellow presents the image of Basil the Blacksmith happily at home, sitting in his chair by the fire so that behind him on the wall

> Darted his own huge shadow, and vanished away
> into darkness
> He, too, a shadow on earth and vanishing soon into
> darkness.

Sumner protested this last line. "Does this come in *naturally* here?" he asked. It clearly does not, and Longfellow struck it out.

Yet if the line is not natural in that place, it is natural to the sentiments of the poem. Perhaps the sentiments are of the essence: that life, no matter how warm and rich and content, is bound at the last to vanish into silence. Longfellow is one of the many nineteenth-century writers who found belief desirable but not possible. His world and he him-self produced a wave of sentimental religious expressions devoid of any precise doctrines. Taken on the surface, this sentimentality is cloying and jejune. But it is possible to see it as stoic protest, as a powerful emotional force in its day simply because people knew it was not true and that death ended everything. The innocent and happy Acadians, serene in their medieval catholic faith, assumed gigantic mythological force in 1847 because educated readers in the mid-nineteenth century knew that such happy and unquestioning faith was not possible for themselves. Longfellow provides a poetic expression of the religious nostalgia that inspired Henry Adams to write *Mont-Saint-Michel and Chartres*. And how was either the moral individual or the moral society to survive without the restraints and the hopes provided by a confidently believed religious faith? He was not sure.

Longfellow's grand vision of an Edenic America where Evangeline wanders looking for Gabriel is darkened by his profound sense that the inhabitants of this rich and beautiful continent have already been thrust out of paradise. The solution is not redemption; neither Evangeline nor the United States can live happily ever after, for matters have gone too far for that, and anyway, all the strivings of human life are destined at last for oblivion, or as he said in his poem "Mezzo Cammin" a few years after *Evangeline*, "The cataract of Death far thundering from the heights." Only by brave resignation can human beings face the realities of this fallen world. If there is any lesson here, it is that our common destiny should impose upon us kindness and compassion for one another. Evangeline does what she must according to the dictates of a love based on sympathy for others who, like her, have known ultimate loss — and so must we.

Longfellow could be serene in the face of his friendly but carping critics. By the time he wrote this poem, his own vision of life was fixed, and he knew what it was, even if they could not see it through the thicket of their commentaries.

Richard Marius

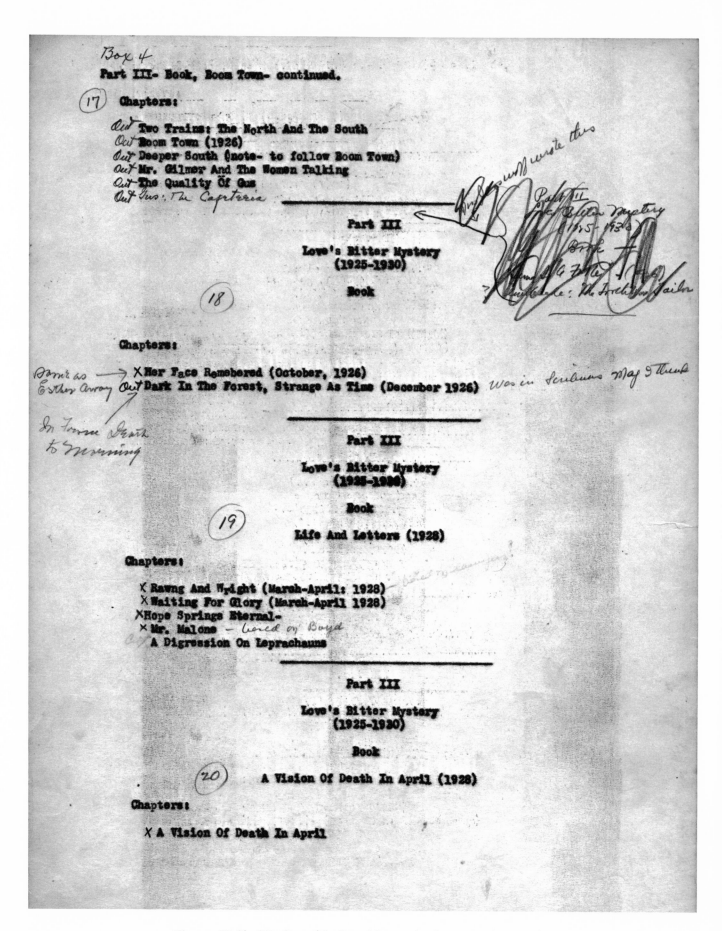

Box 4

Part III- Book, Boom Town- continued.

(17)   Chapters:

Old Two Trains: The North And The South
Out Boom Town (1926)
Out Deeper South (note- to follow Boom Town)
Out Mr. Gilmer And The Women Talking
Out The Quality Of Gus
Out Gus: The Cafeteria

                                    Part III

                              Love's Bitter Mystery
                                  (1925-1930)

                (18)   Book

              Chapters:

Same as → X Her Face Remebered (October, 1926)
Esther away *Out* Dark In The Forest, Strange As Time (December 1926)   *Was in Scribners May I think*

In Forest Dark
to Morning

                                    Part III

                              Love's Bitter Mystery
                                  (1925-1930)

                                      Book

                (19)   Life And Letters (1928)

              Chapters:

X Rawng And Wright (March-April: 1928)
X Waiting For Glory (March-April 1928)
X Hope Springs Eternal-
X Mr. Malone - *Loved or Boyd*
  A Digression On Leprachauns

                                    Part III

                              Love's Bitter Mystery
                                  (1925-1930)

                                      Book

                (20)   A Vision Of Death In April (1928)

              Chapters:

X A Vision Of Death In April

Thomas Wolfe, "Outline of the Last Manuscript," annotated typescript.

13

Manuscript Evidence:
A Case of Authorship Vindicated

WHEN THE AMERICAN NOVELIST Thomas Wolfe died in 1938, the literary world mourned the loss of one of the modern masters of prose fiction, cut off at the age of thirty-seven in the midst of his powers. He did, however, leave behind a huge manuscript of a novel that he called "The Web and the Rock," which with the advice of his editor Edward Aswell he had planned to cut down and revise. The material was in a sufficiently complete state, however, that Aswell was able to do the cutting and revision himself, and dividing the material into three parts, he published three novels out of the stack of pages that Wolfe left behind: *The Web and the Rock*, 1939, *You Can't Go Home Again*, 1940, and *The Hills Beyond*, 1941.

When I was working with the Wolfe papers in the Houghton Library in order to write my critical biography of Wolfe, I discovered the long outline of "The Web and the Rock" that Wolfe had drawn up and also all the evidences of the editorial work that Aswell carried out in order to put the three novels into publishable shape. When I published my book, *The Window of Memory: The Literary Career of Thomas Wolfe*, in 1962, I included Wolfe's fourteen-page outline in an Appendix entitled "The Rough Outline of Thomas Wolfe's Last Manuscript," and I also described how Aswell had cut and rearranged the last half of *The Web and the Rock* (the story of George Webber's love affair with Esther Jack) in order to make it coherent and how Aswell had rewritten some passages in *You Can't Go Home Again* in order to make the prose conform with Wolfe's later style, which predominated in that portion of his manuscript.

These revelations enlightened, and even disturbed, a number of Wolfe readers, although they detracted very little from Wolfe's reputation. Aswell, now dead, came in for more criticism than he deserved, however, and the new perspective on the posthumous novels lessened the admiration for the monumental job of editing that he had performed. Two publications in particular even went ahead to give a distorted picture of Aswell's role in bringing Wolfe's fiction before the public. The first was an article by Patrick Miehe, "The Outline of Thomas Wolfe's Last Book,"[1] in which he declared that Edward Aswell, not Wolfe, was the author of the Outline — and thus implied that the structuring of Wolfe's posthumous novels was really done by his editor. As evidence he cited the facts that the only existing copy of the Outline, a carbon copy, was given to the Houghton Library by Aswell, that Aswell had attached a sheet on which he had written "These are the notes I made in order to help bring order out of chaos while editing the posthumous MSs of Thomas Wolfe,"[2] and that the Outline was typewritten on Aswell's typewriter.

From my familiarity with Wolfe's manuscripts and his methods of work, I knew that this attribution was false, but I had to prove it conclusively because of the circumstantial evidence that Miehe had presented. I knew it was false because the Outline was made up by copying the titles of each "chapter" or episode that Wolfe had clipped together — and each title bore "Part" number and "Book" number as well as "chapter" title. Moreover, each of those title pages was typed on Wolfe's typewriter by his typist, Gwen Jassinoff, identifiable because the typeface has certain characteristics including a broken capital "H." Wolfe's own handwriting appeared on some of these title pages.

Unfortunately for me, the Outline itself was typewritten on another typewriter, whose typeface was similar to Edward Aswell's machine. Similar indeed, but they looked slightly different to me. I took photocopies of pages from the Outline and of other pages of Edward Aswell's office correspondence to two different typewriter companies and asked the experts there if they came from the same typewriter. The answer was no — and the experts pointed out differences in the letters "a," "g," "p," and "q" and the fact that Aswell's typewriter was "out of notion," causing all the capitals to strike above the line. So the proof was clear that the Outline was not copied on Aswell's typewriter.

But I needed more than this. I had interviewed Aswell years before and had asked him whether he had followed Wolfe's Outline in putting the novels together or had used additional material. I looked up my notes of that interview and found that they indicated a discussion of Aswell's "following" the Outline but they did not make a distinct statement that it was Wolfe's Outline. There was no compelling proof of authorship here, only an implication of it.

Many of the annotations on the Outline were in a hand that I recognized as belonging to Elizabeth Nowell, Wolfe's literary agent; there were very few by Aswell, even though he had provided a statement about "notes I made." I decided to go back to the Wolfe papers and look at the correspondence between Nowell and Aswell to see if she had made any reference to the Outline. It was here that I found unmistakable assertions about authorship. In a letter dated 21 September 1938, Ms. Nowell told Aswell that among Wolfe materials in her possession she had "a carbon copy of the list of material in the Web and the Rock, of which Miss Jassinoff said you had the original with the script."[3] She said she would mark it up with comment and mail it to him. I was finally able to write an article, "Thomas Wolfe's Last Manuscript,"[4] pointing out the many evidences of Wolfe's authorship. Mr. Miehe had followed a false trail.

But the new perspective on Aswell's editing of Wolfe's work brought one other person to raise questions about Wolfe's posthumous novels. A Ph.D. candidate named John Halberstadt, after several years' study of the Wolfe manuscripts, made the charge, in an article in the *Yale Review*[5] and in a sensational interview in *The Village Voice*,[6] that Wolfe's last three novels "were not written by Wolfe in the usual sense but were predominantly the work of an editor named Edward Aswell."[7] He even had a public relations agency send a press release to newspapers all over the country in an attempt to create a literary scandal, namely, that Wolfe's last novels were "the creations of one Edward C. Aswell."

Since this was ridiculous and since my book was cited as supporting these charges, I had to set matters straight once more. I wrote a long article in the *Harvard Magazine*,[8] in which I took each detail of Halberstadt's charges and explained how he had distorted or misinterpreted the evidence. To take one example, Halberstadt declared that Aswell had created an entirely new character for Wolfe's *You Can't Go Home Again*. The real situation was this. Aswell had deleted an entire chapter entitled "People of the Night" for fear that libel suits might be brought by people from Wolfe's home town. Again, to avoid the risk of a libel suit, Aswell used the account of a town drunk in that discarded chapter to supply the background for another sleazy character in the chapter "Boom Town": he called them both Tim Wagner. Aswell was actually following a practice that Wolfe had used for years and that was quite evident elsewhere in the manuscript — combining the words and actions of one character with those of another, for a final version that would go into print.

Aswell had made many cuts, revisions, and rearrangements in Wolfe's manuscript in order to bring the three works into publishable form, but the notion of ascribing authorship to him was absurd. In the article, I pointed out how and why Aswell made the changes he did in the stack of manuscript that Wolfe left in his hands. Yet, I was dissatisfied; there was much more to say in this matter. I wanted to put visible manuscript evidence before the reading public.

As a consequence, I went ahead to mount a manuscript exhibition, with the help of the Assistant Curator of Manuscripts at Houghton Library, during a convention of the Thomas Wolfe Society at Harvard. I chose a great many sample pages from the manuscript that would illustrate the full range of the kinds of editing Aswell engaged in as he prepared Wolfe's material for publication. They demonstrated how and why he had to cut large blocks of material — because there were duplications, previous publications, unfinished episodes, undeveloped materials, irrelevantly intrusive materials, or dangers of libel action. The pages showed in detail that Aswell's copy-editing was necessary because of shifts in narrative point-of-view, inconsistency in the names of characters, harshness of language (again to avoid a possible law suit), and adjustment of material that Wolfe had taken from earlier versions but had not yet fitted into his final manuscript.

A look at these typescript pages made members of the Wolfe Society who had harbored any doubts about Wolfe's authorship of the novels feel certain that he had written them.

I then published an article describing the exhibition, with illustrations of many of the typescript pages, "Editorial Influence and Authorial Intention" in *Thomas Wolfe: A Harvard Perspective*,[9] in order to make the visual proof of manuscript evidence available to a larger audience. Even in the twentieth century in the United States, it is sometimes necessary to go to the manuscripts themselves for final proof of authorship.

Richard S. Kennedy

[1]*Harvard Library Bulletin*, 21 (1973), 400-401.

[2]Houghton Library, bMS Am 1883 (1336).

[3]Houghton Library, bMS Am 1883.3 (34).

[4]*Harvard Library Bulletin*, 23 (1975), 203-211.

[5]"The Making of Thomas Wolfe's Posthumous Novels," *Yale Review*, Autumn 1980, pp. 79-94.

[6]Interview by Eliot Fremont-Smith, 25 February 1981.

[7]"Who Wrote Thomas Wolfe's Last Novels?" Letter to the *New York Review of Books*, 19 March 1981.

[8]"The 'Wolfegate' Affair," September-October 1981, pp. 48-54, 62.

[9]Athens, Ohio: Croissant & Company, 1983, pp. 87-108.

14

The Master of the Harvard Hannibal

The named is the mother of all things.
Lao-tzu, c.604-c.531 B.C.

I cannot tell what the dickens his name is.
Shakespeare, The Merry Wives of Windsor, III, ii, 20.

THE MASTER OF THE HARVARD HANNIBAL was named after a frontispiece miniature depicting the *Coronation of Hannibal* in a Harvard manuscript of Livy's *Roman History.* The picture shows the acclamation of Hannibal as emperor by the Carthaginians, an event that does not appear in Livy's original text (where Hannibal is appointed general) but was added by the French translator, Pierre Bersuire. The art historian Millard Meiss gave the illuminator his nickname in 1968 in the second volume of his three-volume study, *French Painting in the Time of Jean de Berry.* Examining how and why this artist received his name tells us something of the nature of authorship, both for the Middle Ages and for today.

Illuminators, like other medieval craftsmen, performed their duties and created their art, on the whole, anonymously. Few signed their work, and if we know the names of any of these painters, like Jean Pucelle of the early fourteenth century, or Jean Bourdichon of the late fifteenth, it is mostly by accident; an occasional name can be gleaned from payment records or inventories. The cult of the artistic personality — and, concomitantly, the artist's name — was really a product of the Italian Renaissance and affected northern Europe only in the sixteenth century.

After it was painted in the early fifteenth century by an artist whose name was then soon forgotten, the Harvard Livy, like most medieval manuscripts, did not attract the attention of art historians until some five hundred years later in the wake of the resurgence of interest in illumination that took place after World War II. How the Harvard Livy attracted attention and what scholars wrote about its distinctive frontispiece represent a typical rebirth of an artistic personality. Dorothy Miner included the manuscript in her influential 1949 exhibition and catalogue, *Illuminated Books of the Middle Ages and Renaissance,* and observed that while there were several hands at work, the one responsible for the *Coronation of Hannibal* belonged to an excellent artist working in a style dif-

Livy, *Les Decades,* illumination by the Master of the Harvard Hannibal; France, early 15th cent.

ferent from the rest of the miniatures. (One might call this remark the Harvard Master's conception.) Marvin Ross, in the catalogue accompanying his 1959 exhibition in Los Angeles, *Mediaeval and Renaissance Manuscripts*, remarked upon the fine representation of contemporaneous costume, a penchant of the Harvard Master's that others will also note. In 1967, on the "eve of the artist's birth," William Wixom, in his book, *Treasures from Medieval France*, said that the frontispiece "is eloquent evidence of a major artist's hand. This is a masterpiece of color, modeling, draftsmanship, and composition." Masterpieces, in today's art history, can never go unattributed. In the following year, finally, Meiss cited the *Coronation* as the painter's eponymous work and, gathering two other manuscripts around him, established him as a distinctive and distinguishable artistic personality: "he was a good storyteller . . . He delights in fantastic headgear . . . [and] favored, among other things, curved wooden ceilings and tie-beams." Once named, and with his recognizable artistic personality aptly characterized, the oeuvre of the Master of the Harvard Hannibal quickly grew. By 1974, in the third volume of his study cited above, *The Limbourgs and Their Contemporaries*, Meiss, adding to his list, among other examples, illumination recognized by Otto Pächt and J.J.G. Alexander, attributed twenty manuscripts to the illuminator. With a more precise notion of the artist's choice of colors, Meiss noted that while he "normally preferred bright reds, greens, blues and yellows, he did choose on occasion a different palette. . . . Areas of polished white are combined with clear blue, pink, lavender and persimmon." Meiss also remarked that in terms of borrowing compositions from other illuminators, the Harvard Master was "a veritable sponge." More recently, in 1982, John Plummer, in *The Last Flowering: French Painting in Manuscripts, 1420-1530*, and activity in the auction rooms (the latest at Sotheby's in London on 29 November 1990, lot 136) have brought the oeuvre to nearly two dozen.

Gathered together, like archaeological fragments of what would otherwise be a lost life, the body of work produced by the man with the funny tag does, indeed, tell a story, albeit a sketchy one. Based on the style of his painting we can tell that the Harvard Master was French and worked from about 1410 to about 1430, beginning his career in Paris. Compositional and iconographic similarities between his work and that of the Boucicaut Master, Paris's leading illuminator in the early fifteenth century, indicate that the Harvard Master began his career within the former's shop, working more as a collaborator, however, than as an assistant since he never assimilated the Boucicaut Master's style. Later works by the Harvard Master reveal that he left the Boucicaut Master's shop and established one of his own, taking on assistants. Liturgical evidence from some of his Books of Hours indicates that he left Paris during the occupation by the English in 1420 and moved north to French Flanders, to Lille or Tournai. Shortly after this we lose sight of him. Thus, although deprived of his actual name, a picture of the Master of the Harvard Hannibal as both man and artist does emerge: his time, the places he worked, his artistic origins and stylistic development, and something, even, of the nature of his success.

We realize that names make a difference when art historians attempt to change them. One scholar would prefer calling the Rouennais illuminator, named the Master of the

Geneva Latini after a manuscript of Brunetto Latini's *Le Trésor* in that Swiss city, the Maître de l'échevinage de Rouen because that designation would more accurately reflect where the artist worked and the primarily lay clientele who hired him. Another scholar would like to rename the Master of the Brussels Initials the Master of the Hours of Charles III de Navarre because the former name, referring to decoration of dubious quality, connotes a secondary painter while the latter, alluding to a more important work whose royal patron has been identified, reflects the artist's purportedly truer and loftier position in the hierarchy of late medieval illumination.

Nothing of what we know about the Master of the Harvard Hannibal comes from his name, of course; but the *recognition* of who this artist was, on the other hand, *is* connected to the name that has been given to him. Why? One of the reasons is that this agreeably alliterative, nearly dactylic label so quickly conjures up the illuminator's style by immediately bringing to mind the very work that encapsulates his artistic essentials. That painting and its style stick in the same mind that will quickly forget the differences, say, between the Master of Morgan 85 and the Master of Morgan 96. Significantly, too, no one has proposed changing the name of the Master of the Harvard Hannibal to anything else.

Roger S. Wieck

III

THE HISTORY
OF THE MANUSCRIPT

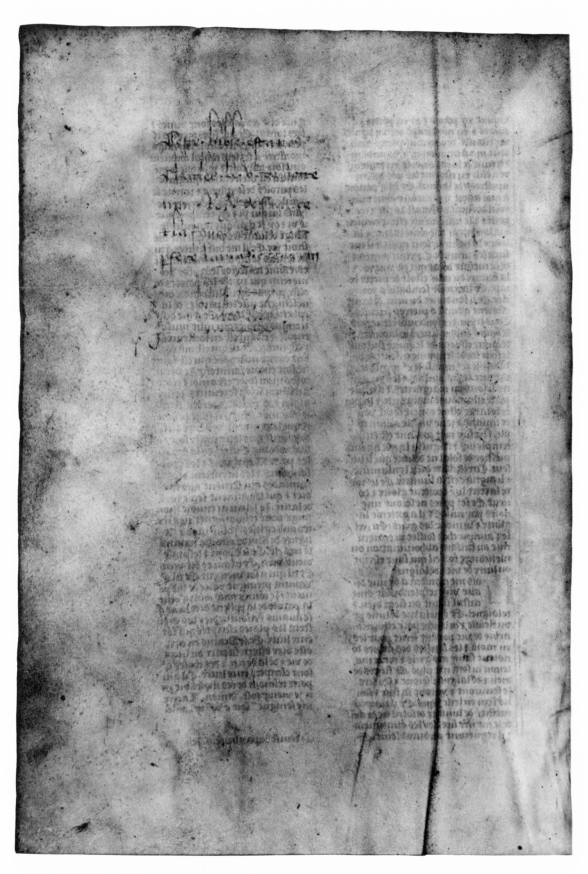

Charles V, King of France, signature and docketing erased from the last leaf of an illuminated *Bible historiale,* France, 1373, an ultraviolet photograph.

15

La Bible historiale de Charles V

L<small>E ROI</small> C<small>HARLES</small> V (1364-1380) est un des rares souverains aux goûts intellectuels que la France ait compté. Réfléchi et lettré, avide de lectures savantes, il avait rassemblé dans ses différentes résidences, tout spécialement dans son château du Louvre et au donjon de Vincennes, un nombre de manuscrits très considérable pour l'époque. Par suite des vicissitudes politiques et de l'achat, en 1424, par le régent anglais Jean de Lancastre, duc de Bedford, de ce qui restait de la bibliothèque du Louvre, cet ensemble se trouve aujourd'hui dispersé, et les épaves qui en ont été retrouvées sont conservées dans de nombreuses institutions, notamment à la Bibliothèque Nationale, dont la "librairie" du "Sage roi" est considérée comme la préfigure. Ce goût des livres se doublait d'un mécénat très actif qui se traduisit par la commande de traductions de textes importants pour la conduite des affaires politiques notamment, mais aussi de manuscrits liturgiques, bibliques, scientifiques, astrologiques, etc., qui requéraient la mobilisation d'un nombre relativement important de traducteurs, de copistes et d'enlumineurs. A ce titre, les manuscrits du roi fournissent un témoignage de premier ordre sur l'activité de la librairie parisienne du troisième quart du XIVe siècle.

Le nombre de volumes actuellement repérés comme ayant appartenu de façon certaine à Charles V atteint à peine la centaine, ce qui représente tout au plus dix pour cent des ouvrages décrits dans les inventaires du roi. La grande majorité de ces manuscrits fut identifiée par Léopold Delisle qui a décrit dans ses *Recherches sur la librairie de Charles V*, parues en 1907, cent quatre volumes pouvant être rattachés selon lui à la librairie royale: en réalité, si l'on élimine les identifications douteuses et les livres entrés du temps de Charles VI, c'est à soixante-dix-sept seulement que s'élève le nombre des manuscrits mentionnés par Delisle dont la provenance des collections de Charles V peut être considérée comme certaine. Depuis, vint-et-un manuscrits ou fragments de manuscrits supplémentaires ont pu être reconnus comme étant de la même origine. La pluspart d'entre eux ont été retrouvés dans les fonds du Département des Manuscrits de la Bibliothèque Nationale. L'un d'eux, provenant d'une collection écossaise, vient d'enrichir tout récemment ces mêmes fonds: il s'agit d'une traduction datée de 1359 de deux traités d'astrologues arabes, Zahel et Messehallach, qui constitue le plus ancien témoignage connu à ce jour du mécénat littéraire de Charles V (B.N., N. a. fr. 18867).

Aucun manuscrit de Charles V ne se trouvait, du temps de Delisle, dans les collections des Etats-Unis. On en dénombre aujourd'hui quatre: le plus ancien et le plus fameux est le petit livre d'Heures en grisaille des Cloisters qu'il y a tout lieu d'identifier avec les Heures enluminées par Jean Pucelle pour la reine Jeanne d'Evreux qui en fit don à son petit-neveu Charles V en 1371. Acheté en 1954, ce minuscule chef-d'oeuvre provient des collections Rothschild. Le second est le fragment des Heures de Blanche de Bourgogne, duchesse de Savoie, retrouvé en 1910 par Dom Blanchard à l'évêché de Portsmouth et acquis en 1969 par la Beinecke Library de l'Université de Yale (MS 390). Enfin la Houghton Library de l'Université d'Harvard a le privilège de détenir deux autres manuscrits de la librairie royale: le premier est la *Bible historiale* dont nous reparlerons plus loin; l'autre est la deuxième partie d'un exemplaire de la traduction du *De Civitate Dei* de Saint Augustin composée entre 1371 et 1375 par Raoul de Presles pour Charles V (MS Typ 201). Ce dernier manuscrit, offert en 1982 par Philip Hofer, et pendant d'un volume conservé à la bibliothèque municipale d'Angers, est considéré comme ayant été exécuté pour Jean de Berry, mais fut très certainement commandé par son frère aîné, comme le prouve la présence dans le manuscrit d'Angers, d'un écu gratté soutenu par deux lions, supports propres à Charles V, et comme le confirme le style des illustrations, dues à la collaboration de trois enlumineurs parisiens fréquemment associés dans les manuscrits destinés au roi, le maître de la Bible de Jean de Sy, le maître du Livre du sacre et le maître du Couronnement de Charles VI, ces deux derniers artistes collaborant également dans la *Bible historiale* mentionnée plus haut. Il est très probable que cet exemplaire de la traduction de Raoul de Presles, de format nettement plus grand que l'exemplaire royal conservé à la Bibliothèque Nationale (Français 22912-22913), correspond à l'article suivant des deux plus anciens inventaires de la librairie du Louvre: "*Un livre de la Cité de Dieu, en deux volumes très grans, couvert de soie à queue, à IIII fermoirs d'argent chascun.*" Le "petit" exemplaire de la Nationale était, selon les inventaires, recouvert du même tissu précieux, qui semble bien avoir été réservé aux livres expressément exécutés pour le roi, et il y a donc de fortes chances pour que Charles ait fait copier, enluminer et relier en même temps les deux exemplaires, ce que confirme la similitude de leur décoration et de leur programme d'illustrations. Ce n'est pas la seule fois que Charles V aurait commandé deux "éditions" différentes d'une oeuvre rédigée à son intention: la traduction des *Ethiques* et des *Politiques* d'Aristotle par Nicole Oresme fit semblablement l'objet, à la même époque, de deux copies quasi jumelles mais de formats différents.

L'appartenance de la *Bible historiale* fMS Typ 555 à Charles V est encore mieux établie. Les deux volumes de cette Bible présentent tous les caractères externes qui distinguent les manuscrits commandés par le roi et les membres de la famille royale: écriture (qui semble bien être celle d'un de ses scribes favoris, Raoulet d'Orléans), décoration peinte (oeuvre de deux enlumineurs, le maître du Livre du Sacre et le maître du Couronnement de Charles VI, auxquels le roi s'adressait régulièrement pour l'illustration de ses livres), ornementation filigranée, où l'on reconnaît un motif particulier aux manuscrits royaux de cette période, et consistant en une bande verticale ornée de demi-fleurs de lis alternativement or (ou rouge) et azur partant des initiales. La réunion de ces différentes particularités constituait déjà une forte présomption en faveur de la destination royale des deux volumes. Pourtant, c'est vainement que l'on chercherait à identifier ces derniers dans les inventaires que nous avons conservés des manuscrits de Charles V. Le seul article d'inventaire qui pourrait convenir aux deux volumes d'Harvard (Delisle, *Recherches*, t. II, p. 6, n° 20) ne fournit pas les mots repères qui seuls permettraient une identification certaine. Heureusement, il existe dans le manuscrit même un élément décisif qui permet de trancher définitivement en faveur de la présence de la Bible dans les collections de Charles V. Lorsque j'examinai celle-ci en 1970, je découvris à la fin du deuxième volume (fol. 275) les traces d'une inscription grattée qui se révéla sous la lampe à ultra-violets être les restes d'un ex-libris autographe de Charles V. Cet ex-libris se trouve au verso du fol. 275 du deuxième volume, et peut être déchiffré comme suit (les parties entre crochets carrés sont illisibles mais peuvent être restituées à partir d'inscriptions similaires):

> *Ceste Bible est à nous*
> *Charles le Ve de notre*
> *nom, Roy de France*
> *et la fimes [faire]*
> *et p(ar)fere [l'an M.CCC.LXX III]*
> *[Charles]*

Dans sa formulation, son orthographe et son écriture, cette inscription offre une parenté évidente avec les autres ex-libris autographes que le Sage roi écrivit à différentes époques dans un certain nombre de ses manuscrits. Ceux qu'avait repérés Delisle sont au nombre de neuf, et, pour ceux d'entre eux qui sont datés, s'échelonnent entre 1365 (Londres, British Library, Cotton, Tiberius B VIII, *Livre du sacre*) et 1378 (Bible bolonnaise de la cathédrale de Gérone). J'ai pu pour ma part en retrouver quatre autres, dont celui d'Harvard, grâce à la lampe de Wood (*Les Voies de Dieu*, B.N., Français 1792, fol. 89^v; *Grandes Chroniques de France*, B.N., Français 2813, fol. 263^v; *Bible historiale*, Arsenal, ms. 5212, fol. 417^v, et *Bible historiale* de Harvard). La présence d'un cinquième peut encore être décelée à la fin du deuxième volume du "petit" exemplaire de la traduction de la Cité de Dieu par Raoul de Presles (B.N., Français 22912, fol. 445^v). D'une longueur de six lignes, cet ex-libris, très soigneusement gratté, est malheureusement illisible. Il est frappant de constater la proportion importante de manuscrits bibliques dans lesquels Charles V a éprouvé le besoin d'inscrire sa marque de propriété: cinq manuscrits sont dans ce cas, deux Bibles latines (Arsenal, ms. 590, et Gérone, cathédrale) et trois Bibles historiales (B.N., Français 5707, Arsenal 5212 et Harvard, Houghton Library, MS Typ 555). Ceci concorde bien avec l'intérêt très marqué que le souverain manifesta toujours pour les Ecritures.

François Avril

Bibliographie:
Sur la Bible MS Typ 555:

R. S. Wieck, *Late Medieval and Renaissance Illuminated Manuscripts, 1350-1525, in the Houghton Library* (Cambridge 1983), pp. 2 et 136-137.

Sur la "librairie" de Charles V:

L. Delisle, *Recherches sur la librairie de Charles V* (Paris 1907), 2 vol. et un album de planches.

La Librairie de Charles V, exposition; Bibliothèque Nationale (Paris 1968).

Provenance de la Bible d'Harvard:

Charles V, roi de France; peut-être la Bible en français offerte par Charles VI au duc Louis de Bourbon en 1397 (Delisle, *Recherches*, t. II, p. 6, n° 6); Pierre et Jérôme de Villars, archevêques de Vienne (1588-1599 et 1599-1626); Gayot de la Régasse, 1697; Cardinal François-Paul de Neufville de Villeroy, archevêque de Lyon (1714-1731); Prince Michel Pétrovitch Galitzine (sa vente, Paris, 3 mars 1825); Henry Perkins (sa vente, Londres, Gadsden et Ellis, 3 juin 1873); M. Benzon; acheté à Quaritch par T. Shadford Walker (sa vente, Londres, 23 juin 1886); acheté de Quaritch par William Augustus White; légué en 1968 à Harvard par son petit-fils Francis Minot Weld.

16

A Psalter from Saint-Riquier

MS Typ 311 is a beautiful Latin liturgical psalter, dating from the second quarter of the thirteenth century.[1] It contains:

Folios 1ʳ-6ᵛ   Calendar
        7ʳ-129ʳ   Psalms 1-150, (*Psalterium Gallicanum*)
        129ʳ-136ʳ   Six Canticles
        136ʳ-137ʳ   Te Deum
        137ʳ-137ᵛ   Benedicite omnia opera
        137ᵛ-138ᵛ   Three Canticles
        138ᵛ-140ᵛ   Athanasian Creed
        140ᵛ-144ʳ   Litany and prayers
        144ʳ-150ʳ   Office of the Dead
        150ᵛ-152ʳ   Three Marian sequences (with musical notation)
        152ʳ-154ᵛ   Various prayers

The prayers that form the last item represent later additions, made at various times, to the original collection. This collection — if we omit the three Marian sequences — belongs to a well defined category described by V. Leroquais, in *Les Psautiers manuscrits latins*, as "Psautier-livre d'heures."[2] The manuscript was made for (if not produced at) the abbey of Centula, also known as Saint-Riquier, from the name of its supposed founder (Richarius), near Abbeville, in northern France.[3] The connection with Saint-Riquier is established by the calendar and the litany that flank the psalms. The calendar has five references to the monastery's founder and patron: (26 April) *Depositio sanctissimi patris nostri Richarii*; (3 June) *Relatio sancti patris nostri Richarii*; (9 October) *Translatio sancti Richarii*; (16 October) *Octava sancti Richarii*; (2 December) *Commemoratio reliquiarum beati Richarii* [feast of all the saints whose relics were preserved at the abbey]. In the litany (f. 141ᵛ) the names of *Richarius* and *Vigor*, placed at the head of the "Confessors" — even before the names of popes and church fathers — receive a double invocation.[4] Hariulf, the eleventh-century historian of Saint-Riquier, describes how the relics of St. Vigor, former bishop of Bayeux, were acquired by his abbey, and we know from the other texts what pride it took in this possession.[5] St. Vigor's feast, accompanied by an octave, is found in the calendar on 1 November. Names of other

History of ownership, partly defaced, in a 13th cent. Psalter from St. Riquier, an ultraviolet photograph.

saints intimately linked either with the history of Richarius, like Caydoc and Adrian (Frichorus),[6] Madelgisile and Maurontus,[7] or with the history of the abbey, like Angilbert, its rebuilder in Carolingian times (Hariulf calls him *reaedificator*)[8] are found both in the calendar and in the litany. Other names of saints point to nearby monastic houses,[9] or to Amiens in whose diocese Saint-Riquier was situated.[10]

Whether MS Typ 311 was actually made at Saint-Riquier, or produced elsewhere for the abbey, must remain an open question. Historiated initials, varying in size, occur at the beginning of Psalms 1, 26, 38, 51, 52, 68, 80, 97, 101, and 109. They represent:

Psalm 1	David and Goliath
	David playing the harp
Psalm 26	The anointing of David as king by Samuel
Psalm 38	David pointing to his mouth ("that I may not sin with my tongue")
Psalm 51	The slaying of Ahimelech and others by Doeg (I Sam. 22:18)
Psalm 52	A fool ("The fool said in his heart")
Psalm 68	David saved from shipwreck ("Save me . . . from the waters")
Psalm 80	David playing on bells ("Raise a song, sound the timbrel")
Psalm 97	Monks singing ("let the earth rejoice")
Psalm 101	David praying before an altar ("Hear my prayer, O Lord")
Psalm 109	The Trinity

MS Typ 311 shares this set of illustrations with numerous other manuscripts of the period. The series represents a conflation of two earlier artistic traditions, one based on a tripartite division of the psalter — where historiated initials accompany Psalms 1, 51, and 101 — the other, where the initials mark the first psalm of Matins for each day of the week, beginning with Sunday (Psalms 1, 26, 38, 52, 68, 80, 97, 101). This last series, however, betrays the fact that the original artistic model, on which MS Typ 311 in conjunction with a whole group of thirteenth-century psalters depends (Günter Hazelhoff[11] lists more than 150 manuscripts), originated not in the monastic, but in the secular tradition of the cathedral and parish churches. A division of psalms originating in a monastic scriptorium would have placed the illustrations at Psalms 20, 32, 45, 59, 73, 85, 101, following the arrangement decreed by St. Benedict's Rule. (Psalm 109 is the first psalm for Vespers on Sunday in both the secular and monastic traditions.) Since Hazelhoff fails to include a single thirteenth-century psalter that reflects the monastic division, we can only conclude that once the "secular" artistic series began to circulate, it was accepted everywhere as standard, even in monastic scriptoria. Thus the layout of MS Typ 311, by itself, does not suffice to show that our manuscript was not produced at Saint-Riquier.

Only an intense comparative study of all the artistic features of MS Typ 311 with the few surviving manuscripts of Saint-Riquier, but especially with the numerous other psalters of the period, is likely to provide the necessary clues as to where it was made. The decoration of the manuscript is superb, the use of gold leaf at times astonishing. Particularly noticeable are the line-fillers that ornament every page, and also the numerous tiny, delicate, and meticulously drawn figures of birds, animals, and plants, normally white on a blue — but sometimes on a brown — background, that occur in profusion in the smaller initials. The cumulative impression suggests an accomplished atelier, armed with a whole repertory of "fillers," and used to turning out manuscripts of this kind. That this atelier was situated in the former province of Picardy, whose capital was Amiens, is suggested by one particular element of the decoration. On f. 60 we find David shown in a boat. The illustration to Psalm 68 ("Save me . . . from the waters") normally shows a naked David half immersed in water. In a few manuscripts (six as opposed to close to one hundred) David is shown in a boat. All these manuscripts, as Hazeloff points out, belong to Picardy, where Saint-Riquier itself was situated.[12] So the atelier where MS Typ 311 was made could have been located at Amiens (or Arras, about equidistant from Saint-Riquier), unless we need to envisage a skilled scribe-artist making the rounds of various abbeys and churches in the region. Given the wealth of surviving material, it would be surprising if further research, particularly into the different series of line-fillers found in manuscripts of the period, did not bring out new evidence regarding the manuscript's place of origin.

MS Typ 311 was produced for the abbey of Saint-Riquier. What of its later history? V. Leroquais has provided abundant evidence to show that psalters did travel in the Middle Ages and were then adapted to suit their new homes: one English psalter went to Evreux and another to Melun, one Paris psalter came to rest with the Benedictines of Arles, and another at the abbey of Sainte-Croix of Poitiers.[13] Evidence for such dislocations can be gleaned from the erasures, additions, and substitutions in the lists of saints' names in the calendars and litanies that accompany the psalters. Both the calendar and the litany of MS Typ 311 are singularly devoid of any such changes.[14] One near-contemporary hand added the name of St. Bridgid (1 February) in the calendar on f. 1ᵛ, but veneration of the abbess of Kildare was so widespread that this addition may prove no more than the remedy for an oversight on the part of the original scribe. In the litany, on f. 141ᵛ, a later hand substituted the name of Bernard for one of the original names but, interestingly, did not add Bernard's name to the calendar on 20 August. This suggests that, at the time the substitution was made, more practical use was being made of the litany than of the calendar. The pristine condition of the calendar, where the latest — chronological — feast recorded is that of St. Francis (4 October), canonized in 1228, shows that as time went by and as Saint-Riquier adopted new feasts into its liturgy, the calendar had ceased to serve a practical purpose.

The office for the dead occurs in numerous psalters of the type that Leroquais terms "Psautier-livres d'heures." The series of lessons, together with responsories and versicles, can vary greatly from manuscript to manuscript, and such a series is indeed a help in localizing manuscripts. The particular series found in MS Typ 311, on folios 144ʳ-150ʳ, agrees with the usage of Saint-Riquier, which we also know from the Saint-Riquier Book of Hours (Abbeville, Bibl. munic. MS 17). This series remains close to the Roman one and differs considerably, for example, from that of Amiens.[15]

The three Marian sequences found on folios 150ᵛ-152ʳ deserve some attention.[16] The combination of a psalter with a hymnal is not unusual, but in such cases the hymnal normally covers the liturgical year. What seems much rarer is a psalter that includes only Marian chants or proses.[17] A gradual from Nevers gives a list of 17 Marian proses with the interesting note: *Ordo iste prosarum que secuntur continetur in uno psalterio ex utraque parte chori et sunt de beata Virgine.* There is also evidence of Marian sequences or proses being added to books associated with the monastic office of Prime. A manuscript from Cornillon, a priory of Chaise-Dieu, contains a martyrology, a Rule of St. Benedict, and a necrology — all used at Prime — to which were added a set of Marian proses with notation.[18] The three Marian sequences in MS Typ 311 also have notation, each melody ending with a melismatic *Amen*, normal for the period. Over the centuries the Virgin was honored in several places at Saint-Riquier. According to the chronicler Hariulf (II.7), Angilbert had built a small church to Mary to the south of the main church, linking the two together by a long cloister. By the twelfth century, however, this church had ceased to be a part of the monastic complex and had become the parish church.[19] The seventeenth-century Maurist plan of Saint-Riquier shows an oratory of the Virgin (*aedicula B. M. Virginis*) at the end of the main apse of the big monastic church.[20] The present structure dates from the time of abbot Eustache Le Quieux (1480-1511) — after the big fire of 1487 — but probably replaced an earlier similar chapel that may well have been contemporary with our psalter and likewise dedicated to the Virgin. According to the abbreviated chronicle of 1492, hymns to the Virgin were sung in this Marian oratory "hora consueta et ante Primam" in the days of Nicholas Bourdon, famous cantor and musicologist of Saint-Riquier — who died in 1452 at the age of 80.[21] If celebration of a Mass of the Virgin before Prime, or her veneration at this office, was a tradition at Saint-Riquier, we may have the key to the presence of the sequences in the psalter. We also know that Abbot Gervinus I (1045-1075) caused a crypt to be made under the church in which he placed four altars, the main altar being dedicated to the Virgin.[22] Masses to the Virgin were undoubtedly celebrated here. Thus our psalter may have been associated with either the oratory or the crypt, and this may explain the inclusion of the Marian sequences.

Although the calendar was not kept up to date, the various prayers (mainly to the Virgin, but also to Saints Yvo, Sebastian, and Christopher) added at the end (folios 152[r]-154[v]) show that the psalter continued in use until at least the fifteenth/sixteenth century — the date of the latest script observable. But none of these added prayers suggests a different home for the manuscript.[23] Based on the evidence of its liturgical contents alone, we might conclude that Typ 311 continued its quiet existence at Saint-Riquier through the centuries.

Only one piece of evidence contradicts this picture. On the verso of the first flyleaf is a note, written in broad letters and in a faded brown ink, four lines of which have been erased but nevertheless remain legible in ultraviolet light; these lines are bracketed in the transcription below. This note reads:

> Ce livre a esté trouvé dans une concavité prati
> quée entre deux murailles d'une tres ancienne mai

son de la Ville d'Arras dans la Rue des trois visages,
appartenante a monsieur Mathon, Receveur general des
[Etats d'Artois et donné par le dit Sieur Mathon a nô
tre Révérend Père en Dieu Frère Jean Durlin Abbé
de Dompmartin pours lors Député Ordinaire des Etats
d'Artois, lequel en a enrichi nôtre Bibliothèque comme]
d'une antiquité curieuse. l'Année 1700.

Ultraviolet light also reveals a line written vertically down the right-hand edge of f. 1^r:

Bibliotheca Dompmartinensis, 1701

The note suggests a dramatic story: the discovery of the psalter at Arras, in a cavity situated between two walls of a house that belonged to Sieur Mathon; its presentation by Mathon in 1700 to Jean Durlin, abbot of Dommartin, a Premonstratensian abbey situated less than 25 kilometers due north of Saint-Riquier, and finally the recording and inclusion of the psalter as "une antiquité curieuse" in the library of Dommartin. What historical verification is possible here?

Jean Durlin was abbot of Dommartin from 1676 to 1701.[24] A French chronicle of Dommartin, covering the years 1672 to 1789, has come down to us in Abbeville, Bibliothèque municipale, Ms 95.[25] The contemporary chronicler, Fr. André Guilleman, makes no mention of Mathon or his gift in 1700, but he does inform us that in August of this year Jean Durlin ceased to be Député ordinaire of the Etats d'Artois, a position he had held for 12 years. In the following month, September, Durlin was chosen "Député en cours aux Etats d'Artois," and later in the year he set out for Paris to take up his position at the court. He never returned to Dommartin since he died in Paris on 6 May of the following year. His heart was sent back for burial at the abbey. If the account it gives is true, the gift of the psalter to Dommartin which the note records must therefore have occurred before August 1700.

As regards Arras, the archives of Dommartin record the acquisition by Jean Durlin of a house on Rue des Trois Visages, at some date between 1696 and 1700.[26] Even more interesting is the information that a Guillaume Mathon (1642-1706), "receveur général des centièmes des Etats de la province d'Artois" (a position he can be proven to have held from 1692 onward) had caused a new house to be built on this same street, close to the date mentioned in the note transcribed above. This information emerges from Guillaume Mathon's will, dated 1 August 1705, in which he lists — among the various properties bequeathed to his son, Antoine-Guislain-Guillaume Mathon (1686-1743) — his new house ("nouvellement construite"), at 6, Rue des Trois Visages, Arras.[27] A newly constructed house surely suggests the demolition of some earlier building on this old street of Arras. Incontrovertible circumstantial evidence thus seems to confirm the likelihood that the remarkable discovery recorded in the note of 1700 actually took place.

And yet the note is not without its problems. We know that Saint-Riquier had had friendly relations with Dommartin over the centuries, stretching back to 1143.[28] In 1634 a spiritual confraternity was established between the two houses. It seems strange that when the psalter was discovered, in 1700, it was not immediately recognized for what it was, namely a Saint-Riquier psalter. Even if Mathon could not decipher the writing, the religious community at Dommartin would surely have had no difficulty in identifying the psalter's true home. The statement that they viewed it as "une antiquité curieuse" to be placed in their own library has a slightly odd ring.

And there are other elements generating suspicions. Jules Hénocque, in volume 2 of his vast history of Saint-Riquier published in 1883, mentions having seen a very rich psalter, formerly belonging to Saint-Riquier. He alludes to it in his chapter on Jean de Foucaucourt (1303-1312), the abbot responsible for reforming the Saint-Riquier calendar and for having a splendid illuminated missal made for the monastery. It is in this context that Hénocque mentions "un psautier très rich, appartenant à peu près à cette époque."[29] At the time he was writing, this psalter belonged to a family named "de la Houplière du Château-Neuf, commune of Quend."[30] Hénocque tells us that he identified this sumptuous psalter as a Saint-Riquier manuscript on the basis of its calendar.

Further on in the same volume Hénocque transcribes some entries from a calendar and litany that he entitles: "Calendrier du XIIIᵉ siècle. Fêtes propres au monastère de Saint-Riquier, d'après un calendrier manuscrit d'un psautier provenant du monastère."[31] One is naturally tempted to conclude that these transcriptions must come from the psalter then at Château-Neuf. But tucked away in an (un-indexed) note of volume one is a reference to another Saint-Riquier psalter, which Hénocque had also consulted: "Un psautier du douzième ou treizième siècle, appartenant à la famille de M. Canu de Saint-Riquier."[32] Although probably made from this local and more accessible psalter, the transcriptions agree almost letter for letter with what we find in MS Typ 311. Hénocque does not refer to the Canu psalter as "très riche," and all the evidence suggests that the psalter belonging to Château-Neuf is the one now in the Harvard library.[33]

Hénocque states that this psalter "avait été donné au chapitre d'Arras," but he does not give us his reasons for making this statement. Nor does he refer to the note concerning the discovery of the psalter and its presentation to Dommartin, which is puzzling, particularly since he describes the historical links that existed between Saint-Riquier and Dommartin, including the confraternity of prayers drawn up in 1634. There seems a clash, moreover, between Hénocque's assertion that the manuscript came from the Chapter of Arras and the note of 1700, which refers only to the discovery of the psalter in a private house at Arras. Was the note on the flyleaf of MS Typ 311 in place there when Hénocque had the volume in hand? If it was not there at the time we would have grounds for viewing it as a forgery inserted after 1883, although finding a satisfactory motive for such a forgery, dovetailing so neatly with verifiable events connected with the Rue des Trois Visages, might be more difficult. Perhaps we should take a new look at the manuscript to see whether any other explanation can be made.

There is evidence of a rough excision toward the beginning of the manuscript, not of whole pages but of pieces of parchment that had been inserted. Stubs, with traces of writing on them, survive before and after f.8. Let us suppose that what was removed carried an indication that the Arras Chapter had possessed the manuscript at one time. We next need to ask whether, when Hénocque saw the manuscript, the four lines referring to Dommartin in the note on the flyleaf, together with the *Bibliotheca Dompmartinensis* on f. 1ʳ, might not already have been erased. If so, Hénocque would have had no reason to think of this Premonstratensian abbey, and the ascription to the Arras Chapter would have been more important to him than the partially erased note recounting later adventures of the manuscript in Arras.

If we start with the supposition that the note is authentic, we can begin to speculate on possible reasons for the erasure of the lines that demonstrate former possession of the volume by Dommartin. The most likely explanation would seem to be connected with the course of the French Revolution. In 1789 the French Assembly nationalized all religious and monastic property, and decreed that inventories of ecclesiastical goods were to be made in preparation for their sale. Land and precious objects were to be sold for the benefit of the state, and the contents of monastic libraries were to be transferred to the municipal libraries of neighboring cities or towns. This explains why some French municipal libraries are so richly endowed with former monastic manuscripts, like Troyes with its collection from Clairvaux, Douai with the manuscripts from Saint-Vaast, etc. The intended depository for the libraries of Saint-Riquier and surrounding monasteries, like Dommartin and Valloires, was Abbeville.[34] If very few Saint-Riquier manuscripts are to be found there today, this is probably because many of the abbey's former possessions were on deposit at the "hôtel de la Gruthuse" at Abbeville when, in January 1795, this building caught fire and burned down.[35] Other circumstances sometimes account for the failure of books and manuscripts to reach their intended depositories. As regards Saint-Riquier, at the time of the confiscation in 1791, it was being rumored that the monks "vendoient sans autorisation et à bas prix les livres de leur bibliothèque." The directoire of Abbeville met to consider how to deal with this flouting of the new decrees: "c'est une infraction formelle aux décrets de l'assemblée nationale et . . . il est très instant de venir au devant des déprédations qui se commettent journellement . . . ."[36] This situation may suggest how some monastic books came into private hands. One can also conjecture that one of the last of the monks, forced to leave his monastic home, may have quietly taken some treasured possession with him when he returned to his native village.

If the note on the flyleaf is authentic, it is therefore to Dommartin rather than to Saint-Riquier that we must turn to find an explanation for the psalter's eventual possession by a private family. Right up to the time of the Revolution the monastery appears to have taken great pride in its library. Thus when the Jesuits were expelled from France in 1764, the librarian of Dommartin went to Paris to acquire many volumes (and even some Poussin paintings) that had been confiscated from Jesuit houses.[37] At the time of its suppression Dommartin had thirty monks, but since ten are listed as engaged in parish work outside the abbey, the resident community amounted to twenty.[38] When the monastic property was put up for auction in 1791 it was the last abbot, Dom Gislain-Joseph Oblin (1787-1791), who bought most of it, setting himself up as owner of most of the former monastic buildings and as a farmer on the former monastic lands, promising to pay the nation a yearly rent of "1000 livres." Some of the monks remained with him to share his new life. While such an arrangement might have been acceptable to the authorities, it was bound to foster resentment among the local population, imbued with Revolutionary ideas. In the course of the following year, 1792, anger against Oblin became inflamed, and his companions escaped one by one to avoid the rising hostility. Finally the former abbot was warned, in October 1792, that an attack was imminent. He was able to escape just in time to the house of a friend at Tortefontaine and thus to avoid being captured by the mob. But the man who had been left in charge of the property was unable to prevent the buildings being stormed and ransacked, including the library which at that time still retained all its books. The national guard was called to try to impose order, but it arrived too late.[39]

In the circumstances it is difficult to know exactly when or how the Saint-Riquier psalter was taken from the Dommartin library. One may suspect that it came into private hands either through one of the last monks or at the time the property was plundered, and was then passed along until almost a century later we find it in the possession of a family at Château-Neuf.[40] Looking at the map of the region, one is struck by the proximity of Château-Neuf to Dommartin, little over 20 kilometers away as the crow flies. The family de La Houplière was already a tenant at Château-Neuf before the French Revolution, and Lefèvre de la Houplière bought the property when it was auctioned in 1791.[41] No direct links can be established, however, between this family and Dommartin and, given the distance, it seems unlikely that the family was in any way involved in the events of 1792. But once the psalter was in discerning private hands it is easy enough to understand how the lines implying former possession by Dommartin came to be erased.

The most tantalizing question about MS Typ 311 nevertheless remains unsolved. How did this beautiful psalter from Saint-Riquier come to be hidden away in the house on the Rue des Trois Visages at Arras, before the year 1700? Here we have a nice puzzle around which to construct a medieval detective story.[42]

Paul Meyvaert and Michel Huglo

[1]For an earlier printed description see *The Philip Hofer Collection in the Houghton Library: A Catalogue of an Exhibition of the Philip Hofer Bequest in the Department of Printing and Graphic Arts, Harvard College Library* (Cambridge, 1988), pp. 18-20, signed R[odney] G. D[ennis]. The present binding (brown calf, blind-tooled) is French and dates from the nineteenth century.

[2]V. Leroquais, *Les psautiers manuscrits latins des bibliothèques publiques de France* 1 (Macon, 1940-1941) pp. li- lxii.

[3]The only major overall study of Saint-Riquier is the now outdated work by abbé Jules Hénocque, *Histoire de l'abbaye et de la ville de Saint-Riquier*, 3 vols. (Amiens 1880, 1883, 1888) [cited henceforth as Hénocque, *Histoire*]. A useful bibliography was more recently drawn up by Albert Labarre, "Saint-Riquier, Bibliographie concernant l'abbaye, la ville etc." *Bulletin de la Société des Antiquaires de Picardie*, 47 (1957-1958) 165-204. On p. 179 Labarre states that Paris, B. N. nouv. acq. lat. 2310 contains the list of manuscripts of Saint-Riquier. This is not the

case, as L. Delisle had noted in his brief description of this manuscript ("Catalogue . . . qui ne renferme pas la liste des manuscrits"), and as M. François Avril, of the Cabinet des manuscrits, Bibliothèque Nationale, has now kindly confirmed in a letter of 14 May 1991. Abbeville, Bibliothèque municipale, Mss 173-179, also contain a catalogue of the Saint-Riquier library, but only of the printed books. Thus no catalogue of the manuscripts possessed by Saint-Riquier when it was suppressed in 1791 has come down to us.

[4]On the importance of double invocations in litanies for determining the original home of a manuscript see V. Leroquais, *Les bréviaires manuscrits des bibliothèques publiques de France*, 1 (Macon, 1934) p. lxxiv.

[5]See Hariulf, *Chronicon Centulense* II.9 [ed. F. Lot] (Paris, 1894) pp. 61-67: "De reliquiis quas de diversis provintiis in hunc sanctum locum congregavit [Angilbertus] et de capsis quibus habentur reconditae." Numerous other chapters also refer to the monastery's relics.

[6]In his chronicle of Saint-Riquier (I.6) Hariulf explains that Chaydocus and Frichorus were Irish missionaries who, at the time of Queen Brunichild, evangelized the Ponthieu and were instrumental in converting Richarius to a more religious life. Saint-Riquier claimed to possess their relics among its treasures. Hariulf explains how Frichorus' name came to be changed to Adrian: "eo quod rictu linguae barbarae ineptum visum est, a prioribus mutatum vocator et scribitur Adrianus." [ed. F. Lot, p. 15]. This feature helps to classify and date some Saint-Riquier documents (see below note 14). Both names are now recognized to be Breton rather than Irish.

[7]Madelgisile (in French St. Mauguille) is another saint whose relics were venerated at Saint-Riquier, after being for a time rejected by some in the community. On this interesting case see Dom Eligius Dekkers, "Un cas de critique hagiographique à Saint-Riquier: Les reliques de Saint Mauguille," *Saint Riquier* 1 (Abbaye Saint-Riquier, Somme, [1970?]) pp. 59-67. Mauxontus, son of (St.) Rictrude, is claimed by Saint-Riquier sources as the spiritual son of Richarius: (5 May) "Castro Duaci, S. Maurontii abbatis..qui legitur in baptismate S. Richarii filius" (Saint-Riquier martyrology: see below note 14).

[8]Angilbert had been a great collector of relics (see above note 5), but his own title to sainthood came to be hotly debated in the second half of the last century — had he been the lover of Bertha, Charlemagne's daughter, or legitimately married to her, becoming a monk only after her death? Dom Mabillon had not hesitated to include Angilbert in his *Acta sanctorum Ordinis S. Benedicti* (vol. 4, Pt 1., pp. 108-120 [2nd edition, pp. 103- 115]), mainly on the basis of the *Vita et miracula Angilberti* by Anscherius, abbot of Saint-Riquier (1097-1136) — a *Vita,* however, that deserves little credence.

[9]For example 1 April and 12 December, *Walaricus* (St. Valry), abbot of Samer [Pas-de-Calais].

[10]For example 16 May, *Honoratus*; 1 September, *Firminus conf.*; 25 September, *Firminus mart.*; 28 October, *Salvius*; 11 December, *Fuscianus* and his companions.

[11]Günter Hazelhoff, *Die Psalterillustration im 13. Jahrhundert. Studien zur Geschichte der Buchmalerei in England, Frankreich und den Niederlanden* ([Kiel], 1938).

[12]The manuscripts showing "David im Boot" (and not merely "David im Wasser"), according to Hazelhoff, are Paris, Bibl. Mazarine 36 (Corbie), Paris, B. N. lat. 10,435 (Amiens-Corbie), Paris, B. N. lat 16,260 (Picardie), Amiens, 124 (Amiens-Corbie), Florence, Riccardiana 435 (Nordostfrankreich). The illustrations of this psalm in I. P. Mokretsova and V. L. Romanova, *Les manuscrits enluminés français du XIIIᵉ siècle dans les collections soviètiques 1200-1270* (Moscow, 1983) — showing mostly psalters made in Paris — all agree in presenting David (clothed or unclothed) in the water, but not in a boat.

[13]V. Leroquais, *Les psautiers manuscrits latins des bibliothèques publiques de France* 1 (Macon, 1940-1941) pp. lxiii- lxxi.

[14]To get a perspective on where the calendar of MS Typ 311 stands within the tradition of Saint-Riquier itself one would need to compare it with the list of Proper Feasts [PF] of the Abbey copied by André Duchesne — from an unidentified source — in Paris, Bibl.nat. ms. lat. 12893, f. 250ᵛ (published by Ferdinand Lot, "Nouvelles recherches sur le texte de la Chronique de l'abbaye de Saint-Riquier par Hariulf," *Bibliothèque de l'Ecole des Chartes* 72 [1911] 269-270). Mabillon in his *Annales O.S.B* (vol. 5 [Lucca, 1740] 87) shows that he knew this list, since he refers to it with the same title as Duchesne (*index solemnitatum ad Centulam proprie pertinentium*). He attributes it to the time of Hariulf

(*scriptus tempore Hariulfi*). A comparison should also involve the Saint-Riquier martyrology [MR] published as *Centul.* in the notes of the Bollandists to their edition of the martyrology of Usuardus (*Acta Sanctorum*, vols. 7 and 8 of June: reprinted in Migne, PL 123 and 124). The surviving liturgical books, like Abbeville MS 17 and Wien, N. B. 1933, should also be taken into account (see M. Huglo, "Un missel de Saint-Riquier," *Ephemerides liturgicae* 73 [1959] 401-412). Thus in PF for 2 December we read *Festivitas omnium sanctorum Centula degentium*, while MS Typ 311 uses a different nomenclature *Commemoratio reliquarum beati Richarii.* PF and MR agree (30 May) *Caidoci, Fricori et Magdegisili*, while MS Typ 311 and Abbeville MS 17 change one name and the order *Madelgisili, Caidoci et Adriani.* (On the meaning of this change see above, note 6). It is particularly surprising that none of the dedications of churches and altars found in PF occur in the calendar of MS Typ 311, and only one of them — (30 May) the dedication of the crypt to the Virgin and to St. Richarius — is mentioned in MR. It is also interesting to note that PF includes a *solemnitas* for Abbot Gervinus I on 3 March, but his name is omitted in MR and replaced by Wingaloeus [= Guingaloeus of Landevenec] in MS Typ 311. One senses a debate within the Saint-Riquier community about whether Gervinus should be honored at the altar.

[15]On the various series connected with the office for the dead see the forthcoming publication of Knud Ottosen's Aarhus thesis, *Responsories and Versicles of the Latin Office of the Dead*, p. 101.

[16](1) F. 150ᵛ, *Hodierna lux diei / Celebris in matris Dei* (Cl. Blume, *Analecta Hymnica*, 54, *Die Sequenzen*, No. 219 [pp. 346-349];

(2) F. 151ʳ, *Clemens et benigna / Iugi laude digna* (U. Chevalier, *Repertorium hymnologicum* I, No. 3391, III, No. 24677, V, No. 3391;

(3) F. 151ᵛ, *Verbum bonum et suave / Personemus, illud Ave* (Cl. Blume, *Analecta Hymnica*, 54, No. 218 [pp. 343-345].

It is obvious from all the references provided in these works that the three sequences are found in numerous manuscripts. Whether any of them happen to be psalters would require a more detailed study.

[17]If the indices of V. Leroquais (*Les psautiers manuscrits latins*) can be relied on, none of the 244 manuscript psalters he describes contain any of the three sequences of MS Typ 311.

[18]On the Nevers and Cornillon manuscripts see Michel Huglo, "Les livres liturgiques de la Chaise-Dieu," *Revue Bénédictine* 87 (1977) 78 and note 1.

[19]After the French Revolution the Municipal Council decided to demolish this building and transfer the title of parish church to the main monastic church of Saint-Riquier. Recent excavations by Honoré Bernard, Director of excavations at Thérouanne and Saint-Riquier, have brought to light portions of the Marian church of Angilbert. Bernard presented the first results of the excavations (made at a depth of 4 meters below actual ground levels) during the archaeological Congress of Saint-Riquier, held in September 1987. The Musée du Syndicat d'Initiative of Saint-Riquier houses a fragment of the Carolingian pavement from this Marian oratory which closely resembles floor remains of the Palatine Chapel now preserved in the Domschatz of Aachen.

[20]This plan is reproduced in Hénocque, *Histoire*, 2, opposite p. 251. See likewise the plan showing Angilbert's church of the Virgin and its relation to the main church in Hénocque, *Histoire* 1, opposite p. 146.

[21]See Joannis de Capella (Jean de la Chapelle) *Chronica abbreviata . . . Sancti Richarii* [ed. E. Prarond] (Paris, 1893) pp. 157-58: "Nicolaus Bourdon . . . fuit primo cantor, deinde praepositus huius ecclesiae. Ipse . . . expertus musicus, vocem habens organisatam in omni prolatione; ita quod, ut communis fama laborabat, in his partibus non erat tenorista, contratenorista similis, nec ei secundus, devotus et frequentans missam quotidianam beatae Mariae virginis, in sua capella cantans in persona et docens musicalia ad praeconium et laudem intemeratae virginis, quotidie dictamina componens, et alios discipulos suos regens et dirigens; ita quod de novo, propria scientia, ordinavit musicalia prosarum *Ave gloriosior, Mittit ad Virginem* et aliarum quas nunc canunt reliogiosi in dicta capella hora consueta et ante Primam."

[22]In PR we read: (19 Oct.) *Dedicatio cryptae sub domno Gervino*, and in MR: (19 Oct.) *Coenobio Centula. Dedicatio orientalis cryptae in honorem Beatae Mariae et sancti Richarii, sacerdotis gloriosi.*

[23]The addition of a prayer to St. Christopher

(f. 154ᵛ) is worth noting in view of the colossal gothic statue of St. Christopher — opposite a similar one of St. James — that stood in the Saint-Riquier church. For a reproduction of this statue see Hénocque, *Histoire*, 2, Plates 2 and 3 (between pp. 384 and 385).

²⁴On Dommartin, see *Dictionnaire d'histoire et de géographie écclesiastique* (vol. 14, 635-636); also Albéric de Calonne, *Histoire des abbayes de Dommartin et de Saint-André-au-Bois* (Arras, 1875) [cited as de Calonne, *Histoire*], pp. 70-73 for the abbacy of Jean Durlin.

²⁵Published by A. de Caïeu, "Chronique Française de l'Abbaye de Dompmartin de 1672 á 1789," *Mémoires de la Société Impériale d'Emulation d'Abbeville* 2ᵉ s., 12 (1867-1868) 507-632. The chronicler from July 1672 to September 1716 was Fr. André Guilleman. A perusal of his entries suggests that the presentation of a volume as a gift to the monastic library was unlikely to get recorded.

²⁶This emerges from a note in de Calonne's *Histoire* (p. 72, note 1): "1696 . . . Vente de la maison refuge que l'abbaye de Dommartin avait à Hesdin, rue de Jérusalem, près du rempart et acquisition d'une autre, rue du château. Quelques années après acquisition par l'abbé Durlin d'une maison à Arras, rue des Trois-Visages, près le jeu de paume (*Archives de Dommartin*)." On the Rue des Trois Visages see Jean Lestocquoy, *Arras du temps jadis* 3 (Arras, 1946) pp. 69-71; also A. d'Hèricourt and A. Godin, *Les rues d'Arras, dictionnaire historique* 2 vols. (Brussels, 1976).

²⁷See Eugène Mathon, *Généalogie de la famille Mathon* (Saint-Omer, 1934). The information concerning Guillaume Mathon and his son, drawn from this work, was kindly supplied by Catherine Dhérent, Directeur of the Archives of the Pas-de-Calais, whom we cordially thank for her help.

²⁸On the relations between Saint-Riquier and Dommartin see Hénocque, *Histoire* 1, pp. 433, 440-41, 462; 2, p. 232; 3, pp. 215, 399.

²⁹Hénocque, *Histoire*, 2, p. 7. This page is the only one referred to in the index under "Psautier, très-riche"!

³⁰On the de la Houplière family see below, note 41.

³¹Hénocque, *Histoire*, 2 (Amiens, 1883) pp. 430-31.

³²Hénocque, *Histoire*, 1 (Amiens, 1880) p. 74, note 1. The family Canu was known to Hénocque. He alludes to a property being sold in 1819 to "Demoiselle Buteux de Franqueville, mariée en premières nôces à Dominique Canu, père de M. Dominique Canu, notre contemporain, et aïeul de MM. Fernand et Gustave Canu" (vol. 3, p. 504). So Dominique Canu may have been the owner of the other Saint-Riquier psalter. One wonders what has become of it!

³³Hénocque, *Histoire*, 2, pp. 430-31, where the author makes no allusion to what he had written on p. 7 but simply heads his transcriptions from the calendar and litany with the title: "Calendrier du XIIIᵉ siècle . . . Fêtes propres au monastère de Saint-Riquier, d'après un calendrier manuscrit d'un psautier provenant du monastère."

³⁴The abbey of Valloires is situated only a few kilometers from Dommartin. Fourteen of its manuscripts are presently in the Abbeville library, which possesses only one from Dommartin.

³⁵Mme. P. Hazebrouck, librarian of the Bibliothèque municipale of Abbeville, is warmly thanked for providing this information in a letter of 18 July 1991.

³⁶See Jean Estienne, "Quelques incendies de Saint-Riquier," *Bulletin de la Société des Antiquaires de Picardie* 48 (1959-1960) 12.

³⁷de Calonne, *Histoire*, p. 889, note 1.

³⁸*Ibid.* p. 86, note 1.

³⁹For all these events see *Ibid.* pp. 85-93. A more detailed and objective account of the last days of Saint-Riquier and of Dommartin, based on existing French archival sources, would be welcome. In particular one could wish for a full study of the fate of the monastic libraries at the time of the French Revolution.

⁴⁰Just as the other Saint-Riquier psalter ended in the hands of the Canu family?

⁴¹On the relationship between Château-Neuf and the family de la Houplière, which goes back to the time of the French Revolution, see Alfred Dufételle, *La Marquenterre: monographie de Quend* (Abbeville, 1907) pp. 17-18; also Roger Rodière, "Statistique féodale du baillage de Rue et quelques village voisins," *Bulletin de la Société d'Emulation d'Abbeville* 17 (1938-1942) 142-143. These references were kindly supplied by Mme. P. Hazebrouck, Bibliothécaire at Abbeville. While the name of Château-Neuf has disappeared from the present Michelin map [51] it

occurs as a group of farm-houses to the immediate right of Vieux-Fort-Mahon on the map of 1887 kept in the Map Room of Harvard University Library [Map Room, No 5830 = France 1:50,000 (1887-97); see sheet 6 (1887)].

[42]An alternative explanation that would make the note on the flyleaf a forgery seems almost impossible to maintain. It could only have been made after the publication of the history of Dommartin by A. de Calonne in 1875 and of the genealogy of the Mathon family by Eugène Mathon in 1934, since these works taken jointly provide the link between Jean Durlin, Mathon and Rue des Trois Visages at Arras. But what could have been the purpose of such a forgery? Wolfgand Speyer, in his *Bücherfunde in der Glaubenswerbung der Antike* (Göttingen, 1970) has explored the theme of books being discovered in tombs and other odd places, both in antiquity and in the Middle Ages. Such "discoveries" were usually intended to disguise the true origin of a work, by laying down, as it were, a different scent to legitimize a work or its possession. In the case of the Saint-Riquier psalter the questionable circumstance that might have needed explaining, or covering up, was how a private family or an individual happened to be in possession of a manuscript that legally had been claimed by the state. All the evidence suggests that the legalities of 1791 weighed little on the conscience of those who possessed former monastic property at the end of the last century.

Marks of ownership in a MS of St. Augustine, *De Civitate Dei*; Italy and France, late 13th cent.

17

Buying and Selling a Manuscript of De Civitate Dei

Fᴏʀ ᴀ ʟɪʙʀᴀʀɪᴀɴ, I ꜱᴜᴘᴘᴏꜱᴇ, the first question is "where are the books?" but for another investigator the question "where *were* the books?" may be equally important: how were the great collections gathered and dispersed? Who wanted them? When and why? Who could afford to read those texts and look at those pictures? The flyleaves and first page of one extremely handsome manuscript of Augustine's *De Civitate Dei* carry somewhat more than the usual number of names, letters, numbers, old and new marks of ownership and classification. I suggest we look at them in chronological order. This manuscript began its travels before it was completed. Its round gothic script is Italian and its decoration is Parisian, either by the celebrated miniaturist Honoré or by a member of his staff (opinions differ) and it seems not to have been written by an Italian scribe working in Paris, but rather to be one of a group of undecorated manuscripts brought to Paris from Italy. The date 1282 has been suggested.

The earliest mark of ownership, a docketing and press-mark, "Augustinus de civitate dei. A," in what appears to be a late fourteenth-century hand is, unfortunately, the only important mark still unidentified. François Avril is not persuaded that the hand is French, so we know nothing whatever of the book's whereabouts during the Middle Ages. The first page of text carries in French and Latin the autograph signature of the poet Phillipe Desportes, (1546-1606), Abbot of Tiron, who assembled a large library at his house in Vanves, just south of the old Paris city wall. Jacques Lavaud, Desportes' biographer, gives an excellent description of this library and singles out among many works of Augustine: "ibi continentur S. Augustini libri XXII de Civitate Dei . . . XVᵉ s.(sic)." Desportes' library was not expressly mentioned in his will, so it passed to his brother Thibaud, who died after 1627 without issue, his wife's brother inheriting. The same page of our MS that bears Desportes' signature has at the top right corner, rather faintly, "Collegii Paris. Soc. Jesus," in other words the Bibliotheca Claramontana of which prominent mention was made in the first essay in this catalogue, and indeed we know from Delisle, Père Jacob, and others that the great part of Desportes' books and seven manuscripts passed to that library, apparently in the 1620's, and constituted one of their earliest major acquisitions. Other manuscripts from Desportes' library went to the Chancellor Séguier and finally to the Bibliothèque Nationale.

Written vertically in the gutter of f. 1ʳ are the words "Paraphé au desir de l'arrest du 5 juillet 1763. Mesnil," a statement revealing the suppression of the Society of Jesus that followed immediately upon General Lorenzo Ricci's stirring and untranslatable response to a Roman ultimatum, "Sint ut sunt aut non sint." All properties of the order were confiscated, among them the books of Clermont. In respect to these, the courts ordered that the manuscripts be turned over to "dependable hands," namely those of the Benedictines of St. Germain des Prés who were then to catalogue them, writing the number of leaves on the first page, and prepare them for sale. The number "284" on our MS is a little off but is revealed by later evidence to be, in fact, that leaf-count. Two scholars, Clément and Bréquigny, produced in 1764 a *Catalogus manuscriptorum codicum collegii claramontani*, which I have never seen, but which lists our Augustine as number 473, a number that appears on the manuscript's pastedown. A catalogue of the printed books was also made. Harvard's copy, the gift of Thomas Hollis, carries, stamped on the front board, the owl of wisdom upside down, a device Hollis often employed when binding books relating to the Jesuits.

The manuscripts were never offered at a public sale. Gerard Meerman, a Dutch scholar and collector, offered 15,000 *livres* for all 856 manuscripts — 17 *livres* per manuscript. The offer was accepted, and the books were crated and started on their journey to Holland. At this point the Librarian of the Bibliotheque du Roi took an interest and offered 6,000 *livres* for 178 MSS relating to the history of France (ours not among them). Meerman demurred. The manuscripts reached the city of Rouen, where they were impounded. At last Meerman agreed to return forty-two, but he kept seven out, offering four others. In April 1765 the transaction was completed and the main body of the manuscripts, including ours, proceeded to Holland. Gerard Meerman received the order of St. Michel, which he, infuriated about the manuscripts he had given up, declined ever to wear. When he died in 1771, his son Jean Meerman inherited. Jean Meerman died in 1824, and his books and 1,086 manuscripts were duly catalogued: *Bibliotheca Meermaniana*. The *De Civitate Dei* was listed as no. 454 and described as a fifteenth-century codex of 284 leaves, so we may assume that both of these early errors had their origin in the catalogue of Clément and Bréquigny.

The doings surrounding the Meerman sale of July 1824 are wonderfully described in Munby's *Phillipps Studies*. Sir Thomas bought heavily, mainly through the bookseller Thomas Rodd. He paid 34 florins for the Augustine. After the sale he wrote his wife that two or three "villainous booksellers" had driven up the prices, whereas what seems to have happened is that several booksellers made agreements to control the prices and Phillipps missed out on certain manuscripts he desired. There followed a long series of negotiations during which Sir Thomas attempted to avoid paying duty. He contemplated taking up residence in Holland. In one of his letters to British officials he asserted: "Believe me the Universities, the British Museum and all other public bodies lose rather than gain by the mean and niggardly conduct of Government. It is not for myself that I wish the duty taken off, but for the sake of literature." He paid the duty, and in 1825 thirty-six large crates left Brussels for England. Our manuscript, correctly described as thirteenth-century, received the Phillipps number 6768, a clerical mistake confusing it with another Augustine text, and then its definitive number 4600. This large discrepancy in numbers may indicate how rapidly the Phillipps collection was growing.

When Sir Thomas died in 1872, his books went to his daughter Katherine Fenwick and then to her son Thomas Fitzroy Fenwick. The great dispersal, which is only now concluding, had already begun. In 1887 most of the Meerman manuscripts went through a separate treaty to the King of Prussia. No. 4600, however, was not among them. In October 1920 Thomas Fenwick approached an American named Alfred Chester Beatty, later Sir Chester, with the thought of selling a large block of manuscripts to an American institution. Beatty had recently begun collecting for himself. In December he visited Fenwick. On New Year's Eve 1920 he acquired our manuscript and twenty-three others as well as two fragments for £11,954, about £480 per manuscript. Fenwick wrote to him that "parting from old friends is always painful."

By now we have reached modern times. E.G. Millar described the Augustine as number 68 in his luxurious *Library of A. Chester Beatty* (1930). Three years later came the two great Chester Beatty sales at Sotheby and Co. Our manuscript was no. 51 in the sale of 9 May. The Sotheby price list informs us it was acquired by Mr. Goodyear for £120. But who was Mr. Goodyear? No collector or bookseller of that name could be discovered, and in fact, although his name can be seen once or twice more in price lists of that year, he disappears thereafter for good. Curiously enough every manuscript he bought is in the Houghton Library. It pleases me to state that Mr. Goodyear was the *nomme de guerre* of America's greatest book collector, still, at that time, unknown enough to attend sales anonymously, bidding for himself and unencumbered by agents' fees. He was, of course, Philip Hofer.

Rodney G. Dennis

et hic tenendū est . quod fit equius : quodqʒ seriosius : quā id quod debilius faciliusqʒ . Vtraeqʒ tamen formae seruandae sunt : ob ea quae facilius in opere adducuntur .

Qualuī est equinoctialis quinqʒ talui est per Meroem quatuor ꝟ semis cū tertia . Vnde ratione habet ad ipm quā treginta ad uiginti ꝟ noue .

Qualuī est eqnoctialis quinqʒ talui est per Syene quatuor ꝟ semis cū duodecima . Vnde ratione habet ad cū quā sexaginta ad qnquaginta ꝟ quinqʒ . hoc est quam duodeam ad undeam .

Qualuī est eqnoctialis quinqʒ talui est p rhodii quatuor Vnde ratione habet ad ipm epicetarti .

Qualuī est eqnoctialis quinqʒ talui est p thyle duo cū quarta . Vnde ratione habet ad ipm quā uigīti ad noue .

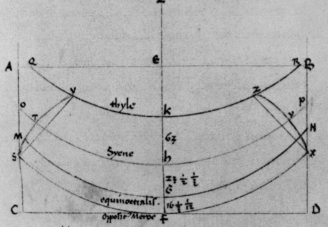

CLAVDII PTOLEMEI COSMOGRAPHIAE LIBER PRIMVS EXPLICITVR.

Diagram describing the globe in conical sections in Ptolemy, *Geography*; Italy, early 15th cent.

18

Ptolemy's Geography *in the Renaissance*

THE *Geography* OF THE ALEXANDRIAN scientist Claudius Ptolemaeus (fl. A.D. 127-148) became in the early fifteenth century a focal point for that rich network of cultural movements we refer to as the Renaissance. The recovery of Greco-Roman literature and science, new techniques for a more realistic imitation of nature in the arts, the exploration of the globe: all of these lines of activity came to intersection in Ptolemy's handbook for mapping the sublunar spaces of the cosmos. In Quattrocento Italy the *Geography* was principally known through the Latin translation made by Jacopo Angeli da Scarperia. Houghton's copy of this text is one of the three oldest of the nearly 100 known manuscripts and, given its provenance, must have played a major role in making Ptolemy known to Florentine artists and scholars in the first half of the fifteenth century.

It was in Florence that the first serious revival of Greek studies in the Renaissance took place. From 1397 to 1399, the Byzantine emigré Emmanuel Chrysoloras taught Greek to a group of young Florentines, many of whom were later to become major figures of the humanist movement. One text that had particularly interested the group was Ptolemy's *Geography* (or *Cosmography*, as Jacopo Angeli preferred). Geography was, naturally, a subject of keen interest in a city of international merchants — merchants who within living memory had found themselves cut off from the Silk Road and Indian Ocean trading systems by the expansion of Ottoman power: the Portuguese were not the first to think about alternate routes to the Indies. So it is no surprise that the young Florentine merchant-banker Palla Strozzi, a member of the Greek study group, had sought out a Greek manuscript of the *Geography* while in Constantinople and had brought it back to Florence for use in Chrysoloras' classes. Ptolemy's work consisted of a complicated set of instructions for drawing maps of the world and its regions, and described three primitive methods for making cartographic projections. Some Byzantine copies contained, in addition, a set of 27 maps that were not the work of Ptolemy himself but had been executed in accordance with his method; an example is the famous *codex Urbinas graecus 82* of the Vatican Library, which is probably the copy owned by Palla Strozzi himself.

To produce a Latin translation of this text became an immediate ambition of Chrysoloras' Florentine disciples. The medieval period had known translations of Ptolemy's astronomical works, but his *Geography* had been neglected. Chrysoloras himself had made a partial version of the text before 1400, probably for class use, but his formal Latin prose was too rough to be published to the learned world. Leonardo Bruni, the most famous of

Chrysoloras' students, began a translation of the text around 1405 that remained unfinished. Finally, around 1406/1409 Jacopo Angeli da Scarperia — another Chrysoloras student who was now a member of the papal chancery — was encouraged by Cardinal Peter Filargis of Candia to revise and complete Chrysoloras' version for publication. Later, when Filargis became Pope Alexander V (1409-1410), Jacopo was able to present him with the dedication of the finished work. Jacopo's original Latin version did not contain the maps; these were added only later, during the 1410s, through the combined efforts of Francesco di Lapacino and Domenico di Lionardo Boninsegni, both members of the circle around the bibliophile Niccolò Niccoli. (Lapacini was in fact Niccoli's second cousin; both later became administrators of his will.)

In his preface Jacopo remarks that certain few ages, whether owing to the stars or to climatic change or to both, seem to produce men of outstanding intelligence. He mentions the efflorescence of philosophy and oratory in the age of Plato and Demosthenes, the literary genius of the Augustan age, the divines of the patristic age, and the Antonine age, which had brought forth Ptolemy. These golden eras, Jacopo added, are found not only in the case of liberal arts and divinity, but also in minor disciplines, such as war, sculpture, and painting. "And, to compare great things with small, does not this present age of ours sparkle with genius, especially in our city of Florence, where the liberal arts have been awakened to great glory from their long sleep?" From this observation, one of the earliest to notice the stirrings of the Florentine renascence, Jacopo passes on to describe the differences between the Greek and Latin approaches to geographical studies. The Latin method, whose greatest representative Jacopo considers to be Pliny the Elder, is unambitious, unmathematical, and anecdotal; it neglects problems of depicting scale, the calculation of longitude and latitude, and techniques of celestial measurement. And "none of our Latin writers explains how our globe, which is spherical, can be described on a two-dimensional surface." It is for this reason, says Jacopo, that a Latin translation of Ptolemy is necessary. After an elaborately disingenuous apology for the plainness of his Latin style, sweetened with flattery of the pope, Jacopo ends with an explanation of the title of the work. He does not miss the opportunity to play on Alexander V's name, alluding both to Alexander the Great and to the Alexandrian scientist's reputation as an astrologer: "A kind of divine presentiment of your soon-to-be-realized empire impelled you to desire the work, so that you could learn clearly from it how ample would be the power you would soon hold over the entire world."

Houghton's manuscript of the Jacopo Angeli translation is of extraordinary interest for the history of this text in Quattrocento Italy. The script has been dated by Prof. Albinia de la Mare to 1410-1415, making it the earliest known copy of this translation. The manuscript was written, moreover, by a scribe trained in, or influenced by, Poggio Bracciolini's newly-invented humanistic script, which after the invention of printing was to become the model for our modern Roman type founts. Poggio himself has written a number of *notabilia* and corrections into the margins. It is very likely that Poggio supervised the production of the codex, borrowing the exemplar directly from the translator, his colleague in the papal chancery.

Poggio was an intimate friend of several disciples of Chrysoloras, including Jacopo Angeli, Niccolò Niccoli, and Leonardo Bruni. He was also a close associate of the Florentine banker and statesman Cosimo de'Medici, into whose possession the Houghton manuscript came sometime after 1418. The manuscript must have continued to be an object of study and discussion in Cosimo's circle of humanist friends. In his *De infelicitate principum* of 1440, Poggio described an occasion in the 1430s when, coming to Florence on a visit, he went to the house of Niccolò Niccoli and found him inspecting, together with Cosimo de'Medici and Carlo Marsuppini, a copy of the *Cosmographia*. If the anecdote is not a mere literary invention, it is quite likely that the codex in Poggio's story is to be identified with the Houghton manuscript.

After the death of Niccolò Niccoli in 1437, his rich collection of manuscripts became, by a provision of his will, the core of what has been called, with some exaggeration, the first public library of modern Europe. This library was housed in the Dominican convent of San Marco in Florence, which had been recently refounded thanks to the efforts of Cosimo de'Medici. Cosimo, who was one of the administrators of the Niccoli bequest, also added to the San Marco collection a number of his own books, among them Houghton's Ptolemy codex.

Another administrator of the Niccoli bequest to San Marco was Paolo del Pozzo Toscanelli, a Florentine astronomer and doctor who had been a close friend of Niccoli and Poggio. Toscanelli had devoted long study to Ptolemy's geographical treatise — very likely making use of Cosimo's copy — and it was his knowledge of Ptolemy that enabled him to make key contributions to two central achievements of Renaissance culture: the rediscovery of the techniques of linear perspective in painting, and the discovery of the New World by Christopher Columbus.

Since the time of Giotto, Florentine painters had sought techniques for a more accurate representation of three-dimensional space on two-dimensional surfaces. During the 1420s in Florence, the realistic imitation of nature in art made a sudden leap forward with the discovery (or rediscovery) of vanishing-point linear perspective. This discovery is usually credited to the Florentine architect Filippo Brunelleschi. Brunelleschi's technique (as later codified by Leon Battista Alberti in his *De pictura* of 1436) involved mapping optical rays leading from the eye of an observer to objects in a visual field onto a two-dimensional grid pattern. This is precisely the technique of Ptolemy's third method for cartographic projection as described in Book VII of the *Geography*. Verbal echoes of Ptolemy in Alberti's treatise leave little doubt as to the source of the innovation. Samuel Edgerton and other scholars have argued that Toscanelli, who was a close associate of both Brunelleschi and Alberti, was the person most likely to have introduced the Florentine artists to Ptolemy's techniques.

But Toscanelli's true fame comes from his role in Columbus's discovery of America. Thanks to the work of Jacopo Angeli and the humanists of Niccolò Niccoli's circle, Florence became the greatest center of cartographic study in Renaissance Italy. Illustrated codices of Ptolemy were among the most eagerly-sought products of her famous scholarly bookshops. And the man who came to embody Florence's preeminence in geographical expertise was Paolo Toscanelli. In 1474 Toscanelli, now an old man, received an inquiry from the Portuguese royal court about the possibility of reaching the Orient by sailing west. The Portuguese since the early part of the century had been exploring the West coast of Africa in the hopes of finding a sea route to the Indian Ocean, but had been temporarily discouraged by recent setbacks and, perhaps, by the growing knowledge of Ptolemy. According to Ptolemaic maps, the southern part of Africa was joined to a large land mass — the "terra incognita" of legend — that blocked the sea route to the Indies. In Toscanelli's famous reply to the Portuguese he sent King Alfonso V a map — now lost, but apparently constructed according to Ptolemaic principles — and a covering letter in which he confirmed the possibility of reaching the Indies from the west. He also made a wildly inaccurate estimate of the distance to be covered — too short by 7000 miles — an estimate for which Ptolemy was beyond doubt his chief authority:

> . . . I am sending his Majesty a chart done with my own hands in which are designated your shores and islands from which you should begin to sail ever westward, and the lands you should touch at and how much you should deviate from the pole or from the equator and after what distance, that is, after how many miles, you should reach the most fertile lands of all spices and gems. And you must not be surprised that I call the regions in which spices are found "western," although they are usually called "eastern," for those who sail in the other hemisphere always find these regions in the west. But if we should go overland and by the higher routes we should come upon these places in the east. . . . From the city of Lisbon westward in a straight line to the very noble and splendid city of Quinsay [China] 26 spaces [longitudinal lines] are indicated on the chart, each of which covers 250 miles . . . So there is not a great space to be traversed over unknown waters.

In Fernando Colón's hyperbolic biography of his famous father, it is said that Columbus, too, corresponded with Toscanelli and received a copy of the same letter written to the Portuguese court years earlier. This story is doubtful, but what is not doubtful is that Columbus possessed a copy of the Toscanelli letter. For in the Biblioteca Capitular y Colombina of Seville, there is still preserved a Venetian incunable of Pius II's *Historia rerum ubique gestarum* (Vitrina Colón, V-114-27) on whose flyleaf the letter is copied in Columbus's own hand. Scholars who have tried to understand the intellectual origins of Columbus's Enterprise of the Indies have credited Toscanelli's letter with enormous influence upon Columbus's thinking. The judgment of the greatest geographer of the age that there existed a western route to the Indies — and, it might be added, his comforting estimate of the small distance to be covered — cannot but have had great impact on the explorer. Indeed, the judgment of Alexander von Humboldt, made in 1836, can still be quoted with approval: "[Toscanelli] was, as Ferdinand Columbus said, the most powerful cause of the spirit with which the admiral launched himself upon the immensity of an unknown sea."

James Hankins

Bibliography

Poggio Bracciolini, *De infelicitate principum*, in his *Opera omnia*, ed. Riccardo Fubini, 4 vols. (Turin, 1964-1969), I, p. 392.

Ferdinand Columbus, *The Life of the Admiral Christopher Columbus by His Son Ferdinand*, tr. Benjamin Keen (New Brunswick, 1959).

Albinia C. de la Mare, *The Handwriting of Italian Humanists*, vol. I, fasc. 1 (Oxford, 1973).

Samuel Y. Edgerton, *The Renaissance Rediscovery of Linear Perspective* (New York, 1975).

Harrassowitz Fischer [and Giovanni Mercati], "De Cl. Ptolemaei vita operibusque, Geographia presertim eiusque fatis," in *Claudii Ptolemaei Geographiae codex Urbinas Graecus 82* (Rome, 1932), Tomus prodromus, pars prior.

Alexander von Humboldt, *Examen critique de l'histoire de la géographie du Nouveau Continent et du progrès de l'astronomie nautique aux quinzième et seizième siècles* (Paris, 1836-1839), I, pp. 210-256.

Samuel Eliot Morison, *Admiral of the Ocean Sea* (Boston, 1942).

_____, *Journals and Other Documents on the Life and Voyages of Christopher Columbus* (New York, 1963).

Mostra Colombiana Internazionale (Genoa, 1950-1951), pp. 241- 242.

Pauline Moffitt Watts, "Prophecy and Discovery: On the Spiritual Origins of Christopher Columbus's Enterprise of the Indies," *American Historical Review* XC (1985), 73-102.

Bertold L. Ullman and Philip A. Stadter, *The Public Library of Renaissance Florence* (Padua, 1972).

Gustavo Uzielli, *La vita e i tempi di Paolo dal Pozzo Toscanelli, Ricerche e studi* (Rome, 1894).

Roberto Weiss, "Jacopo Angeli da Scarperia," in *Medioevo e Rinascimento: Studi in onore di Bruno Nardi* (Florence, 1955), II, pp. 801-824; reprinted in Weiss' *Medieval and Humanist Greek* (Padua, 1977).

_____, "Gli inizi dello studio di greco a Firenze," in *Medieval and Humanist Greek*, pp. 227-254.

Description of Houghton MS Typ 5

CODEX: I (cart., added by binder, s. XVIII) + I (mbr., original) + 232 (mbr., foliated in 1949) + I (mbr.) + I (cart.). 254 x 160 (written area 190 x 90). 26 long lines per page, dryruled. Gatherings: A-Z^{10} AA^4 [signatures in pencil, added probably after 1947]; catchwords for each gathering, centered horizontally at the foot of the page. Round humanistic script, according to A. C. de la Mare written ca. 1410-1415 by a scribe trained or strongly influenced by Poggio; a number of *notabilia* and corrections have been added in Poggio's own hand; a note on f. 16^r is possibly in the hand of Niccolò Niccoli. Early humanist vinestem initials, picked out in blue, green, yellow and red, on folios 1^r, 3^v, 30^v, 66^r, 102^v, 163^v, 186^v, 208^v; chapter initials painted in blue. Diagrams on folios 5^r, 5^v, 26^v, 27^r, 28^r, 30^r. Bound ca. 1768 with wooden boards, russet sheepskin spine.

PROVENANCE: Library of the Dominican convent of San Marco, given after 1440 by Cosimo de'Medici. It is not mentioned in the inventory of Cosimo's books from 1418. On the verso of the front parchment flyleaf are the remains of the San Marco shelfmark ("ex parte occidentali") and the accession note, erased, but partly visible under ultraviolet:

Cosmograp[hiae *superscriptus*]
Libri astrol[ogiae] claudii tholomei [conuentui] scti
marci de flor[entia] ——————————— [quem] emit
Cosm[us de medicis] ——————

Alienated from San Marco sometime between 1768, when it is listed in a manuscript inventory now at the Laurentian Library in Florence (Laur. S. M. 945), and the suppression of religious congregations in 1808 during the French occupation. Purchased by Sir Thomas Phillips (no. 6552) through the London Bookseller Payne, of Townsend, who probably had it from an Italian collector (see the note, s. XIX[1], on the rear cover: "Carte manoscritte 236"). Purchased by Harvard in January 1947 from the Robinson Trust with funds supplied by Philip Hofer.

CONTENTS: folios 1[r]-2[v]: [the dedication] BEATISSIMO PATRI ALEXANDRO V PONTIFICI MAXIMO IACOBVS ANGELVS, *inc.* AD tempora Claudii Ptolemei viri Alexandrini cogitanti michi — loquentem audiamus. Folios 2[v]-3[r]: [Table of contents of Book I]: CLAVDII PTOLEMEI COSMOGRAPHIAE PRIMVS HAEC HABET. Folios 3[v]-232[v]: [Ptolemy's *Geography*, in eight books] CLAVDII PTOLEMEI LIBER PRIMVS COSMOGRAPHIAE INCIPIT FELICITER. In quo differt cosmographia a chorographia. Cosmographia designatrix imitatio est — usque ad utrosque polos Zodiaci. F. 232[v]: [colophon] CLAVDII PTOLEMEI VIRI ALEXANDRINI COSMOGRAPHIAE OCTAVVS ET VLTIMVS LIBER EXPLICIT FELICITER.

BIBLIOGRAPHY: *Catalogus librorum manuscriptorum in Bibliotheca Phillippica* (Middlehall, 1837), p. 97; *Houghton Library Report, 1946-1947*, p. 3. *Illuminated and Calligraphic Manuscripts* (exhibition catalog, Cambridge, 1955), p. 21, no. 60; F. Pintor, "Per la storia della libreria medicea nel Rinascimento," *Italia medioevale e umanistica* III (1960), 189-210; W. H. Bond and C. U. Faye, *Supplement to the Census of Medieval and Renaissance Manuscripts in the United States and Canada* (New York, 1962), pp. 250-51; B. L. Ullman and P. A. Stadter, *The Public Library of Renaissance Florence* (Padua, 1972), pp. 52-53, 211 and 316; R. S. Wieck, *Late Medieval and Renaissance Illuminated Manuscripts, 1350-1525, in the Houghton Library* (exhibition catalog, Cambridge, 1983), p. 118 and plate 120; J. Hankins, *Italian Humanists in Ten Manuscripts from Houghton Library* (exhibition catalog, Cambridge, 1989), pp. 1-2; P.O. Kristeller, *Iter Italicum* (London and Leiden, 1963-1990), V, p. 233; A. C. de la Mare, "Cosimo and His Books," in *Cosimo de'Medici, Pater Patriae, 1389-1464*, ed. F. Ames-Lewis (Oxford University Press, forthcoming).

The Text of Jacopo Angeli's Preface

As Jacopo Angeli's preface has been printed only twice, in rare incunabula (Vicenza 1475 = Hain-Copinger 13536 and Bologna [1477] = Hain 13538), and as the text in Houghton's manuscript is probably taken directly from the author's archetype, I have thought it worthwhile to reproduce here the text of this important document of Renaissance science. I give the variants of the earliest printed edition of 1475 (from Houghton Inc. 7139) in the apparatus. The orthography is that of the manuscript; capitalization and punctuation are mine.

f. 1ʳ]

Beatissimo patri Alexandro V pontifici maximo Iacobus Angelus.
Ad tempora Claudij Ptolemei uiri Alexandrini cogitanti michi
illud occurrit ut, quemadmodum in rebus ceteris quae a natura
gignuntur, secula aliquando ipsa, seu ex celestium siderum meatu
quae in inferiora uim mutant seu ex ipsius aeris terraeque   5
temperie seu ex utroque — quod tamen causam unam habere potest —
ubertatem quandam insolitam pariunt, sic et in preclaris obtigisse
ingenijs uisum est. Apud enim diuini Platonis seculum permultos
egregios floruisse philosophos nouimus, permultos etiam
oratores eadem quae Demosthenes tulerunt tempora. Quot   10
prestantissimi claruere uiri diui Augusti imperio? Diuinarum
scripturarum principes qui in nostra religione habentur et apud
grecos et apud nos, nonne ex una tamquam matre uel nido una
genuerunt secula? Nec in liberalibus tantum diuinisque
doctrinis animaduertisse hoc licet, sed in re ipsa militari   15
minoribusque aliis disciplinis sculptorum pictorumque aliarumque
artium quas etas quedam una excellentissime sibi usurpauisse est
cognita. Et si parua componere magnis licet, hoc ipsum nostrum
seculum, in ciuitate precipue nostra Florentina, quot emicuit
ingenijs quae propemodum sopita liberalium studia maxima sui   20
gloria suscitauerunt? Tulerunt et auctorem omnium mathematicorum
doctissimum hunc Ptolemeum diui Antonini tempora, quae abunde
clarissimis et aliis /1ᵛ/ floruere ingenijs, quorum opera
immortalitati ipsi seculum illud consecrauit. Alii quidem alia.
Ptolemeus uero ipse quam multa diuinitus edidit, inter quae   25
et orbis situm diligentissime et cetera a mathematicis non
discendens exhibuit. Hic enim alio quodam modo quam nostri
Latini, inter quos Plinius Secundus cosmographorum palmam ferre
uidetur, rem hanc tractauit. Illi enim, licet habitabilem
uniuersi orbis situm descripserint, non tamen ex eorum preceptis   30

plane captari potest qua arte totius orbis pictura formari
ualeat, ut proportio cuiusque partis ad totum uniuersale
seruetur. Preterea nemo ab illis doceri potest (nisi grossiori
quodam modo) quae seu quantae inclinationes sint ad quatuor celi
plagas eorum situum quos in pictura figere decreuerimus, nedum   35
quippe longitudinem locorum a fixo quodam totius nostrae
habitabilis termino ductam — quae tamen rara inuentio est — sed
nec latitudinem ponunt. Nostrorum etiam nullus precepta
tradidit habitabilem ipsum orbem in plures picturae tabulas
posse diuidi, mensura cum toto eque seruata. Eorundem etiam   40
nemo prodit qua ratione orbis ipse noster, qui sphericus est,
in superficiem planam deducatur. Non quod nostros, qui
prestantissimi in ea traditione uiri extiterunt, arguendos
tantisper censeam, sed quod suis contenti limitibus historicorum
more rem suam summa industria et complexi sunt et prosecuti —   45
qui et alia quedam habent quae ab auctore hoc Ptolemeo
uidentur pretermissa.

   Vt autem ea quae ab illo absoluta diuino /2ʳ/ quodam
ingenio sunt cum nostris etiam habeatur, in latinum ipsa curaui
transferre sermonem. Opus nempe impeditum, etsi, ut de suo   50
inquit Mela, eloquentiae minime capax, eo hoc magis erit quod
precepta ipsa traduntur quae in eleganti etiam materia, non nisi
dicendi genus ab elegantia ferme semotum, posse admittere
uidentur. Preterea cum circa celestes maxime uersentur circulos
obque id cum obscuriora etiam sint, suauia minus, sicuti sunt,   55
ita et iudicantur. Quare sacrum presensque numen, expectata
religionis uerae salus, quem nulla diuinarum et humanarum
rerum archana latent, quem ad pessundandum orbis qui nunc tibi
subicitur regnum humana pietas et diuinum allicit premium,
quemue ad hoc nostrum desiderandum opus supernum quoddam   60
presagium futuri iam iam imperij tui impulit, ut plane hinc
cognosceres quam amplissimam potestatem totius orbis mox esses
adepturus, ueniam dabis, pontifex maxime, Hieronymi presertim
diuini interpretis memor, qui de interprete Cicerone, quem
eloquentiae aureum flumen appellat, se admirari loquitur quod   65
interdum in transferendo ita hesitet ut qui a Cicerone dicta
nesciat, a Cicerone dicta non credat.

   Ceterum *Geographiam*, hoc est terrae descriptionem, auctor hic
noster hoc omne opus grece nuncupat. Quam appellationem uir
seculi nostri eruditissimus Manuel Constantinopolitanus,   70
suauissimus litterarum grecarum seculi nostri apud nos
preceptor, dum in latinum eloquium id transferre (ad uerbum

licet) pariter incipit, /2ᵛ/ non mutauit; sed nos in
Cosmographiam id uertimus. Quod uocabulum licet etiam
grecum sit, tamen apud Latinos ita usitatum est ut iam pro   75
nostro habeatur, credamusque uirum eum, si id quod transtulit
emendasset, omnino illud in *Cosmographiam* mutaturum fuisse.
Nam si Plinius ceterique Latini qui terrae situm descripserunt
opus suum *Cosmographiam* appellant et auctores ipsi cosmographi
dicuntur, nescio cur Ptolemei opus, qui idem tractat, eodem   80
uocabulo apud nos appellari non debeat. Si uero uelint
Ptolemeum ipsum ut diximus longe a nostris differe
cosmographis — nam assertiones huius operis quam maxime ex
celestibus sumit — tum magis nobiscum sentiunt cum in
cosmographiae uocabulo plus quiddam quam ipsa notetur terra,   85
quae geographiae nomen tribuit. *Cosmos* enim grece, latine
mundus, qui terram celumque ipsum, quod per totum hoc opus
tamquam rei fundamentum adducitur, plane significat. Quod
ergo geographiam dicunt greci in omnibus cosmographorum
operibus, exemplo nostrorum hoc maxime in opere cosmographiam   90
uisum est proprius dici.

   Sed de his satis. Iam iam Ptolemeum ipsum latine loquentem
audiamus.

---

   16 -que¹] qui *ed.*   19 uestra *ed.*   22 doctissimum
om. ed.   diui] diuini *ed.*   26 et *scripsi*: ut *MS, ed.*   27 enim]
uero *ed.*   28 Latini *om. ed.*   34 inclinationis *ed.*   35 quos
scripsi: quod *MS, ed.*   36 totius *post* habitabilis *ed.*   43 uiri
extiterunt *transp. ed.*   50 et similiter *ed.*   56 etiam *ed.*
60 quemne *ed.*

upon the table dissolved his reverie, and
we all sat down in good humour. There
were present besides Mr. Arthur Lee who was
an old companion of mine when he studied at
Edinburgh — Mr. now Sir John Miller. Dr. Lettsom
(the Quaker Physician) and Mr. Slater the drug-
gist. Mr. Wilkes placed himself next
to Dr Johnson, and behaved to him with
much attention politeness that he gained
upon him insensibly. No man eat more
heartily than Johnson or loved, what was
nice and tasty. Mr. Wilkes was at great
pains in helping him to some fine veal.
Pray give me leave Sir — It is better here —
a little of the brown — some fat Sir — a little
of the stuffing — some gravy — Let me have
the pleasure of giving you some, butter —
Allow me to recommend a squeeze of this
orange — or the lemon perhaps may have
more zest. — Sir Sir I am obliged to you
Sir — cried Johnson bowing and
turning his head to him with a look for
some time of "surly virtue" but in a short
of complacency. Foote being mentioned, Johnson
said

James Boswell, *Life of Johnson*, autograph; Dr. Johnson has dinner with John Wilkes.

19

Boswell's Life of Johnson
The Houghton Manuscript Leaves

In 1927 Lt. Colonel Ralph Heyward Isham made his massive purchase of Boswell papers at Malahide Castle, near Dublin. At the time, he thought, as did the seller, the sixth Lord Talbot de Malahide (James Boswell's great, great grandson, the last direct descendant), that the sale included all the Boswell manuscripts still in existence. Lady Talbot, who knew something about the papers and had a lively interest in them, also believed this. She represented her husband in all of the transactions. In August of 1927 she and Colonel Isham made a list of the collection and agreed upon a price for each item. The Colonel paid £450 for 16 leaves of Boswell's *Life of Johnson*. These few pages were now acclaimed to be the only surviving manuscript fragment of the great biography.

Three years later, however, in the spring of 1930, Colonel Isham received astonishing news from Lady Talbot. She had found more papers of Boswell in an old croquet box in the wood cupboard by the drawing room fireplace: journal fragments, "Hebridean Notes" (actually the manuscript for his published *Tour*), various "oddments," and 110 more manuscript leaves of the *Life* (the ones now in the Houghton Library).

The Talbots were aware of Colonel Isham's desperate financial condition, his losses in the Stock Market Crash, and his overpowering publishing demands, for he had earlier proclaimed that he was giving the "Boswell papers" to the world in a magnificent "Private Edition" — the most eminent scholar-editor, the greatest book designer, finest type and paper. He promised eighteen volumes to his subscribers: six had been published before the tragic death of his editor, Geoffrey Scott, in August 1929. Eight days after Professor Frederick Pottle had taken over as editor, Wall Street crashed. By the spring of 1930 Pottle and Isham were struggling to bring out Volumes VII, VIII, and IX.

Lady Talbot wrote that she did not think Colonel Isham was in a position to meet the prices she and Lord Talbot had set: £3000 for the leaves of the *Life*, £500 for the *Hebrides*, and £500 for the "oddments." The "journal fragments" should, of course, be considered part of the original purchase and she would mail them to the Colonel at once. Lord Talbot, she said, had decided to sell the *Life* manuscript at auction. She wondered if Colonel Isham would sell back the 16 leaves for the price he had paid, to add to the lot.

This was an agonizing situation. Isham had assured his subscribers that his collection contained "Boswell's papers in their entirety." Somehow, he had to buy all the items found in the croquet box. As for the 16 leaves of the *Life* that he had bought in August 1927, he couldn't have sold them back to the Talbots even if he wished to, because, in November 1927, after his return from Malahide, he had raised money by selling two leaves of the *Life* to Dr. Rosenbach, the great Philadelphia bookseller, (at $1800 each) and four more at the same price in 1928.

Colonel Isham arranged another auction of his own books and received another loan from his sympathetic friend, James Van Alen. In this way he was able to buy the croquet box material, and publication of the "Private Edition" continued. Volumes X, XI, and XII were brought out in 1931, Volumes XIII through XVI in 1932, Volume XVII in 1933, and Volume XVIII in 1934 — completing the great project.

During the course of 1934, Dr. Rosenbach sent Arthur Houghton a description of the 110 leaves found in the croquet box and this astute young collector purchased them on 12 February 1935 for $45,000 — the day before Isham accepted Rosenbach's offer of $35,000! Arthur Houghton was now known as the proud possessor of the largest manuscript portion of *The Life of Johnson* in existence.

During the Second World War, however, there was a new find at Malahide. When the loft of a horse barn was cleared out to store grain in case of invasion, a new hoard of Boswell papers was discovered, including 900 leaves of the manuscript of the *Life of Johnson*. After the War, Colonel Isham, with great difficulty and with help from different quarters, was able to purchase the grain loft material. This was sold to Yale in 1950, a year after the University had acquired all the rest of Colonel Isham's vast Boswell collection, making Yale the center of Boswell research and publication.

Arthur Houghton's 110 manuscript leaves of the *Life of Johnson* were deposited in the Houghton Library on indefinite loan in December 1978. They were presented to the Library on 26 December 1989.

Although now only a tenth of the master manuscript of the *Life*, the Houghton leaves are a treasure in themselves. They give a continuous and entertaining account of Boswell's eventful visit to England in 1776, from the 15th of March to the 16th of May. During this time Boswell was studying Johnson's every move and recording every word — in London, on their jaunt to Oxford and Lichfield, and back again in London.

One of the finest scenes in the whole biography is Boswell's introducing Johnson to the celebrated John Wilkes, radical politician and rake, someone the Doctor totally despised. Johnson and Wilkes had attacked each other in their writings. "Two men more different could perhaps not be selected out of all mankind," Boswell wrote.

Edward Dilly, the bookseller, was giving a dinner on May 15th, the evening before Boswell's return to Scotland. Wilkes was to be there, and Boswell had "an irresistible wish" to bring Johnson. The host feared he would lose the Doctor's friendship. Boswell, revelling in the drama of the encounter, assured Dilly that he would "negotiate" and all would be well. His "negotiation" began by telling the Doctor of the farewell dinner at Dilly's. Johnson was pleased to accept. Then Boswell, knowing Johnson would refuse outright if he knew Wilkes would be present, played upon his spirit of contradiction; "Provided the Company is agreeable to you," he said.

Johnson exploded: "What do you take me for? Do you think I am so ignorant of the world, as to imagine that I am to prescribe to a gentleman what company he is to have at his table?"

"I should not be surprized to find Jack Wilkes there."

"And if Jack Wilkes *should* be there, what is that to *me*, Sir?"

"Thus," the manuscript records, "I secured him."

On the "much-expected Wednesday," though, nothing went well. When Boswell arrived at Johnson's house to escort him to dinner, he found him "buffeting his books . . . covered with dust." Dilly's dinner was forgotten, "it went out of my head. I have ordered dinner at home with Mrs. Williams." Boswell knew that unless this blind, peevish, obstinate woman gave permission, Johnson "would not stir." He rushed to Mrs. Williams. He earnestly entreated her with all his powers; she "gradually softened," and finally released the Doctor.

Boswell "flew back" to Johnson, who "roared" for a clean shirt and was very soon dressed, and off they went in a hackney-coach. "I exulted as much," the manuscript records, "as a fortune-hunter who has got an heiress into a post-chaise with him to set out for Gretna-Green."

Once at the party, Johnson inquired, "Who is the gentleman in lace?"

"Mr. Wilkes, Sir —"

Johnson, "confounded," picked up a book, "sat down upon a window-seat and read." "The cheering sound of 'Dinner is upon the table' dissolved his reverie and we *all* sat down without any symptom of ill humour."

Wilkes placed himself beside Dr. Johnson and proceeded to charm him with "attention and politeness."

This succulent leaf of the manuscript, numbered "599," is the chosen illustration.

There are interesting parallels between Boswell, pursuing for twenty years his passion to write a life of his hero, and Isham, fighting with as much passion and for as many years to acquire Boswell's papers and "give them to the world."

In 1934 both stories inspired the imagination of Arthur Houghton, Harvard '29. He acted impetuously, with the genius he had throughout his life of making a lightning major purchase at the right moment.

The 110 leaves of the *Life of Johnson*, now in the Houghton Library, are a treasure that great libraries and collectors would give a fortune to possess.

Mary Hyde Eccles

69

To Night.

Swiftly walk o'er the western wave
    Spirit of Night!
Out of the misty eastern cave
Where, all the long & lone daylight
Thou wovest dreams of joy & fear,
Which make thee terrible & dear
    Swift be thy flight!

Wrap thy form in a mantle grey
    Star-inwrought!
Blind with thine hair the eyes of day
Kiss her until she be wearied out—
Then wander o'er City & sea & land
Touching all with thine opiate wand—
    Come, long sought!

70

When I arose & saw the dawn
    I sighed for thee
When Light rode high & the dew was gone
And noon lay heavy on flower & tree
And the weary day turned to his rest
Lingering like an unloved guest
    I sighed for thee

Thy brother Death came, & cried
    Wouldst thou me?
Thy sweet child Sleep the filmy-eyed
Murmured like a noontide bee
Shall I nestle near thy side
Wouldst thou me? & I replied
    No, not thee!

Death will come when thou art dead
    Soon too soon
Sleep will come when thou art fled
If neither would I ask the boon
I ask of thee, beloved Night
Swift be thine approaching flight
    Come soon, soon!

Percy Bysshe Shelley, *To Night,* from a notebook.

20

The Provenance of the Harvard Shelley Manuscripts

Harvard's poetic manuscripts of Shelley are unique among major institutional collections: they consist primarily of fair copies of Shelley's shorter poems, and they relate closely to two individuals — Edward Augustus Silsbee (1826-1900), a retired Salem merchant ship captain and admirer of Shelley, who donated the two notebooks that contain fair copies of many of Shelley's shorter poems, and George Edward Woodberry (1855-1930), from another Massachusetts seafaring family, who was an undergraduate at Harvard in 1877 when the larger of the Silsbee notebooks was first brought to the campus.

When news of Silsbee's gift to Harvard of the larger Shelley notebook reached England, Harry Buxton Forman wrote for information about it. His curiosity arose from his competition with Silsbee in the 1870s to acquire the Shelley manuscripts and Shelleyana in the possession of Claire Clairmont, Mary Shelley's step-sister. Silsbee had acquired at least the larger of the two Shelley fair-copy notebooks — perhaps both of them — from Claire and/or from her niece Pauline (Plin) Clairmont between October 1872 and 1876, while he was visiting Claire's home in Florence, where Pauline Clairmont lived with her aunt as a paying guest. During this campaign to learn more about the poet he worshipped (and to gain possession of Claire's Shelley relics), Silsbee seduced Pauline, but balked when she made her further cooperation contingent on his marrying her. (Gossip about this incident reached Henry James, inspiring his fine novella *The Aspern Papers*.)

Silsbee, who first deposited the larger notebook at Harvard in 1877, had definitely acquired it during his first sojourn in Florence. After Claire's death on 19 March 1879, Silsbee returned there and entered a bidding war with Forman's representatives for the remaining Clairmont papers, including letters by the Shelleys and some of Claire's own journals. (During this return to Italy, Silsbee temporarily removed the larger notebook from Harvard's custody, since he would have wished to impress Plin Clairmont with his constant attachment to it.)

In 1910, after the deaths of both Pauline Clairmont (1891) and Silsbee, Forman gave his version of the acquisition in his Introduction to *Letters of Edward John Trelawny*.

> When by good hap I acquired that splendid "pig-in-a-poke" the Clairmont collection of Shelley documents and relics of various kinds, . . . it grieved me not to

find the book of manuscript poems which Claire Clairmont possessed. . . . Of the mutilated manuscript volume, containing Shelley's fair copies of many of his published poems, which should also be here, there is a sad tale to tell. An American who had been residing in the same house at Florence with the Clairmonts had been bidding against me for the collection; but as his rather free bids turned out to be only in bills at long date, the executrix decided to accept my cash rather than his paper, in which she lacked confidence. This man, however, had "borrowed" and not restored the precious manuscript book, — which now graces the classic precincts of Harvard College, while I am "left lamenting."

Since Silsbee had deposited the larger notebook at Harvard before Claire Clairmont's death, Forman's charge cannot be true as he framed it. The notebook that Silsbee was accused of purloining may possibly have been the second, smaller account book. But inasmuch as this one contains pencilled notes both by Claire Clairmont herself and by Silsbee about what Claire had told him of the poems, it is more likely that he had received it, too, while Claire Clairmont was still alive.

In 1887 George E. Woodberry wrote a bibliographical pamphlet describing the larger Shelley notebook. Though in it he confused the handwriting of Percy Bysshe Shelley with that of Mary W. Shelley, his notes were reprinted without substantive change in 1929 in a facsimile of the *Harvard Shelley Notebook*. Woodberry later went on to edit for Houghton Mifflin the fine four-volume Centenary Edition of Shelley's poetry (1892) and its derivative one-volume Cambridge Edition (1901), becoming the most knowledgeable American Shelleyan before World War I. At his death in 1930, he bequeathed his manuscripts of Shelley's poems and letters to the Harvard College Library.

For further information, see *The Harvard Shelley Poetic Manuscripts*, ed. Donald H. Reiman (New York and London: Garland Publishing, 1991).

Donald H. Reiman

21

The Gillman-Harvard Manuscript of The Death of Wallenstein

"SCHILLER'S *Wallenstein* IS SO GREAT, that there is nothing else like it of the same sort," Goethe commented to Eckermann on 23 July 1827. A year later, on 15 June 1828, when he became acquainted with the translation of Samuel Taylor Coleridge, Goethe wrote to Thomas Carlyle: "Now that I see it again so unexpectedly in the language of Shakespeare, it arises before me in all its parts once again like a freshly varnished painting. I rejoice in it as of old and in a new and peculiar fashion." *The Death of Wallenstein* constitutes the final part of a dramatic trilogy Schiller wrote on the life of Wallenstein, the principal general of Emperor Ferdinand II in the Thirty Years War.

The original Berlin *Wallenstein* manuscript was lost in the Second World War. Three copies from that manuscript were made, one of which is the Gillman-Harvard Manuscript. A scribe prepared the copy at the request of Schiller's publisher Cotta to be dispatched to London for future translation into English. Schiller carefully proofread the copy, made some additions in his own hand, affixed his signature and the date, 30 September 1799, and attested its correctness and authenticity, for he believed that an English publisher would desire such certification. Since neither translator nor publisher had yet been determined, Schiller did not know the identity of the person who would use the copy. It turned out that Samuel Taylor Coleridge used the copy in making his now famous translation of *The Death of Wallenstein*. The manuscript has a double distinction as the unique source for some of Schiller's variants and as the text used for the Coleridge translation into verse. The present title derives from the fact that Coleridge gave the manuscript to Dr. James Gillman, in whose household he lived from 1816 until his death in 1834.

Ferdinand Freiligrath began his search for this Schiller *Wallenstein* manuscript when he found a reference to it in *The Life of Samuel Taylor Coleridge* (1838) by Dr. Gillman. Freiligrath, a German revolutionary poet who found refuge in England twice, admired both Schiller and Coleridge. He placed an inquiry about the whereabouts of the *Wallenstein* manuscript in the *Athenaeum* of 11 March 1861; his notice elicited a reply by James Gillman, son of Dr. Gillman, in the 18 May issue, which stated that the manuscript was still in his possession. Freiligrath was proud that he had brought the *Wallenstein* manuscript to light with his "divining rod," and thus was able to publish some of the variants in Schiller's hand.

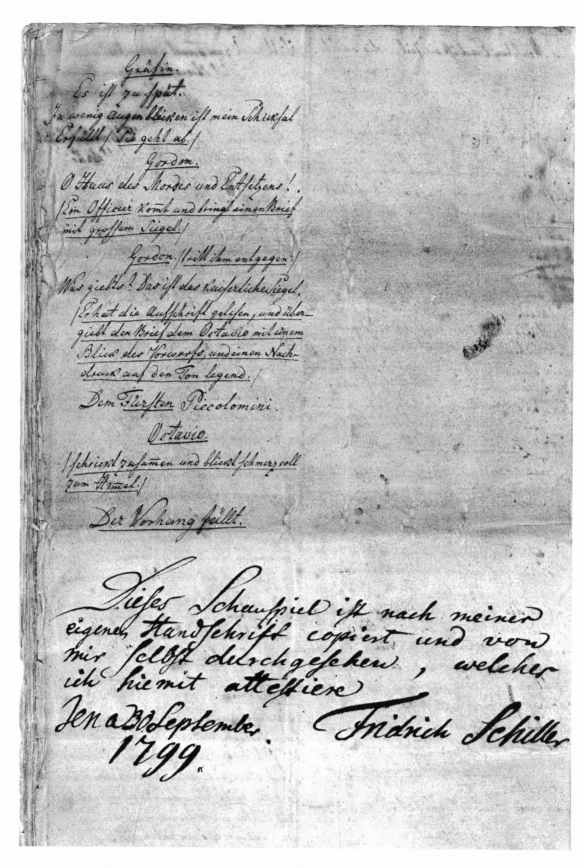

Gräfin.
Es ist zu spät.
In wenig Augenblicken ist mein Schicksal
Erfüllt. (Sie geht ab.)
Gordon.
O Haus des Mordes und Entsetzens!
(Ein Officier komt und bringt einen Brief
mit grossem Siegel.)
Gordon. (tritt ihm entgegen.)
Was giebts? Das ist das kaiserliche Siegel.
(Er hat die Aufschrift gelesen, und über-
giebt den Brief dem Octavio mit einem
Blick des Vorwurfs, und einen Nach-
druck auf den Ton legend.)
Dem Fürsten Piccolomini.
Octavio.
(schrickt zusamen und blickt schmerzvoll
zum Himmel.)

Der Vorhang fällt.

Dieses Schauspiel ist nach meiner
eigenen Handschrift copiert und von
mir selbst durchgesehen, welches
ich hiemit attestiere
Jena 30. Septemb.   Fridrich Schiller
1799.

Johann Christoph Friedrich von Schiller, *Wallenstein,* act III, scribal MS with autograph
corrections and attestation.

Once more in 1902 a German scholar, Hans Roscher, was permitted to examine the manuscript in the home of Mrs. Watson, James Gillman's granddaughter. He published the results of this examination in his dissertation (1905). Although he recorded many of the variants Schiller had made in his own hand, he did not make a complete transcription, which would hardly have been possible under the circumstances in which he had access to the manuscript.

Thereafter the manuscript disappeared from record until its listing in Catalogue 981 (1930) of the London rare book and autograph firm James Tresgaskis & Son. Swift action then brought the manuscript to the Harvard College Library, where it was accessioned on 23 May 1930. John Livingston Lowes took notice of that purchase in the second edition of his study of Coleridge, *The Road to Xanadu*, which appeared the same year. He also called attention to a note to Coleridge by Georg Wilhelm Heinrich Blumenbach, the poet's companion in his Harz wanderings, and to some jottings by Coleridge. This note, tipped to the terminal free end paper, has since been identified as a page from Coleridge's notebooks.

All variants found in the Gillman-Harvard manuscript of the passages in vol. 8 of Schiller's *Werke* (Nationalausgabe, 1949) together with all variants from other manuscripts are printed in the *Harvard Library Bulletin*, vol. XI, number 3, Autumn 1957: Walter Grossmann, "The Gillman-Harvard Manuscript of Schiller's *Wallensteins Tod*," pp. 319-345.

Walter Grossmann

и Франція стакуются съ Германіей, Конгрессъ, вѣроятно, этомъ
состоится. Но Конгрессъ банкротовъ способенъ ~~~~ ничего не
~~~~ дать пролетаріату!

× ×
×

Claude Farère, о которомъ я упоминалъ на дняхъ, выбранъ
въ Академію. Какое отвратительное ~~учрежденіе~~ скопище старыхъ
шутовъ!

Барту, который (въ качествѣ плохого писателя) тоже, какъ извѣстно, былъ академикомъ,
~~отвѣтилъ~~ на анкету: „чего бы вы желали для себя?"
отвѣтилъ: „мнѣ желать нечего: я въ юности мечталъ о
каррьерѣ министра и академика, а къ сорока годамъ сталъ тѣмъ
и другимъ!" Нельзя съ бо́льшимъ сарказмомъ охарактери-
зовать себя самого!

30 марта

Это, конечно, изъ „Правды". Ни кадетъ, ни меньшевиковъ,
ни эсеръ не помянуто: дѣйствуютъ „заодно" лишь
троцкисты и зиновьевцы! Есть въ этомъ сообщеніи
нѣчто непроходимо глупое, а въ глупости — нѣчто

Leon Trotsky, Journal entries for May 1935.

22

The Travels of the Trotsky Archive

WHAT *is* THE TROTSKY ARCHIVE? When, in 1927, Leon Trotsky was expelled from the Communist Party by Joseph Stalin, his rival for leadership, and then soon deported to Alma Ata, the capital of Kazakhstan in Soviet Central Asia, he took with him all the papers that were to form the nucleus around which the so-called exile correspondence was accumulated. Throughout the ensuing thirteen years of wandering exile, the voluminous files of an ever-widening correspondence, manuscripts of publications, and related documents travelled by train and ship with Trotsky, his wife Natalia, and their associates.

One can go no farther without introducing Jean van Heijenoort, the very young French mathematics graduate who joined the exiled Trotsky in 1932. He was one in a long series of political idealists who volunteered their services to Trotsky and worked with him throughout his exile. From the outset van Heijenoort worked intensively with the organization and interpretation of the contents of the Trotsky Archive. Beginning in 1953 (by now a professor of philosophy and mathematics at New York University) he presided over the Archive as a Bibliographer in the Harvard Library, overseeing the detailed cataloguing of the collection so that by the time it was opened in 1980 it was readily accessible to scholars.

How did Harvard acquire the collection? After Munich in 1938, when Trotsky was already in Mexico, he became convinced that war in Europe was imminent and that Stalin would increase his relentless pressure for the elimination of the man and his papers, which Trotsky knew to be of central importance to the future interpretation of the history of the period. As a consequence, he thought about American institutions to which the archives could be consigned for safety and for subsequent preservation as a unique source for historical research. After negotiations had been entered into with three United States universities, Harvard bought the archive in 1940, shortly before Trotsky's assassination. It had been decided to ship to Cambridge all the files up to the end of 1936, leaving the later papers in Mexico as the current working files. Then, immediately following Trotsky's death, his widow decided to shift all the remaining papers to Cambridge as well. Thus the entire archive arrived at Harvard in the fall of 1940. From the start of the negotiations it had been stipulated that the files of Trotsky's correspondence and other papers would be closed to scholars for forty years, to be opened in 1980. Before long, Natalia Trotsky gathered additional material, mostly from Europe, to add to the archive, together with her own considerable body of papers. In 1953, shortly after my arrival in the Harvard Library, Jean van Heijenoort and I went to Mexico to arrange with Mme. Trotsky for the purchase of these documents. Finally, we need only note that since then, thanks to the indefatigable work by van Heijenoort, some half-dozen archives of important Trotskyist groups in Europe have been added to the collection, culminating with his own extensive files.

And now for a quick story of the odyssey of Trotsky and his papers. After Trotsky had been at Alma Ata for nearly a year, Stalin decided to banish him. The second stop in the long and perilous journey was the Isle of Prinkipo in the Sea of Marmara, where van Heijenoort joined the company and began his seventeen-year career as Trotsky's secretary and archivist, doubling all along as an armed bodyguard. In 1933 when the Turkish authorities no longer wanted to harbor the exile, it became necessary to move again. Fortunately, the Daladier government in France agreed to receive the wandering group, and in July 1933 the party arrived at Saint-Palais, a village at the mouth of the Gironde estuary, to live for nearly three months in a house arranged by Trotsky associates in France. By the end of October, fears for their safety required a move to Barbizon on the edge of the Forest of Fountainbleau. After nearly six months here, anxiety arose over the possible disclosure of the Trotskys' identities by local authorities. Following a journey to Chamonix there came a series of unsatisfactory living and working arrangements in a number of villages in the mountains near Grenoble. The French authorities were increasingly eager to see the Trotsky group out of the country.

Fortuitously, just at this time, the Norwegian government offered six-month visas. The wanderers arrived in Oslo in June 1935 and went first to Hønefoss, a town north of Oslo, to stay in the home of a sympathetic member of Parliament. The books and archives duly arrived by the end of July! But the situation rapidly deteriorated as the Norwegian government came under relentless Soviet diplomatic and economic pressure. On 2 September, Leon and Natalia Trotsky were suddenly interned; they were not released until they sailed for Mexico on 19 December 1936, sixteen months later.

Coyoacán, a suburb of Mexico City, was to become the last stop on their hegira, some 15,000 miles and nine years after they had left Moscow in early 1928. With the help of Diego Rivera, a major figure in the Mexican Trotskyist group, the Cárdenas government had issued visas to the Trotskys and their entourage. They left the first house they occupied in May 1939 and moved to another that was quickly transformed into a small fortress, with high walls, look-out towers, and more armed guards. Here they were to reside until Trotsky's death on 21 August 1940; his widow continued to live there until she died several years later.

Jean van Heijenoort left the Coyoacán menage in November 1939 to start a new life in New York. He had spent seven momentous years with Trotsky, but before leaving his company, van Heijenoort organized the entire Trotsky archive for its journey to safety in Cambridge. There, fourteen years after he had packed the collection for shipment, he was to resume his long and intimate association with the archive, an association that continued until his own untimely death in 1986.

Douglas W. Bryant

IV

THE NATURE
OF THE MANUSCRIPT

Rufinus, *Historia Monachorum,* pages with the written area adjusted one line
downward, an ultraviolet photograph; England, 12th cent.

23

A Twelfth-Century Manuscript in Reshaped Boards

Two constant factors pertain to bookmaking throughout the ages. One is that styles change, sometimes slowly and sometimes rapidly. The other is the desire to produce a unified object, most particularly one that, when opened, reveals facing pages of like appearance. The second half of the twelfth century, when the Romanesque style was moving toward the Gothic, was a period of major development in all aspects of the book — writing, lay-out, binding. In one twelfth-century manuscript at Harvard the fact of change and the desire for unity collide, and the collision has interesting results. The manuscript, somewhat rough in appearance, was probably written in England. It contains several texts in two-column format: Rufinus, *Historia monachorum*; St. Jerome, *Vita Malchi monachi captivi; Vita Sancti Frontonii*; St. Athanasius, *Liber de exhortatione monachorum*; *Vitae patrum*, V-VI; St. Macarius, *Epistola ad filios*; and a brief *Life of the Virgin*. There are 159 leaves not counting end-leaves. The binding, whittawed leather over oak boards, is early. There are four scribes, of whom A, folios 1ʳ-45ᵛ, and D, folios 49ᵛ-159ᵛ, are the principal ones. B, folios 45ᵛ-48ᵛ, and C, folios 49ʳ-49ᵛ, enter briefly at a point of transition in the production of the completed work.

What strikes the reader of this manuscript first is that during the first forty leaves and one column of the forty-first, the lowest text line in each column is written in blacker ink and in a different hand from the rest. This curious situation led the author of an earlier description of the manuscript to assert that these lowest lines were "written in first by a master scribe as a guide to the scribe who copied the bulk of the text" and thereby posit a method of writing that on reflection seems uncomfortable and precarious in the extreme. Add to this the fact, not in itself conclusive, that the hand of the lowest lines seems a little later than that of the text that is being corrected. The situation was somewhat clarified several years ago by Paul Meyvaert, who noticed in each column a certain smudginess above each top line of text, a smudginess that resulted from erasure and that, on closer scrutiny, showed that each of the original top lines was erased and rewritten by the second hand at the bottom of the previous column. The result of this systematic tampering with a perfectly well-written text is a slight but noticeable lowering of the *mise-en-page*. Who made this correction? It was scribe D. Why did he do it? Let us look at the binding.

The hinge of the front board is a little loose, and we can see not only the entrance of the four thongs into the outside of the board, a position we associate with the thirteenth century or later, but traces, snipped off, of four earlier thongs that tunnelled into the thickness of the board in accordance with earlier practice. The edges of the boards themselves are not squared in the typical twelfth-century way, but rather shaped downward from the outside or "chamfered." The leaves of the manuscript are flush with the boards except at the upper edge, where the boards protrude about 1.5 cm., again in accordance with a style thought generally to have been emerging around 1200. Beneath the threads that tie the early gatherings rather tightly one can occasionally see old sewing holes that correspond to the early thonging in the boards. It is not possible to tell exactly where this stops.

To return to the text, one observes that the first four leaves of quire VII, beginning on f. 49^r, have prickings in the inner margins as well as the outer, the only instances of this in the manuscript. This is presumably the work of scribe C, who wrote only the first page and a half of the quire, and it suggests that, as is frequently the case, the rulings were made by the scribe himself. Scribe D, when he enters on f. 49^v, closely imitates both the writing and ink color of his predecessor and also the dimensions of the written area. As he proceeds, however, the height of the written area expands from 19.1 cm in the seventh quire to 19.7 in the twentieth, and at the same time he gradually reduces the lower margin from 6.7 cm. to 4.8. By the time he finished a situation of visual disunity existed. If we assume that the *Historia monachorum*, folios 1-42, was originally bound in a square-edged twelfth-century binding, that it was then disbound in order to enlarge the volume, that the boards were reshaped, the manuscript resewn with the upper edge trimmed, the new thongs entered in the new manner into the old boards — if we assume all that, then perhaps we can see why the radical reshaping of the early pages was undertaken, and thus observe one manuscript revealing two styles of book-making during a period of marked transition.

Two additional observations may be made about this manuscript. The first concerns the vellum leaves, four at the front and four at the back added at a later time to "fill out" the binding. These leaves have been washed, but one can faintly see a good deal of music in white mensural notation of the fifteenth century, and this music, still unidentified, brought out strongly by ultraviolet photography, is being worked on now by a graduate student in the music department.

The other point of interest came out when this manuscript was receiving its ultraviolet photography at the Fogg Art Museum. On a whim, we opened the manuscript, the twelfth-century part, in the middle, placed it under infrared light and looked at it on the television screen. Suddenly we saw the vellum opening as the scribe saw it before he began to write: the tracing and bounding lines were there, but the text had disappeared. Infrared photography could not see the writing, which was done with an iron-based ink, but it could see the bounding lines. That meant that these lines had not been drawn, as is universally assumed, with a plummet, which is made of lead and would also have been invisible to infrared. The ruling instrument was charcoal or wood-based, or possibly a mixture of materials such as graphite. This is a small point, but now we know something more about medieval pencils.

Rodney G. Dennis

24

Discard or Masterpiece?
Mallarmé's Le "Livre"

"THE BLANKS, INDEED, TAKE ON IMPORTANCE," wrote Mallarmé in his preface to *Un coup de dés*. But a concrete poem that sculpts blankness at the same time that it prints text is not the same as a pile of scribbled sheets left behind at a poet's death, especially if, feeling himself already captive on that threshold, he has had time to instruct his wife and daughter to "burn everything; there is no literary heritage here, my poor dears." Or is it?

The women did not obey the paternal word. The "half-century-old pile of notes" was not burned. It was placed in the hands of an eager young doctor, an habitué of Mallarmé's famous Tuesdays, soon to become the husband of the poet's daughter. Out of that pile came *Igitur*, published by the son-in-law shortly after his wife's death, almost thirty years after the poet's. Other short works were pieced together and published by the same hand. A patterned blue folder of notes may or may not have sat by undisturbed all that time. Or it may have been constituted by the son-in-law from the leavings of other works. The blue folder passed through several hands, always treated with reverence, until, in 1969, at an auction in which all eyes were on the sale of the letters of Victor Hugo and Juliette Drouet, an agent bought it for the Houghton Library for $4,922. A gasp filled the room. Harvard had stolen a French national treasure.

The experience of working with what has come to be known as *Le "Livre"* is one of encountering both profound mystification and profound demystification. This object, this bunch of scruffy, crossed-out, mismatched, almost illegible, and at first glance totally incomprehensible bits of cheap paper has been elevated into a draft of "The Book," the one Mallarmé said the entire world was designed to end up as. The fetishism of metonymy — I am touching the very paper that the Master himself once touched — is magnified by the fact that there exists no finished work, no proof of intention, nothing but the sense of privileged contact, in a room in which only pencils and laptops are allowed, with the traces of a genius at work. What forces have created the belief that this thing is a work of genius? How many human beings in the world can expect a pile of their discarded notes to burn with this kind of appeal? What sort of privilege does one have to have already acquired in order to draw attention to oneself by whispering?

I open a box, in which I find ninety-four white paper folders. Each folder is labeled with a Houghton sticker. Inside the first folder are three sheets of blank "white news" paper, the kind we used to call "math paper," folded in half. The paper shows signs of

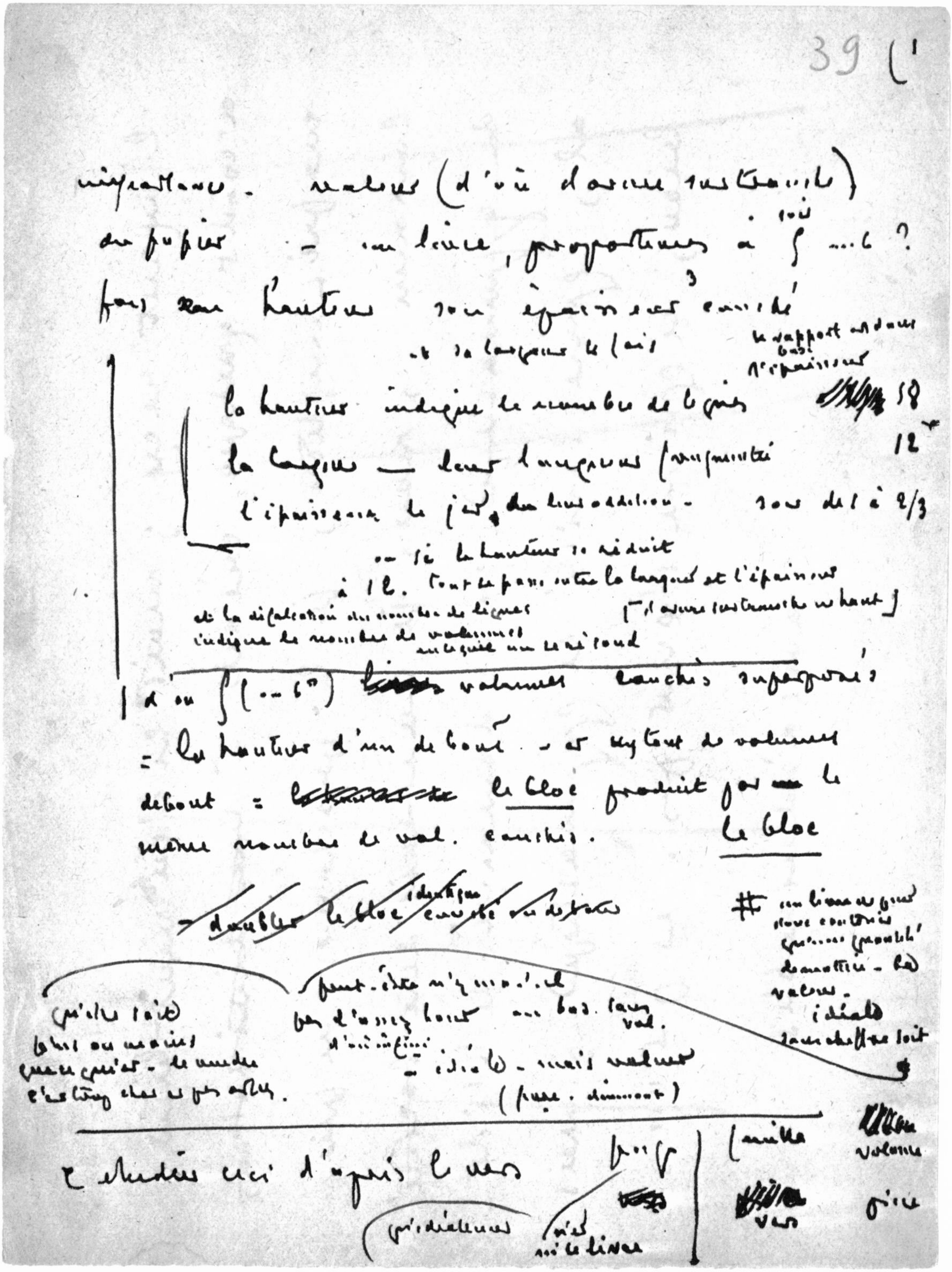

Stéphane Mallarmé, *Le "Livre,"* autograph.

considerable age. It is not acid free. The browning manilla against the crisp white of the Houghton folder makes a lie of the synonymy in French between "blank" and "white." In the lower left-hand corner of each of the six rectos is a tiny number in pencil, circled, 1 through 6. This is the only writing in the first folder.

I open the second folder. One folded sheet (smaller). Again, a circled 7 and 8. But, in addition, a larger number 1, and, on the left side of the inside, fourteen words in pencil, three in pen, all crossed out in pen. Dimly decipherable: "childhood, double, crowd, crime, sewer (or is it "spouse"? — *égout* or *époux*?), conscience . . ."? The tiny circled numbers have been added by the Houghton cataloguer, the larger number by Jacques Scherer, editor of the published transcription of the manuscript. It is he who gave it its present title. As I stare at the almost indecipherable scratches on the page, my respect for Scherer grows. It must have taken him years, merely to make out the words.

Third folder. Heavily revised draft of a letter to Charles Morice on Edgar Allan Poe. The letter has been published in the Pliade edition of Mallarmé's complete works. ". . . The intellectual armature of the poem is dissimulated and holds — takes place — in the space that isolates the stanzas and among the blank of the paper: significant silence that it is no less beautiful to compose, than verse . . ."

Fourth folder. Half sheet. Draft of a thank-you note on one side, pencilled numbers on the other. 480 = 96 x 5, etc.

Fifth folder. Piece of paper (in whose handwriting?) saying, "Place of the two pencilled sheets which are found in the preface to Igitur." The son-in-law, Bonniot, who wrote that preface, had thus at some point removed the two sheets.

Sixth and seventh folders. The two sheets.

These two sheets contain fragments of sentences and a diagram of words that will recur often in these notes:

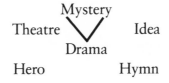

"If this is that, that is this" (a theory of metaphor?) "The Hero . . . the Hymn (maternal) that creates him and is restored to the theatre it was . . . city and life = homeland . . . the development of the hero, wrongly divided in two . . ." (a theory of identity?) "Drama is caused by the Mystery of what follows — Identity (Idea) Self" (a theory of theatre?)

Is this a vision of total synthesis? A Casaubon fantasy of what underlies all mythologies? A phallogocentric hallucination in which human life can be reduced to the drama of a single man? *Igitur* was perhaps such a vision, as was, in Mallarmé's reading, *Hamlet*.

Eighth folder. New kind of paper (lined). Another diagram of Drama, Hero, Hymn, Idea, Book, Mystery, world, year, man.

Ninth folder. Five heavily revised pages are contained within a folded sheet on which is written, in red pencil:

N.O.

Literature
Doctrine

These pages were also published by Bonniot, in the 1920s, in a journal entitled *Latinité*. It is my guess that "N.O." stands for "National Observer," a British journal of culture and politics edited by W. E. ("Invictus") Henley, in which Mallarmé published some of his best-known critical prose. These pages probably constitute a draft of an article Mallarmé intended for that journal.

Do we have a masterpiece yet?

I open the remaining folders, one by one. ("One by one": I realize with a start that the phrase comes back to me from the end of *The Aspern Papers* — "I burnt them last night, one by one, in the kitchen," says Miss Tita.) Some folders contain single sheets, some five or six folded together; often there is writing on both sides, with one side crossed out in red pencil. Scherer does not reproduce those sides. Two or three of the folders contain large groupings of pages of various sizes, written with different implements, held inside other folded pages. The fragility of the enclosing pages is alarming. Amid the clicking of the percussive alphabets in the reading room around me, have I just heard another molecule of the fold give way?

About half the pages are covered with calculations: the number of sessions, the number of participants, the number of copies, pages, seats, the price of admission, the size, shape, and format of the volume, syllables, intonations, seasons. The other half, words, fragments of plot, Drama, Hero, Hymn, Mystery. Page after inscrutable page:

> It is always you that I see on the shore
> egg
> church
> two beings at once bird and perfume
> The remains of a grand palace
> all that can be known is that it
> triangular
> elephants
> guillotine
> doubt, *tout est là*
> "the gimmick of starving to death"
> the wind that has blown the door shut
> the priest must not know, for the glory of man, the mystery
> of woman

child between the legs
Reading. Mass. 12 people. 2 francs per person
I myself am faithful to the book
96 instead of 32
2 sessions
360 people
the height indicates the number of lines   18
a square
thickness of the book
chance
series of folds
do the 24 come at the same time, a single reading
the manuscript alone is mobile
2 francs for me
yacht
banquet
syllable
Reading, *tout est là*
the outside pages not joined in the middle
put it in the other way
ten different interpretations
electric light
two readings in a day, with a different audience
twenty sessions per year
Thus, by convoking these 480 people at 1000 francs each
the same Reading at three different times of the year
400 volumes
begin by the end, the middle
concurrent repetitions
the missing 25th sheet,
redistribute pages into boxes
pages folded into each other, new way of reading,
simultaneous, offering new communications among them
a false page could be added by chance

Are the folded pages in my hands *examples* of the folded pages about which I am reading? Or are they just the products of that very French habit of organizing papers by using a piece of paper as a sleeve? *Have* false pages been added by chance? *Could* this be the plan of the Book to which Mallarmé refers in his letter to Verlaine, "the Orphic explanation of the Earth, which is the sole duty of the poet and the literary game par excellence: for the very rhythm of the book, having become impersonal and alive all the way down to its pagination, is juxtaposed to the equations of this dream, or Ode.

"There you have the avowal of my vice laid bare, dear friend, which I have rejected a thousand times, my spirit bruised or tired, but I am possessed by it and perhaps I shall succeed; not in accomplishing this work in its entirety (one would have to be I don't know who to do that!), but to show an executed fragment of it, to provide a place for its glorious authenticity to shine forth, and gesture toward the whole for which one life would not suffice . . ."

Mallarmé could not have set things up better if he had tried. The ways in which indeterminacy and lack here generate fascination exceed anything that could reasonably be ascribed to his intentions. Yet somehow, even about that, a doubt remains. These unburned, untitled, unauthorized, disintegrating pages offer an uncanny realization of "the text speaking on its own, without the voice of an author." Unable to discount either the fantasy of totality or the materiality of dissemination, I can do nothing but come back, again and again, into the Mallarméan fold.

Barbara Johnson

25

St. Bonaventure, Commentary on the Second Book of Peter Lombard's *Sentences*

THE *Sentences* OF PETER LOMBARD brought together in one convenient manual the writings of the church Fathers that were relevant to the theological questions being addressed in the twelfth-century schools. By the thirteenth century, this work had been embraced as an essential textbook of the theology faculty of the university, and one of the tasks of a master of theology was to lecture on this text. The manuscript shown here, MS Lat 265, contains the *Commentary on the Second Book of Peter Lombard's* Sentences by the Franciscan theologian St. Bonaventure (1221-1274).[1] It was copied in Paris in the second half of the thirteenth century. This manuscript can tell us something about how students and masters in thirteenth-century Paris obtained the books that were essential for the functioning of the new university.[2]

Even a quick examination reveals that this was a manuscript that was intended to be used for study, one that was valued chiefly for its text. The parchment is of average quality. It is fairly thin; one side is white, while the other side is usually yellow and mottled; there are occasional holes. Parchment of this quality is typical for books of this type, but it is a far cry from the evenly finished, white parchment found in luxurious illuminated manuscripts. It is copied in a legible, but undistinguished gothic bookhand. This is a quickly written script, and the roundness of many of the letters contrasts with the heavy, angular appearance of more formal gothic scripts. Note also the informal appearance of the feet at the bottom of the minims, which were produced by a quick upward stroke of the pen. Abbreviations are numerous. There is only one small, competently executed painted initial, which provides a very modest decorative beginning to the text.

As in any modern textbook, the margins of this manuscript are full of scribbled notes. Early in its history, someone, perhaps its first owner or one of the scribes, clarified and corrected the text by adding omitted words, changing readings, and expanding abbreviations. Other early readers added comments in both ink and lead point. The contents of this manuscript, and the details of its physical makeup, are clues to its origin, and help to tie it to a university milieu. Hidden among the informal marginal annotations and corrections, moreover, are a series of marks that prove that it was indeed copied in Paris for the use of someone at the university.

For example, in the outer margin of f. 10ᵛ, near the middle of the page, the scribe has written "ii pe." in dark brown ink. On f. 14ʳ, again in the outer margin, one finds "iii p." On f. 214ᵛ, the series concludes with a mark numbered "lvii." "Pe." or "p." here are

Pecia mark in the lower right-hand margin of a leaf of St. Bonaventure,
Commentary on the Second Book of Peter Lombard's Sentences.

the scribes' abbreviations for *pecia*, a medieval Latin word meaning "piece."[3] Some marks in this series, like the first, were probably trimmed when the manuscript was bound. The majority of the original *peciae* marks, however, survive, and one can be found approximately every four folios throughout the manuscript.[4] To understand the origin of these marks, we need to look at how this manuscript was copied.

One of the jobs of the university booksellers known as *stationarii*, or stationers, was to rent exemplars of the works that were most in demand by the university community.[5] These exemplars were copied in small quires known as *peciae*, usually consisting of four folios, which were kept loose instead of being bound. A scribe who wished to make a copy of the text began by renting the first exemplar *pecia*. When he was finished, he returned the *pecia* to the stationer and rented the second and so forth, to the end of the text. Scribes kept track of the *peciae* they had copied by noting down their numbers in the margins. As we have seen, MS Lat 265 was copied from an exemplar in 57 pieces.[6]

The most important advantage of the *pecia* system was that it enabled numerous scribes to work simultaneously from the same exemplar. Copying a manuscript was a lengthy task. A recent study of two different manuscripts has shown that they were copied at the rate of a little more than one folio per day.[7] We can assume that these scribes were working at a fairly typical rate, given the fact that university regulations stipulated that anyone who kept a *pecia* for more than one week could be charged extra. The manuscript we are studying contains 215 folios. If one scribe had copied this manuscript from a traditional exemplar, no one else would have had access to the exemplar for about 30 weeks.[8] As it was, since our manuscript was copied from a *pecia* exemplar, many scribes could have copied this text at the same time.

The overall appearance of our manuscript, and in particular the type of script and parchment, allow us to assert confidently that it was copied in Paris. We can deduce, however, that either its original owner or a very early one was from Italy. In most manuscripts, the small alternating red and blue initials used at the beginning of important sections within the text were added by the scribe. In our manuscript, however, although the script is clearly French, the initials are executed in an Italian style.[9] The first quire of our manuscript was also added early in its history by an Italian owner. This quire includes a table of chapters for St. Bonaventure's *Commentary* on folios 2^r-3^r, followed by an unidentified *questio* discussing form and matter on folios 4^r-6^v.[10] When the scribe reached the end of f. 5^v, he still needed space to finish his text. He therefore completed his text on the second leaf of a bifolium discarded from another manuscript. The first leaf of this bifolium, now f. 1^r of our manuscript, is therefore completely unrelated to the rest of the manuscript, and contains a fragment of a Latin translation of Aristotle's *Ethica nicomachea*.[11] It is clearly Italian in origin, since it is copied on parchment prepared in the Italian fashion, in a formal Italian gothic bookhand.

The *peciae* marks in this manuscript are a vital clue to its origin. On a broader scale, it is the study of manuscripts like this one, copied from *peciae* exemplars, that has enabled scholars to reconstruct how the system of book production functioned at the University of Paris in the thirteenth and fourteenth centuries.

Laura Light

[1] Brief descriptions are found in S. De Ricci, with the assistance of W. H. Wilson, *Census of Medieval and Renaissance Manuscripts in the United States and Canada* (New York 1935-1937) 997 (as MS Norton 1002), and C. U. Faye and W. H. Bond, *Supplement to the Census of Medieval and Renaissance Manuscripts in the United States and Canada* (New York 1962) 244. It was purchased with funds from the Friends of the Library in 1905 from Charles E. Norton (1827-1908).

[2] The fundamental study of the topic is still Jean Destrez, *La pecia dans les manuscrits universitaires du XIIIᵉ et du XIVᵉ siècle* (Paris 1935). Many of his findings have been revised, however, and substantial new information has emerged; see the very important collection of essays: Louis J. Bataillon, Bertrand G. Guyot, and Richard H. Rouse, eds., *La production du livre universitarie au Moyen Age. Exemplar et pecia* (Paris 1988).

[3] Hugues V. Shooner, "La production du livre par la pecia," *La production du livre universitarie au Moyen Age. Exemplar et pecia*, 18.

[4] My examination of the manuscript suggests that forty-eight of the original fifty-seven *peciae* marks remain.

[5] The distinction between *stationarius* and *librarius*, and the various functions of each, have finally been sorted out in Richard H. Rouse and Mary A. Rouse, "The Book Trade at the University of Paris, ca. 1250-ca. 1350," *La production du livre universitaire au Moyen Age. Exemplar et pecia*, 41-43.

[6] Although St. Bonaventure's *Commentary on the* Sentences is included in the earliest surviving list of exemplars rented by a Paris stationer, the number of *peciae* is not specified. See H. Denifle and E. Chatelaine, *Chartularium universitatis Parisiensis* (Paris 1889) 1:647; see also Louis Jacques Bataillon, "Les Textes théologiques et philosophiques diffusés à Paris par *exemplar* et *pecia*," *La production du livre universitarie au Moyen Age. Exemplar et pecia*, 155, and works cited, for a discussion of the date of this *taxatio*.

[7] Shooner, "La production du livre," 19-20, and 31-34.

[8] It should be noted that this manuscript was in fact copied by numerous scribes, an interesting anomaly since many manuscripts copied from *peciae* exemplars seem to have been copied by single scribes. The change of scribes often corresponds with the beginning of a new *pecia*; see for example ff. 56 and 79.

[9] Other organizational devices which are usual for manuscripts of this date were also omitted when this manuscript was copied. Blank spaces remain throughout for the rubrics. Running titles have been added in a later hand in brown ink, and the distinctions have been numbered in the margin.

[10] "[Inc.] Utrum materia in essentia suo substantia omnimoda possidere potuerit produci . . . [expl.] et quo ad alicui substantiale in se ponunt fieri ita et conseruari."

[11] R. A. Gauthier, ed., *Ethica nicomachea, translatio antiquissima libri ii-iii, sive "Ethica vetus." Aristoteles latinus* 26, 1-3, fasc. 2 (Leiden 1972) p.40, line 10 — p.43, line 24, with interpolations similar to those printed by Gauthier, pp. 58-59.

26

Dickinson's Fascicles

To read Dickinson's poems as single lyrics — the way they have been read in the century since her death — is to think of them as critics have variously described them: as riddle poems, so sceneless, even apparently subjectless, that they appear enigmatic in both syntax and reference. To read Dickinson's poems in the fascicles — the manuscript notebooks in which she copied and bound these poems — is to see that they are less alien than we had supposed, or not alien in the way we had supposed. It is to observe scenes and subjects unfolding between and among poems as well as within them. Thus the canonical sense of Dickinson is not the contextual sense of Dickinson.

Yet even read in context, the poems raise questions rather than answer them. For example, they raise questions about how to read the variants, for, surprisingly, variants to words exist in fair copy in the manuscript notebooks. The metrics of the poem insist we choose among the variants (in that the metrical scheme can accommodate one but not two of the variants). But the presence of the variants insists on the impossibility of doing so. In fact Dickinson frequently appears to be understanding variants not as substitutions, but as additions, as parts of the poem. Thus alternatives to words in the line are not treated in Dickinson's poems as having a status *other* than those words. Nor is there a uniform way to read these variants. Sometimes, as in "The [maddest/nearest] Dream — recedes—unrealized—" the variant seems to amplify the word it is modifying, to establish a conjunctive or causal relation to it ("maddest" and/because "nearest"). Sometimes the variant reiterates (rather than adds to) the sense expressed in a whole poem. This is the case in "I gave [myself to Him—/Him all myself—]," a poem that predicates a double economics differently calculated according to how much is given and reciprocated. So understood, the variant first line participates in the poem's conflict about whether the exchange is one of inequality. Sometimes a word in one poem becomes the variant in another in the same fascicle, drawing the poems together (as does "Still Fable" in the line of one poem, which echoes "[Out] fables," in a poem bound two bifolia later). Such associations can make poems appear tentative, incompletely developed, continuations of one another, even when they do not follow sequentially. This is the case when the phrase "That Whiter Host," a variant in the poem "One need not be a Chamber—to be Haunted—," echoes "the 'White Heat'" in "Dare you see a soul at the 'White Heat?'" a poem that precedes it by two bifolia. For the passion that seems vanquished in one poem reappears as a submerged specter signaled by the variant in another, obliquely connecting the two poems. Moreover, within the same poem variants can be seen to work in differ-

Of Bronze — and Blaze —
The North — Tonight —
So adequate — it forms —
So preconcerted with itself —
So distant — to alarms —
An Unconcern so sovereign
To — Universe, or me —
Infects my simple spirit
With Taints of Majesty —
Till I take vaster attitudes —
And strut upon my stem — manners
Disdaining Men, and Oxygen,
For Arrogance of them —

My Splendors, are Menagerie —
But their Competeless Show
Will entertain the Centuries
When I, am long ago,
An Island in dishonored
Grass —
Whom none but Daisies, know.
                    Beetles —

+ Some —

There's a certain Slant of light,
Winter Afternoons —
That oppresses, like the Heft
Of Cathedral Tunes —

Heavenly Hurt, it gives us —
We can find no scar,
But internal difference,
When the Meanings, are —

None may teach it — Any —
'Tis the Seal Despair —
An imperial affliction
Sent us of the Air —

When it comes, the Landscape listens —
Shadows — hold their breath —
When it goes, 'tis like the Distance
On the look of Death —

Emily Dickinson, *Of Bronze — and Blaze —* and *There's a
certain Slant of light*, autograph.

ent ways. In "Of Bronze—and Blaze—" the speaker imagines herself dead, as "[An /Some—]Island in dishonored Grass—/Whom none but [Daisies, /Beetles—]know." In first of these variants a transformation is being enacted as the speaker imagines herself being made dead and anonymous, "An Island" with particularity becoming one without it — even while "Beetles" and "Daisies," which have no logical connection, seem neither interchangeable nor substitutive, nor in any other way related. Rather, in their unlikeness they seem only to co-exist: in the vision of her own death, beings like the speaker, who earlier in that poem analogizes herself to a flower, and beings not like her, mingling indiscriminately.

But if variants to words must often be considered as non-exclusive alternatives, so must poems in proximity within a single fascicle. Consider the relationship between two celebrated poems: "Of Bronze—and Blaze—" precedes "There's a certain Slant of light" in Fascicle 13. In "Of Bronze—and Blaze—" nature's indifference or "Unconcern" to us, manifested in the splendor of the Northern lights, is what the speaker imbibes in relation to herself. As a consequence, she sees that the eternal part of herself — her poems — will achieve immortality:

> My Splendors, are Menagerie—
> But their Competeless Show
> Will entertain the Centuries
> When I, am long ago,
> [An /Some—]Island in dishonored Grass—
> Whom none but [Daisies, /Beetles—]know.

A relation, then, is being specified between "Unconcern" and immortality. If "Of Bronze—and Blaze—" records the indifference to the self that the self should and does adopt, "There's a certain Slant of light" (the poem that directly follows, on the back of this sheet) cannot do this, for the light in the second poem does not naturalize the self but only afflicts it — the speaker there rather internalizing nature's indifference as the "difference" that is betrayal, producing a vision of death. For with respect to the shifting light that "comes," that "goes," that shifting, when "internal[ized]," when taken in and taken personally, turns to despair. "Of Bronze—and Blaze—" does not, then, simply contextualize "There's a certain Slant of light," it also changes its meaning, for when the two poems are read as retorts to each other, the second becomes a denial of the neutral perspective advanced as natural in the poem that precedes it. Or rather the second poem makes clear that the *natural* perspective is not a *person's* perspective, and cannot be made so. Thus something is being negotiated between these two poems: a prospective vision of death that cannot be seen beyond is made the rejoinder to a vision of death viewed, as if retrospectively, from the vantage of the poet's immortality.

In the fascicles, then, variants connect poems. Poems are connected as variants of each other. And there are variant ways to read connections within the fascicles. For though these fascicles could be described as ordered, orders in the fascicle are both plural and shifting. Some fascicles seem governed by a single thematic (as Fascicle 20 does by the topic of obsession). Some fascicles seem connected by their first and last poems. (You can hear this in the verbal echo: "My period had come for Prayer—" and "I prayed, at first, a little Girl.") Other fascicles (15, for instance) seem connected by antithetically paired poems that also affect poems not implicated in the pairing. Still other fascicles (16, for instance) are ordered by more loosely defined thematic clusters — interesting precisely for the ways in which poems occupy several positions in relation to these clusters simultaneously. And of course there are relations between and among the fascicles. For if the poems read individually suggest the autonomy of single lyrics, the poems read in the fascicle context suggest amorphously defined sequences.

One reason that Dickinson may not have published her poems is not that she was unable to, and not that she chose not to, but perhaps rather that she couldn't choose how to publish them — as single lyrics or in the sequences represented by the fascicles. Thus "not choosing" is a thematic question (see Fascicle 16 particularly). It is a textual question. And it is a larger, formal question, although in the variants such "not choosing" is embodied and superadded in broken form.

That the identity of Dickinson's lyrics is compromised in the fascicles leads us to ask: What is a poetic subject? How is it bounded? What are the boundaries around what something is? Dickinson raises these questions because she writes into being subjects (in the sense of topics) that are conventionally written out of poems. But she also raises these questions by reconstructing a subject as something relational (one specific relation in question being that of part to whole — variant to lyric, lyric to fascicle, one fascicle sequence to adjacent fascicles). She raises these questions by amplifying the idea of a subject to include its variants as well as variant ways of conceiving it. Finally, Dickinson raises these questions by producing utterances that are extrageneric, even unclassifiable, and (for that reason, in a way that it seems to me no one yet has quite explained) untitled.

Sharon Cameron

27

On R. W. Emerson's 2 March 1835
Letter to Lydia Jackson

Emerson wrote this letter to his fiancée a month after they became engaged. On the printed page it seems to express the impatient lover's eagerness to be united with his future bride. But what if the last sentence were a belated, hasty addition? In the manuscript, the last two lines look cramped, and in a different inking from the rest: an odd-seeming afterthought where the signature would otherwise be. This casts some doubt on the writer's sincerity of purpose, tempting us to reread the epistle not as a spontaneous outpouring but as the hasty contrivance of a guiltily delinquent correspondent ("I am quite impatient of not writing to you") excusing his delinquency with querulous self-indulgent trivia about his health and work obligations, not to mention the small bit of defensive table-turning at the end ("write a little to your friend"). Without the final sentence, the previous two seem curt and unaffectionate, more concerned about maintaining social proprieties ("remember me to Mrs Bliss & Miss Russell") than the intimacy of their relationship.

This rereading may be too severe on Emerson, a habitually courteous man who probably added the last sentence out of consideration for Lydia's feelings, so as to offset the self-preoccupied tone of the rest of the letter. Yet at the least the manuscript raises questions about what Emerson's communication might mean.

In their correspondence after marriage, Mrs. Emerson sometimes complained about her husband's coolness and reserve. Even in the heat of courtship we can see him molding her to his needs much more often than he accommodates to hers. With the touchiness of the ex-minister, he scolds her for addressing her letters to "Rev." Emerson. He renames her "Lidian" out of distaste for the Bostonian pronunciation of the open "a." He insists that she live in his Concord rather than her Plymouth: "unless Lidian can trundle Plymouth rock a score of miles northward," he writes in playful (but telling?) third personese, "she must even quit it & come & sit down by Concord Battle-Bridge." He delivers this request right after learning that his favorite brother is about to move to Concord. He urges her to put off a visit to Concord so as not to interfere with the composition of his lectures. All this adds probability to the skeptical reading of the 2 March "love letter." Altogether, it would not be hard to put together a fairly incriminating portrait of Emerson, whose courtship of his first wife (who had died four years earlier) was clearly more ardent and unreserved.

At this point, however, the manuscript again supplies a wholesome corrective. As a window onto Emerson's character it does not settle but complicates the issue of his sincerity as a lover. Its very existence as a physical object proves that he cared about his fiancée. So too does the addition of the last sentence — if in fact it was an addition — although we could credit him with greater affectionateness if we could be sure that he wrote the conclusion in the heat of the moment.

Seeing the manuscript, we can more easily imagine Lidian holding the letter in her hand than when we eye the text in print. Very likely it would have given her more pleasure than it gives us distant time-travelers from another century. For one thing, the sincerity of a tangible message from a living person with whom one has just made a lifetime commitment does not rest merely on the strength or flimsiness of the written record as much as it does for the outsider who has only the written record to go on. The fact that Waldo's previous and subsequent letters were considerably more fond and less distracted would also have helped Lidian overlook the emotional shallowness of this one. To be sure, as a lover just pledged to *her* first engagement, yet already at cross-purposes with her future husband's wishes (in the matter of the visit and their eventual home), Lidian might have searched this document much more hungrily than we for signs of deep feeling and more quickly found it wanting; but she would also have been more quick to forgive the offense.

Lawrence Buell

Concord
Monday 2 March 1835

Dear Lidian I am quite impatient of not writing to you but a visit time & strength-consuming to Waltham a heavy cold riding like the night mare my head & throat & two biographies of Burke with 8 volumes of his works to read mark & inwardly digest, — quite eat up my hours & minutes. Meantime his great Shade stalks round & frowns upon my temerity. Yet I tell him what can avail my pins against his ethereal mail adamantean proof. — And if as seems inevitable I only show my own weakness on this occasion I promise him I will atone by hereafter uttering a word truer wiser to his most deserving Name. Thursday night, if I am well will release me from my present strings, & promise me the happiness of more of your Company. So live well walk much write a little to your friend and remembering me to Miss Bliss & Miss Russell. I refresh myself between whiles with thinking that you will live with me soon all the time.

Ralph Waldo Emerson, autograph letter to Lydia Jackson, 2 March 1835.

Farm Implements and Vegetables in a Landscape

stet

The first of the undecoded messages read: "Popeye sits in thunder,
Unthought-of. From that shoe-box of an apartment,
From livid curtain's hue, (a tanagram emerges: a country."
Meanwhile the Sea Hag was relaxing on a green couch: "How pleasant
To spend one's vacation en la casa de Popeye," she scratched
Her cleft chin's solitary hair. She remembered spinach

And was going to ask Wimpy if he h ad bought any spinach.
"M'love," he intercepted, "the plains are decked out in thunder
Today, and it shall be as you wish`." He scratched
The part of his head under his hat. The apartment
Seemed to grow smaller. "But what if no pleasant
Inspiration plunge us now to the stars? For this is my country."

Suddenly they remembered how it was cheaper in the country.
Wimpy was thoughtfully cutting open a number 2 can of spinach
When the door opened and Swee'pea crept in. "How pleasant!"
But Swee'pea looked morose. A note was pinned to his bib. "Thunder
And tears are unavailing," it read. "Henceforth shall Popeye's apartment
Be but remembered space, dry or wet, toxic or salubrious, whole or scratched."

Olive came hurtling through the window: its geraniums scratched
Her long thigh. "I have news!" she gasped. "Popeye, forced to leave the country,
As you know, by the machinations of his wizened, duplicate father, the spinach
King and die-hard politico, heaves bolts of loving thunder
A t his own astonished becoming, rupturing the pleasant

And all that it contains, myself and spinach in particular

Arpeggio of our years. No mo re shall p leasant
Rays of the sun refresh your sense of growing old, nor the scratched
Tree-trunks and mossy foliage, only immaculate darkness and thunder."
She grabbed Swee'pea. "I'm taking the brat to the country."
"But you can't do that—he hasn't even finished his spinach,"
Urged the Sea Hag, looking fearfully around at the apartment.

But Olive was already out of earshot. Now the ap artment
Succumbed to a strange new hush. "Actually it's quite pleasant
Here," thought the Sea Hag. "If this is all we need fear from spinach
Then I don't mind so much. Perhaps we could invite Alice the Goon over"---she scratched
One dug pensively---"but Wimpy is such a country
Bumpkin, always burping like that." Minute at first, the thunder

Soon filled the apartment. It was domestic thunder,
The color of spinach. Popeye chuckled and scratched
His balls: it sure was pleasant to spend a day in the country.

Our mesty, gusty evening,

John Ashbery, *Farm Implements and Rutabagas in a Landscape*,
typescript with autograph revisions.

28

Ashbery and Popeye

RESPONDING TO CONCEPTUAL ART demands an understanding of its "concept" — the insight or theory that it exists to demonstrate. Ashbery, who is usually, as we read him, teaching us *how* to read him, often presents a very odd surface, one that begins with the title (e.g. the title *Untilted*). *Farm Implements and Rutabagas in a Landscape* is a title that belongs on a painting: *The Hay Wain*; *Boats on the Seine*. (Ashbery is an art critic as well as a poet.) The linguistic clashes in Ashbery's title, though, bring us up short: the homely word *farm* sits ill with the technical word *implements* and the coarsely comic *rutabagas*. Under this promise of an (odd) picture we meet an apparently irrelevant narrative of sorts. Ashbery is fond of using a skeleton we're used to, and we see that the skeleton here is unexceptional:

> The first message read. . . . Meanwhile, X was
> relaxing. . . . She remembered Y, and was going to ask Z
> whether A. . . . Suddenly they remembered B. . . .
> P was doing Q when the door opened and M crept in. . . .
> "Actually it's quite pleasant here," thought X.

In Ashbery's poem, this more or less "normal" skeleton has acquired alienating flesh. The *dramatis personae* have been lifted from the Popeye comic strip, and preposterously translated into some familiar (though strangely mingled) genres: a spy story (*undecoded messages*), a prophecy (*Henceforth shall Popeye's apartment be but remembered space*), a nursery rhyme ("On a misty, moisty morning, when cloudy was the weather / I met an old man, all dressed in leather"), a fairytale (*by the schemes of his wizened, duplicate father*), a Virgilian pastoral (*No more shall pleasant rays of the sun*, etc.), a mystery story (*Now the apartment / Succumbed to a strange new hush*), and so on. These improbable and incoherent goings-on are written up in one of Europe's most historic, strict, and decorous verse-forms, the sestina. (In a sestina, the same six end-words are repeated, in fixed recurrent positions, in each stanza; a three-line envoy uses up all six, two per line.) What has this venerable form to do with its Popeye pop-content?

In an earlier poem, *Street Musicians*, Ashbery had described his own writing:

> So I cradle this average violin that knows
> Only forgotten showtunes, but argues
> The possibility of free declamation anchored
> To a dull refrain.

The "forgotten showtunes" in *Farm Implements* are those of the narrative genres, and the "dull refrain" is that of the six sestina end-words. But why Popeye? And why in Spanish? "An allusion," thinks the reader, "but to what?"

This is a question raised by many of Ashbery's poems. Sometimes the allusion is public ("the Good Samaritan"), sometimes half-private (how many readers now remember "On a misty, moisty morning" well enough to hear *One musty gusty evening* as an allusion?), and sometimes altogether private — at least until (as in this case) archives yield a source. In the Ashbery manuscript collection at Houghton the reader can find the obscure original of Ashbery's narrative — Popeye in Spanish, from *El Diario*, the Sunday supplement of *La Prensa*. Indeed, as we see in the comic strip, the Sea Hag *is* relaxing on a couch (orange, not green), saying "¡Es muy grato pasar mi vacación en la casa de Popeye! Hay una atmósfera familiar tan encantadora!" (*El Diario* of this date — Sunday, April 16, 1967 — identifies itself as "El Diario Hispano Más Influyente y Más Grande de América: Mayor Circulación Diaria en los E[stados] U[nidos]."

Who is Popeye to Ashbery, and what especially is *Popeye el Marino* to Ashbery? And what are both to *Farm Implements and Rutabagas in a Landscape*? Ashbery's rude jamming together of the popular culture of his own past (*Popeye* as a comic strip of his childhood) and the same popular culture as it becomes ever more "popular" (done up for Hispanics in the Spanish of *La Prensa*) brings an acute self-consciousness about the language of the comic strip as one sees it in the unfamiliar Spanish. The Sea Hag's debased vocabulary of pastoral *otium* ("How pleasant to spend my vacation in Popeye's house! There's such a charming familiar atmosphere!") reminds Ashbery of both its nobler Virgilian source and of Renaissance pastoral sestinas. The poem exists to expose the whole trickle-down effect of what we are pleased to call "Western culture," to lay bare the strange ragtag-and-bobtail persistence of historic genres like pastoral even as we cartoon and Hispanize them. Ashbery is interested in the persistent appeal not only of pastoral but also of mixed genres where words and pictures cross (from emblem books to comic strips and *fotonovelas*). His poem manifests the general assimilative speed-up of culture in the wake of global communication and ethnic mixture, and the newly rapid attention-shifts stimulated by visual montage, as in TV cartoons (perhaps of Popeye?). All these cultural predicaments lie imprisoned in the genially coercive Procrustean bed of Ashbery's sestina.

Ashbery's aesthetic problem — how are we to assimilate the past to the present, the high to the low, the classic to the popular — is posed nakedly in the end-words of his sestina. We find *thunder* (the pastoral sublime), *apartment* (the urban), *country* (pastoral rusticity), *pleasant* (pastoral ease), *scratched* (vulgarity, damage), and *spinach* (agricultural fact, but, in the comic strip, the source of Popeye's mythical strength). Normally, the end-words of a sestina all cohere — as they do in Ashbery's earlier sestina, *The Painter*, where the end-words are *buildings, portrait, prayer, subject, brush,* and *canvas* — all at least conceivably assimilable to a poem about the creative act.

By the time of *Farm Implements*, Ashbery already conceives of himself as a "piece of traffic" (*We Hesitate*) where many lines of discourse cross, jam up, flow, crash, and honk.

El Diario, Sunday supplement to *La Prensa,* 16 April 1967, Popeye in Spanish.

He is responsible, metaphorically speaking, to airplanes, buses, ferryboats, pick-ups, sea-sleds, helicopters, and whatever else churns about making traffic. Nothing in the way of discourse is alien to him, since it is all part of the great mass of streaming language, perpetually staining, like a spiritual sperm or excrement, the canvas of life:

> Our question of a place of origin hangs
> Like smoke: how we picnicked in pine forests,
> In coves with the water always seeping up, and left
> Our trash, sperm, and excrement everywhere, smeared
> On the landscape, to make of us what we could.
>
> [*Street Musicians*]

Farm Implements and Rutabagas in a Landscape has the dryness of conceptual art, made to shock the common man. "Look," says the poet, "this is the only sort of pastoral we could possibly throw together these days: it has to be American, as populist as we are, but it also has to remember its classical origins." And so Ashbery does something democratic and farcical, even while remembering the real farm implements of Rochester (where he grew up on a farm) and invoking echoes of Virgilian mossy shades.

Ashbery's family was an educated one (his grandfather was a professor of physics) and after Harvard, Ashbery went to Columbia, thinking he might become a university professor himself, writing a Master's thesis on Roussel. Yet popular culture was as much a part of his adult mind as French and English poetry, and his works bear witness to both. Although mass culture is always a part of everyone's growing up, artists have tended to integrate it into poetic art in a subordinate position. Shakespeare delighted in the speech of "rude mechanicals" and drunken porters, but those characters never have whole plays to themselves. Yet it is easier to integrate "the low" in drama than in lyric; and even when it is encapsulated in lyric, it is usually relegated to a speaker other than the chief speaker, who maintains his own separate decorum. In *Farm Implements and Rutabagas* (published in 1970, three years after the comic strip), Ashbery absents himself. All the low doings are projected onto the Sea Hag or Wimpy or Olive Oyl or Popeye. The writer is present only invisibly, as the inserter of the ridiculous low "plot" into a rickety (because not regularly scanned) sestina, a sign of the hidden writer's "high" culture.

In more satisfactory lyrics than this one, Ashbery integrates low and high without separating them so distinctly into content and form. His usual form of integration — letting genres and discourses collide — does occur here, but the discourses do not seem to be those of a single lyric speaker. The purist in Ashbery (the exquisitely educated aesthete, the academic *manqué*, the art-critic, the writer of sinuously Proustian sentences) has had to kill himself off to write the lyrics of the whole contemporary sea of discourse, omitting none of its subaqueous inhabitants, none of its flotsam and jetsam. One of Ashbery's later poems is called *Purists Will Object*; it describes "the human haul" of language, "The shining, bulging nets lifted out of the sea," constructed into "this pornographic masterpiece," culture (anthropologically construed).

Until someone articulates our culture, we live like the fish in the sea before they are hauled in; the poet has to raise experience from its sub-aquatic, sub-literary life to a breathing existence in the air of language. *Purists Will Object* closes with a wry set of questions in which Ashbery speaks from a triple position: he is a citizen, he is a poet bearing the burden of making the common life visible in language, and he is a person in historical time knowing that the raw material of language outlasts all its poets:

> It seems we were going home.
> The smell of blossoming privet blanketed the narrow
>   avenue.
> The traffic lights were green and aqueous.
> So this is the subterranean life.
> If it can't be conjugated onto us, what good is it?
> What need for purists when the demotic is built to last,
> To outlast us, and no dialect hears us?

Farm Implements and Rutabagas in a Landscape, with its demotic scenario out of a Hispanized *Popeye*, is one of Ashbery's nets for snaring the demotic without forgetting the Muse of the sestina. It is, for all its grotesquerie, one more token of Ashbery's willing self-immersion in the sea of words. When he returns, his nets bulging and shining with the newest example of New York language — "¡Es muy grato pasar mi vacación en la casa de Popeye!" with its upside-down initial exclamation point — we are forced to recognize not only how archaic conventional pastoral has become, but also how ineradicable pastoral is from the human imagination. Farcical it may be; but pastoral it is.

Helen Vendler

Jubilate Agno.

Rejoice in God, O ye Tongues; give the glory to the Lord, and the Lamb.

Nations, and languages, and every Creature, in which is the breath of Life.

Let man and beast appear before him, and magnify his name together.

Let Noah and his company approach the throne of Grace, and do homage to the Ark of their Salvation.

Let Abraham present a Ram, and worship the God of his Redemption.

Let Isaac, the Bridegroom, kneel with his Camels, and bless the hope of his pilgrimage.

Let Jacob, and his speckled Drove adore the good Shepherd of Israel.

Let Esau offer a scape Goat for his seed, and rejoice in the blessing of God his father.

Let Nimrod, the mighty hunter, bind a Leopard to the altar, and consecrate his spear to the Lord.

Let Ishmael dedicate a Tyger, and give praise for the liberty, in which the Lord has let him at large.

Let Balaam appear with an Ass, and bless the Lord his people and his creatures for a reward eternal.

Let Anah, the son of Zibeon, lead a Mule to the temple, and bless God, who amerces the consolation of the creature for the service of Man.

Let Daniel come forth with a Lion, and praise God with all his might through faith in Christ Jesus.

Let Naphthali with an Hind give glory in the goodly words of Thanks-
- giving.

Let Aaron, the high priest, sanctify a Bull, and let him go free to the Lord and Giver of Life.

Let the Levites of the Lord take the Beavers of the brook alive into the Ark of the Testimony.

Let Eleazar with the Ermine serve the Lord decently and in purity.

Let Ithamar minister with a Chamois, and bless the name of Him, which cloatheth the naked.

Let Gershom with an Pygarg bless the name of Him, who feedeth the hungry.

Let Merari praise the wisdom and power of God with the Coney, who scoopeth the rock, and archeth in the sand.

Let Kohath serve with the Sable, and bless God in the ornaments of the Temple.

Let Jehoiada bless God with an Hare, whose mazes are determined for the health of the body and to parry the adversary.

Let Ahitub humble himself with an Ape before Almighty God, who is the maker of variety and pleasantry.

Let Abiathar with a Fox praise the name of the Lord, who ballances craft against strength and skill against number.

Let Moses, the Man of God, bless with a Lizard, in the sweet majesty of good-
- nature, and the magnanimity of meekness.

Let

Christopher Smart, *Jubilate Agno*, autograph.

29

Rearranging the Manuscript of Jubilate Agno

IN THE MID-THIRTIES WILLIAM FORCE STEAD, an American don at Oxford and a poet of great sensitivity, made a remarkable discovery: a considerable series of fragments of autograph manuscript — some hundreds of lines — of a previously unknown poem by the eighteenth-century poet, Christopher Smart. Smart had composed the poem during a seven-year confinement in the madhouse, and it exhibits much of the eccentricity to be expected in a work written under such circumstances. It also foreshadows and illuminates Smart's later masterpiece, *A Song to David*, and it contains many flashes of brilliance and beauty peculiarly its own. What survives comprises thirty-two folio pages: three pairs of conjunct leaves and ten single leaves, of which eight can be shown to have originally been conjunct: that is, seven pairs of conjunct leaves and two singletons. The original MS must have been more than twice as long, but no trace has been found of the missing portions.

Stead published the text in 1939 as *Rejoice in the Lamb*, arranging the fragments according to actual dates and references to datable events scattered through its lines. The poem falls into two principal parts. Most of the lines in one part began with the word "Let"; most in the other with the word "For." In Stead's edition the relation of these parts was unclear, especially since his method of arranging them by dates mingled the two. He provided a biographical and critical introduction and voluminous scholarly notes that explained most of its obscurities, but it remained a series of rather discontinuous fragments. Nevertheless its publication proved of great interest to scholars and lovers of poetry; it is quite unlike any other poem of its period, or any other period, for that matter. Passages were speedily anthologized, and Benjamin Britten set to music a considerable portion of its text for choral performance, a work that still appears in the concert repertory.

In 1940 Professor George Sherburn learned that the owner of the original MS, the widow of Colonel W. G. Carwardine Probert, wished to sell it, and Sherburn persuaded William A. Jackson, who would soon be the founding Librarian of the Houghton Library, that it would be a good acquisition even though it had already been published. The price was modest: £100, or slightly more than $400. Through the good offices of the firm of Bernard Quaritch Ltd. the MS came to Harvard and payment was transmitted to Mrs. Probert (international transactions being complicated in those days of World War II). It was purchased with money from the gifts of the Friends of the Harvard College Library and accessioned on 31 October 1941. Since no one was then assigned to the cataloguing of MSS, few were aware of its presence and it remained on the shelves undisturbed for nearly a decade.

In 1948 Jackson, who had been busily acquiring voluminous archives of New England authors as well as quantities of rare books and manuscripts of all kinds, viewed with alarm the growing backlog of important research materials effectively closed off from scholarly investigation because it was uncatalogued, and persuaded the library administration that a department should be established to deal exclusively with MSS. I had the good luck to be invited to become the first Curator of Manuscripts. For the first six months I struggled solo through the sorting and indexing of several small but knotty archives; I did not even want the aid of a typist-secretary until I had a better notion of the kind of cataloguing most likely to be useful to inquiring scholars. Once I had some grasp of what ought to be done, the Manuscript Department doubled in size. But its staff remained at two for the best part of another decade.

Our efforts were almost exclusively directed towards the literary archives and correspondence that formed the greater part of the backlog, but one cannot sort letters day after day, week after week, without something to lend spice to the work. When fed up with archival material, I would turn occasionally to the miscellaneous accessions, which were pleasingly varied and often extremely fascinating. They ranged from illuminated MSS to drafts by modern writers. It was a great relief for a jaded (and not always enthusiastic) archivist. So it was that one day in 1949 I came upon the Smart manuscript, entitled in his handwriting *Jubilate Agno*.

It is well for a cataloguer to read what he is cataloguing. I was soon in the grip of this strange poem. I found Stead's *Rejoice in the Lamb* in Widener stack and took it home to study. A cataloguer must also put his materials in as good order as possible, and I found the sequence of fragments puzzling in the extreme. The answer to the puzzle came most unexpectedly. After an evening spent studying Stead's text I went to bed and slept soundly until the middle of the night, when I awoke with the whole pattern quite clearly in mind. It was suddenly obvious that each "Let" verse must have a corresponding "For" verse to go with it; it was an antiphonal poem with analogues in the Bible and the Book of Common Prayer. There was no more sleep that night, as I leafed rapidly back and forth in Stead and quickly confirmed the hypothesis. I could hardly wait for the chance to return to the library and lay out the MS itself in the sequence that now seemed so inevitable.

Before the library opened to the public I arranged the relevant fragments on a large table in my office, and found the physical congruence so exact as to be uncanny: in the MS, the relevant "For" lines corresponded precisely on their pages with the appropriate "Let" lines on theirs. Shortly after nine A.M., the Curator of the Poetry Room, Jack Sweeney, happened by, and we gazed in wonder at what was now revealed. It was nothing less than a completely new poem. No question about it; a new edition, based on the fresh arrangement, was required, preceded by an explanatory article in the *Harvard Library Bulletin*. The correct arrangement of *Jubilate Agno* now seemed so obvious that I died a thousand deaths in the fear that someone else *must* see it and forestall me; but nobody did.

Now began a series of remarkable and happy coincidences. I must have my own copy of Stead's edition to annotate, but it was out of print. On Plympton Street in Cambridge was Gordon Cairnie's legendary storehouse of poetry, the Grolier Bookshop: I went at once to Gordon, and he quietly fetched a mint copy of Stead from his back room, at the published price. (Ten years later, when Arthur Sherbo wanted to borrow my then heavily annotated copy because he could find none elsewhere, I took Arthur to Gordon, who produced another mint copy from his back room — still at the original price.)

Who would publish this putative new edition? Jackson suggested his friend Rupert Hart-Davis in London, and Rupert leapt at it — he had been on the staff of Jonathan Cape when Cape published Stead's edition, so he knew all about it; and as for America, what about the Harvard University Press? Thomas J. Wilson was then its Director, and it turned out that Tom had been working for Henry Holt when that firm was American publisher for Stead. Everything fell into place as if by magic. My edition, with dual imprint, appeared in 1954. I then had the honor to be singled out by W. H. Auden in his inaugural lecture as Professor of Poetry at Oxford as a scholar whose work had been of some importance in the understanding of poetry: curators and scholars are more often regarded as impediments to the Muse, with their ponderous editions and arcane apparatus. Ben Shahn responded in another way: he created a miniature bestiary in twelve vigorous drawings to illustrate a portion of the poem, published by the Fogg Art Museum in 1957 with a postscript by Jack Sweeney and a note by Philip Hofer.

Jubilate also brought me many friends and much correspondence, beginning with William Force Stead himself. The most amiable of men, he placed his entire scholarly apparatus freely at my disposal. Eventually we spent a pleasant and profitable day together in Oxford in 1953. Our exchanges of letters continued until his death, and he confided many fascinating anecdotes about Oxford poets from Yeats to T. S. Eliot, over whose baptism into the Church of England he had presided in circumstances of strictest privacy. After Stead, there have been many communications and contacts with scholars and enthusiasts interested in Smart. These still continue, despite the fact that one inquirer four or five years ago, directed to my office by the Houghton Reading Room, expressed great astonishment at finding that I am still alive. So I am, as this writing demonstrates, and I am still interested in anything anyone can tell me that further illuminates *Jubilate Agno*.

W. H. Bond

3

THE MAP

Land lies in water; it is shadowed green.
Shadows, or are they shallows, at its edges
showing the line of long sea-weeded ledges   (slow)
where weeds hang to the simple blue from green.
Or does the land lean down to lift the sea from under,
drawing it unperturbed around itself? ?
Along the fine tan sandy shelf
is the land tugging at the sea from under?

                                               (stop)   (contemplative)

The shadow of Newfoundland lies flat and still.
Labrador's yellow, where the moony Eskimo
has oiled it. We can stroke these lovely bays,   (bustle)
under a glass as if they were expected to blossom,
or/as if to provide a clean cage for invisible fish.   (stop)
The names of seashore towns run out to sea,
the names of cities cross the neighboring mountains   (bustle)
—the printer here experiencing the same excitement
) one
as when emotion too far exceeds its cause.
These peninsulas take the water between thumb and finger
like women feeling for the smoothness of yard-goods.

Mapped waters are more quiet than the land is,
lending the land their waves' own conformation:
and Norway's hare runs south in agitation,
profiles investigate the sea, where land is.
Are they assigned, or can the countries pick their colors? ?
—What suits the character or the native waters best. (stop)
Topography displays no favorites; North's as near as West.
More delicate than the historians'/are the map-makers' colors.

Elizabeth Bishop, *The Map,* from *The Complete Poems,* New York, 1970, with
autograph marks.

30

Elizabeth Bishop, The Map

Manuscripts often help to answer questions. Sometimes a manuscript raises a question instead, or even intimates that a question lurks unraised. What might surface from the curiously flat markings with which Elizabeth Bishop minded herself how to utter aloud one of her own poems? "The Map," for instance.

Since poetry is, as Keats said, "the true voice of feeling," there may be pleasure and profit in hearing it voiced by its creator. Needless to say, the critical question is what it always was: when the poet utters it so much more compellingly than we had managed to hear it with our inner-ear, is she or he bringing out what our imperfect attention had failed to register, or foisting in what an imperfect art had failed to register?

There are at least three knots of contradiction, of word-principles running cross-wise.

1. Bishop's public readings. David Kalstone observed in 1977: "she only rarely gives the public readings which keep poets visible." (Or audible?) Yet she bore witness unexpectedly to how important such readings were to her. Had she given them often, they might well not have mattered. Likewise had she given them never. But *rarely*: this was to accord them a signal importance, especially for someone "painfully shy," moved to "overcome her dread of readings." The rewards — not, manifestly for her, the pleasures — of giving a reading must have been substantial if worth subduing pain and dread for.

2. Bishop and Hopkins. Her delight in Hopkins went back to when she was twelve or thirteen and first met his art in an anthology. "I was immensely struck by those lines, and then when I went to school, in 1927 or 1928, the second Bridges edition of Hopkins came out and a friend gave me that. I wrote some very bad imitation Hopkins for a time, all later destroyed — or so I hope." Marianne Moore, reviewing Bishop in 1935, remarked the debt to Hopkins; Bishop had published, the previous year, her maturely imaginative essay "Gerard Manley Hopkins: Notes on Timing in His Poetry" (*Vassar Review*, February 1934). But a paradox of Hopkins's art is still pertinent. On the one hand, Hopkins has not only such insight and such "inscape" but such, yes, *insound* as to be of all our poets the one who most builds in his intonational stage-directions. In Bishop's words: "The lines have said themselves exactly with that poise I label *timing*." But on the other hand, his poems direly needed those diacritical marks. He himself winced: "This is my difficulty, what marks to use and when to use them: they are so much needed and yet so objectionable." The most recent (1990) edition of Hopkins insists that it "differs from all previous ones in the efforts made to indicate wherever possible how Hopkins probably wished his lines to be read." (The word *probably* does die away rather.) Hop-

kins's latest Oxford editor has need for a coercive *surely* when he wishes both to acknowledge and to skirt the critical nub: "like the composer of music or writer of a play he was surely entitled to set down directions for its correct performance." The problem is the old one: why isn't the proto-modernist Hopkins tarred with the same brush as the Victorians who are contemned for being emphatical? William Empson deprecated any "insensitivity in a poet to the contemporary style of speaking": "And that is why the practice of putting single words into italics for emphasis (again the Victorians are guilty) is so vulgar; a well-constructed sentence should be able to carry a stress on any of its words and should show in itself how these stresses are to be compounded." *Should show in itself*: Bishop's "The lines have said themselves exactly." But if so, why Hopkins's marks? Bishop's youthful essay on his timing neither mentions nor reproduces Hopkins's recourse to diacritical marks.

Yet the interest of Bishop's relation to Hopkins in this matter is perversely a reversal: whereas Hopkins knows just how his lines are to go, and needs to supply his marks lest his reader not know, Bishop supplies no marks for her reader but needs them for herself when she comes to — or rather forces herself to — give a public reading.

3. Timing and punctuation. Marianne Moore praised Bishop in 1946: "Among the many musicianly strategies is an expert disposition of pauses." The pauses of a poem have a double disposition, as T. S. Eliot insisted in a letter to the *Times Literary Supplement* (27 September 1928): "Verse, whatever else it may or may not be, is itself a system of punctuation; the usual marks of punctuation themselves are differently employed." This double disposition should accrue as a counterpointing, and can amount to a contradiction or a contrariety of speakings.

Give me "The Map" there. Bishop gave salience to "The Map" by placing it first both in *North and South* (1946) and in *The Complete Poems* (1969). But backing a poem by putting it at the front might suggest some unease as to whether the poem can hold its own. Robert Lowell judged "The Map" to be "self-indulgent." Bonnie Costello found that the poem prompted her to question Bishop's interrogative mode: "At its weakest, the interrogative mode seems a tic, as pat as any assertion it might overturn. In 'The Map' and in 'The Monument', some of the questions seem contrived."

Bishop's instructions to herself are at their oddest and their plainest when she enforces *upon herself* her interrogative mode, three times adding by pen a question-mark to bring home that the text has, yes, a question-mark. But no, not exactly that. For the first question in the poem, in its second line — "or are they shallows" — neither has nor arrives at a question-mark; it is less a question than a musing. Bishop supplies, to alert herself, an interlineal question-mark, and yet could she, could any sensitive utterer of the line, have failed to rise to the passing interrogative occasion?

Bishop's next two sentences are both overt questions — not only is the question-mark there, but it is, in both cases, at the end of the second line of a doublet, unmistakably stationed. Yet Bishop even here needed to pen question-marks, to append them, for her own education or educing. How strange are these tellings of herself. "The lines have said themselves exactly"?

Bishop says to herself, so that she may say aloud to others, that the words "long sea-weeded ledges" must be "(slow)", as if the consonantal and rhythmical thickening and the internal rhyme might have licensed them to be uttered other than slow. She compounds those printed question-marks with penned ones. She tells herself, at a manifest break (the white space being that of a stanza-break though the poem is not in stanzas), "(stop)." She twice instructs herself "(breath)," as if the longer syntactical sequences at those points might not have asked a breath. She twice puts "(stop)" after what is not only a period, a full stop, but one that ends a line withal. Where there is an unignorable enjambement

> — the printer here experiencing the same excitement
> as when emotion too far exceeds its cause.

she suggests by her double marking of the two lines that she might otherwise, in uttering the poem, have managed to ignore it: not only bracketing the lines ")" but adding "one." A rhythmical effect that would not have escaped a half-way attentive reader, the stress on "own" —

> lending the land their waves' own conformation

has to be given its own stress — "ówn" — lest it elude its own creator. And in the last line of the poem, a line that tacitly cries out for a caesura, she marks . . . a caesura.

Some explanatory hypotheses rule themselves out. That Bishop was silly, for instance (Auden's word for Yeats), or that she didn't actually write "The Map" herself but filched it from A.N. Other and therefore had to prime herself as to how to say the thing. Less absurd though scarcely more subtle or inward would be the idea that here lies the real evidence of Bishop's dread of giving public readings, that she couldn't trust herself to make clear vocally what is perfectly clear on the page: that a full stop means stop, that an enjambement means making the two lines one, and so on. Would paralysis, tongue-tied grotesquerie, have been the alternative to thus treating herself as the patient master of an idiot-school or as an underequipped understudy?

"Contemplative," she tells herself (it is the only such tonal self-adjuration in the markings for "The Map"), of a moment that no reader contemplating the lines would hear other than contemplatively.

Bishop doesn't trust her eyes? But then "The Map" is about not trusting one's eyes too much. Randall Jarrell famously, and beautifully, said of Bishop: "All her poems have written underneath, *I have seen it.*" And it is seeing which the commentators on "The Map" have most dwelt upon, "an artist's way of seeing": "an invention derived not only from her empirical eye but also from her mind"; "Yet reality is not merely relative to how we see it"; "Bishop suggests in these lines that what one sees depends on how one looks" (Sybil Estess).

But the poem is less secure about looking and seeing than this might suggest. For one thing, looking at the map is quite other than seeing the landscapes and seascapes themselves. The truthful beauty of the map is not above inducing falsification. And what about that other sense which both competes with and complements seeing?

Mapped waters are more quiet than the land is,
lending the land their waves' own conformation:

The colors are exquisite; the sounds (the sounds of a sound, perhaps) inaudible.

The poem touches upon power, tyranny even. "Are they assigned, or can the countries pick their colors?" Wordsworth — and Bishop is among other things, other feats, a Wordsworthian poet — understood the need to resist the tyranny of eye and ear, understood that often the way to resist the one is to appeal to the temporary safeguard of the other. Reading aloud "The Map" is an odd business, for although a map is printed all right ("the printer here experiencing the same excitement"), and although a map must be *read* or it will prove useless, you cannot read a map aloud. The *relief* of a map . . .

Bishop hated tyranny. She knew its diversity of appearance and of impulse. This included the way in which the creator of a poem may tyrannize over her or his own creation, own conformation, or over an audience. David Kalstone wrote about tone, about "the kind of authority a single voice will claim over the material included in a poem. Anyone who has heard Miss Bishop read will know how *flat* and modest her voice is, how devoid of flourish." How flat: another listener reported, "almost numbingly flat." But then a map is flat, and must be faithful, and must not be too much trusted, must not be supposed to do right by all that it records. More is meant than meets the eye (as with a poem), but what meets the ear? Whereas, in the poem, "Shadows, or are they shallows," appeals to the ear.

"My first poem in my first book was inspired when I was sitting on the floor, one New Year's Eve in Greenwich Village, after I graduated from college. I was staring at a map. The poem wrote itself." Bishop, of Hopkins: "The lines have said themselves exactly." But if the poet dares to say the poem, to walk unblindfolded the plank of its lines, the needed self-admonition may be simply to make sure that the system of punctuation, or rather the two systems of punctuation, be modestly respected. "(stop)"

Christopher Ricks

31

Heightened and Un-heightened Neumes: an Eleventh-Century Missal Fragment

THIS BIFOLIUM CONTAINS PART of the proper of the Mass for the first Sunday in Advent. The first item is the collect, the second the epistle. There follow the two most elaborate musical pieces of the Mass, the gradual *Universi qui te expectant* and the *Alleluia: Ostende nobis*. The last seven lines are the beginning of the gospel. Immediately striking is the contrast between the larger letters of the prayer and the lections and the much smaller ones for the text of the musical pieces. The earliest service books left no space for musical notation, and most of them were never provided with it. In those that were, the musical symbols had to be squeezed into inadequate space. By the eleventh century, most missals were arranged as this one is, so that there is plenty of space for the music, while at the same time the initial pricking and ruling of the parchment could be executed regularly: all lines are the same distance apart.

The issue of space became critical as soon as the types of notation known as "diastematic" came into regular use (eleventh century in West Frankish regions, much later in the East). In these, the relative height of the symbols above the text is a metaphor for the "height" of the melody at that point — a metaphor so familiar to us after over nine centuries that we are apt to think it universal, which it was not. In this example, the heighting of the symbols is still very approximate. The modern reader would hardly be able to guess, for example, that the word "te" in the first line should be sung considerably higher than the end of the preceding "Universi," or that the two notes on "*expectant*" are higher still. Even with the aid of notation, a singer had to have the melody fixed in his memory.

Up through the twelfth century, the number of different notational schools was considerably greater than the number of text types, often determining the provenance of a manuscript even where the text hand is uninformative. This is the so-called Nonantolan notation, found in relatively few sources, all from the area around Modena. Like most eleventh-century notations, it has a number of different symbols. The ordinary single note is found on the second and fourth syllables of "Universi" (the first syllable apparently lacks a note): it is a rising line inclined to the right, ending in a small leftward descender. In some Nonantolan sources, the length of this line indicates fairly exactly the pitch of the note, but that is not the case here. A simple two-note ascending group may be made by placing two of these signs above a syllable ("*expectant*"; also "*Vias*" at the beginning of

Excita dñe qs potentiã tuã ora - tionē . Sed induim̃...

veni . ut abimmiñentib; dñm iĥm xp̃m .

peccatoꝝ nr̃oꝝ periculis G Universi qui te expecta nt

te mereamur . ptegente non confun den tur dñe om̃ ne

eripi . te liberante saluariꝗ Vias tuas dñe de mon...

Fratres . Scientes adhoꝛ... ...

Quia hora est iam nos de ...mi tas tu... et ego te me...

sõno surgere . Nc̃ eñ p... ille ... tu ... v...

pior est nr̃a salus quã cu v de nobis dñi iĥm ne mise...

crediclimus . Nox preces ri cor di am tu am et salu...

sit dies aut apppinquauit . ta re...

Abiciamus ergo opera te da ño bi...

nebraꝝ . &induamurar P ruit ip̃r . Sed o ...

ma lucis . sicut indie hone Cu apppinquasse ih̃r

ste ambulemus . Non i co hy erosolimis & uenis

messationib; &ebrieta . set bethphagẽ admon

tibus . Non incubilibus te oliuet . tunc iĥr

& impudicitiis . Non in misit duos disciptos

contentione . &emula dicens eis . Ite inca

Universi qui te expectant, gradual for the first Sunday in Advent from a
missal fragment; North Italy, 11th cent.

the third line: there the first element is actually written over the "i" of the text, in order to show that the two notes are widely separated in pitch). A descending pair may be shown by bending a single line down to the right ("*qui*"), or by a single note followed closely by a small curved symbol ("*do*mine," line 3).

When several notes are to be sung to one syllable, simple signs may be combined ("expec*tant*," end of line 1, with three consecutive higher-lower pairs, each alternating the rising line with the small curve, then a low-high-low group, in which the first note is a dot, signifying a lower pitch). The longer melisma at the end of line 3 (on "dom*ine*") largely abandons the ascending line in favor of points and small curves. This is perhaps merely a practical matter: the ascending groups of four notes that appear three times in the melisma would, if written as lines, exceed even the fairly generous space available. Points are often used to indicate lower notes, but that seems not to be the case here. This melisma is more diastematic than most of the notation: the vertical positioning of the symbols mirrors quite accurately the relative pitches of the notes.

Most notations also contain a number of special signs — either modifications of normal notes or entirely new shapes. These signify special performance effects, either in rhythm or in some sort of vocal nuance, that are no longer understood. It is curious (and sometimes frustrating) that details of performance were often specified when the actual pitches were not: many melodies are lost to us for that reason. But as long as notation was merely an aide-mémoire, there was enough room in the symbol systems to convey a good deal of performance instruction. This specimen is not notably rich in nuance-indications, but the frequent use of different signs for the same note-progressions shows that the scribe had them in mind. Note, for example, the careful alternation of points and small curves (each symbolizing one note of a descending scale fragment) at the end of line 5, and the variety of note signs over "*tu*am" in line 8. As is often the case, the text scribe has left too little space for the melisma, the signs for which continue over the syllable "-am," which itself has only a single note directly above it. Again, only an accurate recollection of the melody would permit a singer to read the notation correctly.

There are many obscure issues raised by books like these, but the central purpose of preserving music, not so much by specifying the pitches of the melody, but rather by reminding the singer of its contour, and adding indications specifying subtle nuances of performance, is not the least curious. It testifies to an attitude toward music fundamentally different from ours.

David G. Hughes

4.

et sa main t'entraînait aux marches de son temple,
et comme un humble enfant, je suivais son exemple
et sa voix me disait tout bas, Prie avec moi!
car je ne comprends pas le ciel même sans toi!

pourquoi m'entraînez vous vers ces scènes passées,
laissez le vent gémir et le flot murmurer
Revenez! Revenez ô mes tristes pensées!
Je veux rêver, et non pleurer!

Voyez dans son bassin l'eau d'une source vive
S'arrondir comme un lac sous son étroite rive
bleue et claire, à l'abri du vent qui la courir
Et du rayon brûlant qui pourrait la tarir!
un cygne blanc nageant sur la nappe limpide
en y plongeant son cou qu'enveloppe une ride
orne sans le ternir le liquide miroir
et s'y berce au milieu des étoiles du soir,
mais si prenant son vol vers des sources nouvelles
il bat le flot tremblant de ses humides ailes
le ciel s'efface au sein de l'onde qui brunit,
la plume à blancs flocons y tombe et la ternit,
comme si le vautour, ou le chasseur qui passe
de sa mort sur les flots avait semé la trace,
et l'azur éclatant de ce lac enchanté
n'est plus qu'une eau ternie où le sable a monté!
ainsi quand je partis, tout trembla dans son âme,
le rayon s'éteignit, et sa mourante flamme
remonta dans le ciel pour ne plus revenir;
Elle n'attendit pas un second avenir,
Elle ne languit pas de doute en espérance
et ne disputa pas sa vie à la souffrance

Alphonse de Lamartine, *Le Premier regret*, autograph.

32

Lamartine's Graziella *and* Le Premier Regret

THERE ARE BUT FEW MANUSCRIPTS EXTANT of Lamartine's voluminous works. The Houghton Library holds two items of interest, acquired twenty years ago. They are closely linked since the first can be considered as a source for the second.

The first is a poem initially entitled *Le Premier Regret*. Lamartine then changed the title to *Le Premier Amour*, and finally went back to his original title, *Le Premier Regret*. Lamartine's hesitation about the title is indicative of his views on the poem. With the fifth edition of *Harmonies poétiques et religieuses* (1830) and subsequent editions, the poem will bear the title of *Le Premier Regret*. The note of sadness of the love story does seem to call for the title retained by Lamartine. The manuscript is obviously copied from former drafts; there are some interesting variants and corrections. On the fourth folio, in the left margin, appear peculiar smudges, which could well be teardrops, next to the line: "Elle n'attendit pas un second avenir . . ."

The second item derives from the first and consists of two large fragments of Lamartine's most famous novel, *Graziella*. The poet visited the Bay of Naples in 1811-1812, but no mention is made of a Neapolitan young woman, either in his travel-book or in his letters. In 1844, Lamartine returned to the Bay of Naples, and during his stay in Ischia proceeded to write commentaries on his published poems, including *Le Premier Regret*, with an eye to a new edition of his complete works. The commentary to *Le Premier Regret* inspired Lamartine to write *Graziella*. Because the novel exceeds by far the length of a commentary, Lamartine decided to publish it separately in a volume entitled *Confidences* (1849) and finally as a book (1852). Henri Guillemin, a well-known specialist on Lamartine, writes that he saw an incomplete manuscript of *Graziella* (folios 93-120, which correspond to the end of the novel) in the archives of Saint-Point, where the poet lived after he sold Milly. Our two fragments contain the beginning and most of the end of the novel, and there seem to be, therefore, at least two different versions. I have been unable to find the manuscript seen by Guillemin (*Eclaircissements* [Paris, 1961], in the chapter entitled "Antoniella — Graziella," p. 166).

The genesis of the novel *Graziella* is obscure and widely debated. An accusation of plagiarism was thrown at Lamartine, claiming that he had largely used a novel by Comte de Forbin entitled *Charles Barimore* (1843), in which the hero meets and loves a young Italian girl named Nisieda, the daughter of a fisherman, on the island of Procida. The first half of the novel is, indeed, very close to Lamartine's work (see Charles Brifaut's

Souvenirs, 1857). Critics have all noticed the complete absence of reference to Graziella in all of Lamartine's notebooks, travel-books and letters. Finally, the poet published another Neapolitan love-story, named *Antoniella*. So the very existence of Graziella has been questioned by some scholars.

There is no reliable edition of *Graziella*. The late Fernand Letellier worked on one for years, but died before its completion. The manuscripts concerning *Harmonies poétiques et religieuses*, donated to the Bibliothèque Nationale by Lamartine's niece and adopted daughter, do not mention *Le Premier Regret* or *Graziella*. The Houghton Library manuscripts are, therefore, of great interest, as they offer quite a number of variants and corrections.

Jean Bruneau

See principally: *Graziella*, ed. Gustave Charlier, Paris, 1926; Renée de Brimont, *Autour de Graziella*, Paris, ed. 1931; Henri Guillemin, *Eclaircissements*, Paris, 1961; *Graziella*, ed. Jean-Michel Gardair, Paris, 1979; and Lamartine, *Oeuvres poétiques complètes*, ed. Marius-François Guyard, Paris, 1963.

33

Henry James, *The Awkward Age,*
The Novels and Tales of Henry James: New York Edition,
vol. 9 (London: Macmillan and Co., 1913).

SPINE CAVED IN, the leaves starting from the hinges at the top, covers curling, leaves badly crushed at the bottom corner, buckram scraped off in several places revealing the binder's board, gilt lettering and ornament worn off the spine. Serviceable copy, all the same, with a photograph of the Statue of Liberty pasted over the original title-page vignette of the Brooklyn Bridge, typewritten title label pasted at the head of the spine, "Max Beerbohm Rapallo" inscribed and circled in pencil on the free front flyleaf. Otherwise clean and unannotated, lot 126 at Sotheby's December 12, 1960: The Library and Literary Manuscripts of the Late Sir Max Beerbohm, Removed from Rapallo.

So you might describe, particularly if you felt the bookseller's need to convey the condition of an object for sale, the volume classified and shelved in the Houghton Library after the splendid collection of first editions by Beerbohm and among other books from his library, some of them acquired at the same auction and several "improved" with clippings or drawings. Beerbohm had fun decorating his books, a benign book-collector's hobby, and sometimes he made fun of Henry James with his drawings and inscriptions. Particularly cunning is the drawing in one of them of young James in the presence of the Master.

Less benign, however, was his behavior with *The Awkward Age,* as Rupert Hart-Davis exposed it when he published Max Beerbohm's *Letters to Reggie Turner* four years after the volume was acquired by the library. "This craving [for James]," Beerbohm wrote on May 18, 1920, "is in despite of a nasty jar that I lately had. I tried again to read *The Awkward Age,* a book that had utterly floored me some years ago. . . . *This* time I wasn't able to get nearly as far as the middle, and I wasn't in the least ashamed of leaving off — nor even of laying the book down rather violently; nor even of some uncouth words that I uttered in the act of laying the book rather violently down." Hart-Davis footnotes the reference: "This copy . . . rather the worse for its violent treatment, is now in the Houghton Library at Harvard."

(One could question when or how it is that a manufactured article, such as a single copy of a machine-printed book in a publisher's uniform case binding, acquires a personality sufficiently differentiated from other copies so that it could be called unique, manuscript-like if you will. By contrast, upstairs in the stacks and around the corner from

Henry James, *The Awkward Age,* London and New York, 1913, Sir Max Beerbohm's copy.

Beerbohm's *The Awkward Age* is Henry James's own set of the New York Edition, the limited American issue on Ruisdael hand-made paper. It was given to the Library in 1928 by James's nephew Harry, and volume nine is signed "Henry James Lamb House April 1908." It is a bit dust-soiled and the heavy paper is pulling at the top of the spine, but it is just a regular copy of a regular limited edition. No personality there, untouched by human hands.)

Beerbohm continues the anecdote by confessing his infatuation with James's "later manner," but he finds *A.A.* a most inauspicious introduction of it. By comparison with George Meredith in *Harry Richmond*, James in *A.A.* is likened to "a very old mole burrowing very far down under a very poky back-garden in South Kensington." Beerbohm's aggravation with the author provides a new definition for our casual reference to "tossing a book aside."

The most celebrated toss of a book is fictional: "Just as the coach drove off, Miss Sharp put her pale face out of the window, and actually flung the book back into the garden . . . [watching] the Dixonary, flying over the pavement of the little garden, fall at length at the feet of the astonished Miss Jemima . . . 'So much for the Dixonary; and, thank God, I'm out of Chiswick.' " Samuel Johnson, author of Miss Becky's briefly-held emblematic parting souvenir of Miss Pinkerton's academy, is the most celebrated books bully of them all, wrenching them open and knocking them around. What sweet revenge for Thackeray to entrust Johnson's masterpiece to the swift justice of Miss Sharp at the outset of *Vanity Fair*.

Less spirited is William Blades's account, in *The Enemies of Books*, of lads recreating the Battle of Balaclava in a collector's library. The Russians have built a four-foot rampart of folios and quartos while the Britishers have piled heaps of small books for use as missiles. The collector, surprising the battle in progress, receives "quite unintentionally, the first edition of 'Paradise Lost' in the pit of his stomach . . . many wounded (volumes) being left on the field."

Perhaps this will bring to some minds the old days when Widener stackboys would toss books end over end to one another across the long aisles of the library. Better we should remember Walter Jerrold: "Why have we no society for the prevention of cruelty to books?" Or, that we lend our support to the current Houghton Library staff project: "Be Kind to Books."

Roger E. Stoddard

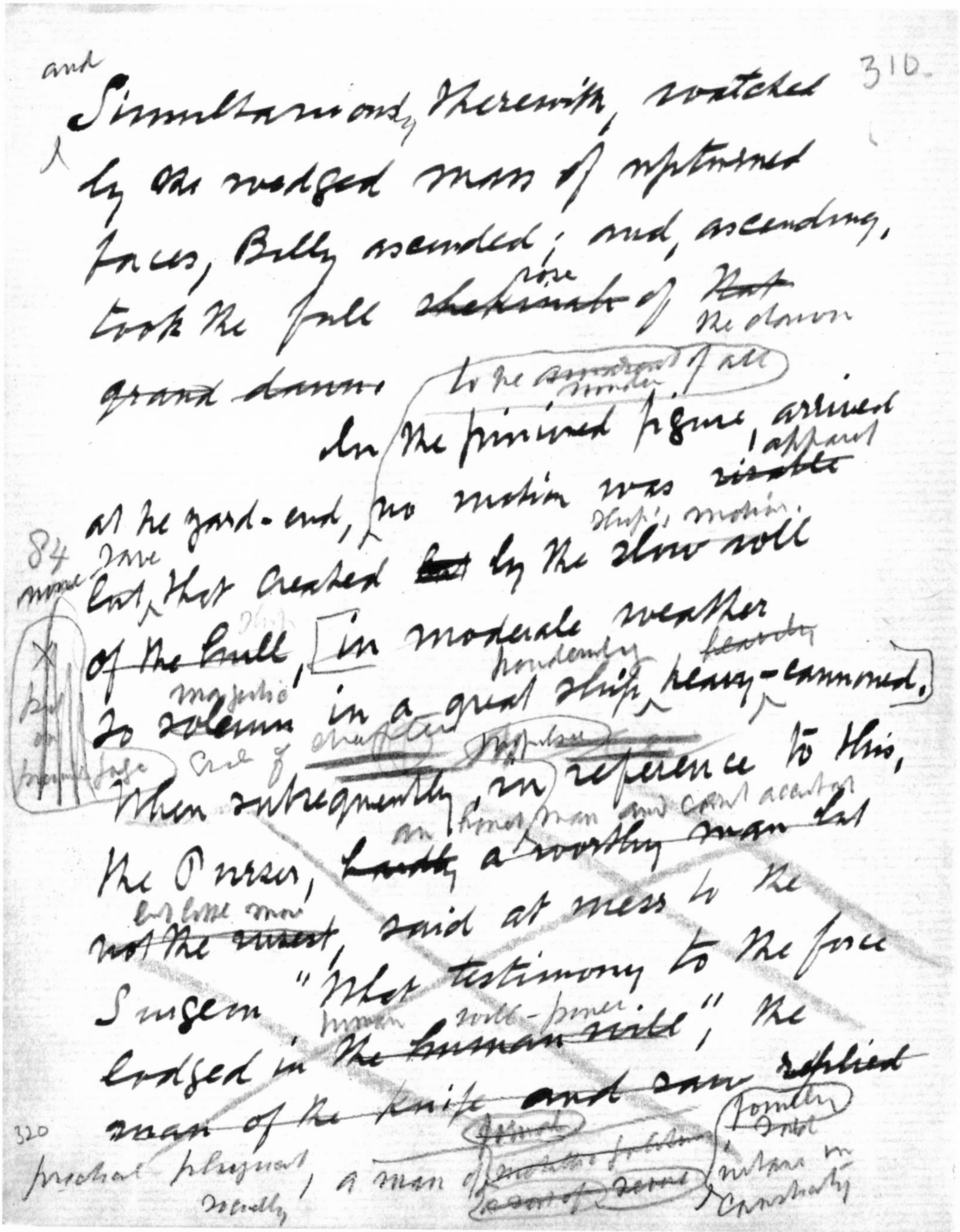

Herman Melville, *Billy Budd,* autograph: Billy ascends.

34

The Billy Budd *Manuscript*

WITH THE *Billy Budd* MANUSCRIPT, the one thing not open to scholarly dispute is that it is indeed a treasure. This final extended prose composition by one of our greatest writers is nevertheless a treasure of a singular kind: a work which, once it reached print three decades after Melville's death, quickly won classic status, yet which has survived to us in a form that — to quote its definitive editors, Professors Harrison Hayford and Merton M. Sealts, Jr. — "may be most accurately described as a semi-final draft."

Far from constituting a fair copy ready for printing, the bulk of the manuscript abundantly confirms Elizabeth Melville's notation, following her husband's death, that this "inside narrative" (Melville's own unamended inscription) remained "unfinished." Nearly every manuscript leaf shows pencilled cancellations, substitutions, interpolated passages enclosed in irregular balloons or inscribed vertically along the margins. Frequently the revised passage is pasted over a portion of the original leaf. A number of leaves are virtually disfigured by revision. To the editors it seems likely that many of these alterations were added during the final weeks of Melville's life, in the summer of 1891. There is no particular ground for concluding that substantial further revisions might not have been made if Melville had lived to see the story into print.

Yet the last manuscript leaf of the story proper (leaf 351) is marked, in Melville's own hand, "End of Book / April 19th 1891." A composition, then, that we may call *unfinished* but not *uncompleted*? In all the profusion of modern commentary on the work's quality and meaning, no one has seriously argued that the story Melville meant to tell has not reached, in these manuscript pages, its proper termination.

In any case, apart from inferences drawn down from Melville's earlier writings, what can be said about *Billy Budd, Sailor* must come from the manuscript itself. There are no accompanying factual documents: no letters, like those Melville dispatched to Nathaniel and Sophia Hawthorne during the writing and after publication of *Moby-Dick*; no extra-textual indications of the author's outlook and purposes; no responses, explicit or inferred, from contemporary readers. A peculiar silence surrounds the *Billy Budd* manuscript. What the French critic Gérard Genette has called the *paratext* of a literary work — the accessory printed information that accompanies and gives an initial direction to our reading of a published text — is, in this instance, a miscellany of negatives. From various cancelled leaves retained by Elizabeth Melville and from cancelled or rejected passages on the reverse of other leaves (there are eight of these, half a dozen others bearing on the reverse unrelated poems or poetic fragments) certain probabilities do emerge which we may follow the modern editors in postulating as facts: that, for example, the story took its rise from a version of the ballad that now forms its beautiful closing passage, or that the role given to Claggart, of which there is no hint in the original ballad draft and head-note, preoccupied Melville during a period of particularly extensive revision and augmentation. Otherwise all we know is bound up in a pen and pencil chirography that takes practice to decipher with confidence and that here and there still leaves us groping in semi-darkness.

The state of the manuscript — which led an earlier editor to conclude that what had been preserved actually constituted two distinct narratives, i.e., a preliminary short-story version as well as the novel itself — required of Professors Hayford and Sealts certain editorial interventions in order to arrive at a satisfactory reading text. For some of these they had no reasonable option: where in the manuscript the original wording had been cancelled but the absence of any substitute word or phrase resulted in a defective sentence, they simply restored the cancellation. Standardizing irregular accidentals — spelling, capitalization, hyphenation, punctuation — may also pass as a reasonable procedure, though an argument may be offered about including the manuscript's paragraphing in the same category, or about making "present-day usage" the basis for such standardization.

A few editorial changes in Hayford-Sealts, however, seem distinctly questionable. Should slightly inexact quotations from one or another poetic source be corrected in every case? Do we not want the passage, however "incorrect," as it sounded in Melville's own ear? Where, next to blanks in the manuscript text (leaves 336, 337), Melville penciled in "Athéiste" as the name of the French ship engaged in battle by Captain Vere, is "correct" French usage a sufficient reason for printing, instead, "the Athée"? By writing "two petty officers" rather than "two sailors" as the accessory mutineers in the 1842 *Somers* case — historical precedent for the central action of *Billy Budd* — Melville was indeed factually "mistaken," but are we sure it was not his intention to give the back-reference a greater narrative weight and thrust? Except for Jay Leyda's exemplary *Viking Portable* text, modern printings (Hayford-Sealts included) regularly mark breaks in the manuscript by chapter numbers. But Melville himself did not, using instead only an umlaut-shaped diacritical marking enclosed between dashes (—"—). Numbered chapters allow for easier critical reference to particular moments in the story; do they not also substantially alter its flow or advance, the way we absorb it as its readers?

"Nor book, nor author of the book, hath any sequel," Melville had written long before in *Pierre* (resolute, as we may imagine him, through every discouragement), "though each hath its last lettering." In the case of *Billy Budd* he seems for once to have been wrong, and on both counts. Of sequels — biographies, new editions, commentaries, casebooks, and opera and play versions as well — there is as yet no end. All we are deprived of, with this "unfinished" manuscript masterpiece, is what would have been its author's "last lettering."

Warner Berthoff

35

Ostracon Harvardianum 2

Ostracon, Egypt, 131 A.D.

Twenty years ago I published a small group of ostraca lodged in the Houghton Library of Harvard University: "Ostraca Harvardiana," *Harvard Studies in Classical Philology* 76 (1972): 245-258. The group includes ten Greek pieces and one in Coptic; all but the Coptic (No. 11) have been reprinted in the *Sammelbuch griechischer Urkunden aus Ägypten* 14.2 (Wiesbaden 1983): 11919-11928. One of these texts has proven of some interest in the light it sheds on the process of reading ancient documents, as I have discovered in discussing it with graduate students over the years. Prompted by the kind invitation to contribute to the volume dealing with the scholarly uses of the manuscripts in the Houghton Library, I take this opportunity to present the text to a more general audience.

The ostracon in question, No. 2 in the aforementioned article, is but an ephemeral tax receipt, one of the millions of such texts that the administration of Egypt produced during the first few centuries of our era when the country was a province of the Roman Empire. Deemed too insignificant for formal expression on a sheet of papyrus, the text's message was scratched on a broken piece of pottery, and the resultant product — now a full-fledged ostracon — falls for its scientific study under the purview of the papyrologist. Ostraca of such a type as this survive in the thousands, and over the years papyrologists have become quite expert in decoding the scrawls and scribbles with which these documents were usually written. For behind the cursive script lies a formulaic system that, once grasped, allows the scholar to transcribe what to the uninitiated must surely seem impenetrable. Such texts are not read letter by letter, since individual letter forms blur one into another, as the scribe, pressed by the demands of his task, was content merely to sketch each word with but a few of its most salient characteristics.

Sometimes, however, even when the papyrologist is well versed in the underlying formulaic system, such texts can be baffling or deceptive. In my article, "The Pursuit of Papyrological Fleas," *Journal of Juristic Papyrology* 20 (1990): 37-38, I discussed one of the Leiden ostraca edited some time ago. The piece in question, a routine tax receipt written in the usual execrable style, appeared to be satisfactorily transcribed until I came upon a similar text, now in the Ashmolean Museum. The latter was written by the same scribe as the Leiden piece but rather more carefully. Comparison of the two pieces allowed me to make such sweeping adjustments in the transcript of the Leiden ostracon that the revision has almost nothing in common with the original edition. Suffice it to say, without knowledge of the Ashmolean text I could never have made the revision.

A similar background informs the decipherment of the Harvard ostracon with which I began this discussion. In the edition it takes the following shape (pp. 247 f.):

$[Καλασεῖρι]$ς πράκ(τωρ). διέγρα(ψεν) Καλασεῖρις
$[±9]$ μη(τρὸς) Σενπετορζμήθ(ιος) μερι(σμὸν)
$[ἁλιάδ(ος)$ καὶ ποταμ]οφυλ(ακίδος) στατ(ίωνος) ιε (ἔτους) ῥυπ(αρὰς)
    (δραχμὰς) γ (τετρώβολον). (ἔτους) ιε
$[Ἀδριανοῦ τοῦ]$ κυρ(ίου) Φαμεν(ὼθ) $\overline{κδ}$. Κάκρην
$[ἔγρ(αψα) ὑπ(ὲρ) αὐτοῦ]$ μὴ εἰδ(ότος) γρ(άμματα).

Kalasiris, Collector. Kalasiris son of . . . and Senpetorzmethis has paid, for the tax concerning the cutter and the river-guard ship and for the *statio*-tax of the 15th year, 3 *rhyparai* drachmas 4 obols. Year 15 of Hadrian the lord, Phamenoth 24 [i.e. 20 March A.D. 131]. I, Kakren, wrote on his behalf, as he is illiterate.

The nature of the taxes involved and other details of interpretation are discussed in the introduction and commentary accompanying the edition. The reader will note that the left side of the text is lost, and he will read in my introduction that "the writing . . . is quite faded in several places, particularly in the last line. Decipherment has been greatly facilitated through the discovery that O. Wilb. 20 was written in the same hand. . . ." For the words "decipherment has been greatly facilitated" I should have written "decipherment has been made possible," for, as the attached photograph reveals, the text appears to be largely illegible except for a few isolated letter combinations, among them the scrawl beginning with δι in line 1 and signalling some form of διέγραψεν ". . . has paid," a sure indication that we are dealing with a tax receipt.

Beyond this basic identification, however, I could not have gone had I not accidentally been looking through the volume referred to above as O. Wilb.: C. Préaux, *Les Ostraca grecs de la Collection Charles-Edwin Wilbour au Musée de Brooklyn* (New York, 1935). Of the 78 ostraca edited in that volume, only eight were included in the plates at the end. Luckily, I discovered that one of these, No. 20, revealed the same script as the Harvard fragment but in a much better state of preservation. Prolonged and at times agonizing scrutiny gradually made it clear to me that the Wilbour piece, "drawn up on 15 March A.D. 131 [i.e. five days before its Harvard analogue] is practically a duplicate of the [latter], and the same taxes are involved in both. The only significant difference is in the name of the taxpayer." — So I wrote in the introduction to the edition.

Texts like the Harvard ostracon are not uncommon. They are usually passed over by scholars in the hope that something more promising will turn up. Had I not felt obliged to edit all of the Greek and Coptic ostraca in the Houghton Library, I too would have pushed the fragment aside, bequeathing it to a more patient and knowledgeable posterity. But then I happened upon the volume of Wilbour ostraca and thereby saved the Harvard piece from oblivion. Whether it, *qua* text, was worth saving, is not for me, a humble editor, to decide. But it has clearly proven itself an instructive example of the role that serendipity plays in the acquisition of human knowledge.

Gerald M. Browne

List of Plates

128. James Boswell, *Life of Johnson,* autograph; Dr. Johnson has dinner with John Wilkes. *78M-48 (1), s.599.

132. Percy Bysshe Shelley, *To Night,* from a notebook. MS Eng 258.2, folios 12ᵛ-13ʳ.

136. Johann Christoph Friedrich von Schiller, *Wallenstein,* act III, scribal MS with autograph corrections and attestation. fMS Eng 947.6, f.26ᵛ.

138. Leon Trotsky, Journal entries for May 1935. bMS Russ 13, T-3731, pp. 84-85.

142. Rufinus, *Historia Monachorum,* pages with the written area adjusted one line downward, an ultraviolet photograph. England, 12th cent. MS Typ 194, folios 30ᵛ-31ʳ.

146. Stéphane Mallarmé, *Le "Livre,"* autograph. MS Fr 270, s.54.

152. *Pecia* mark in the lower right-hand margin of a leaf of St. Bonaventure, *Commentary on the Second Book of Peter Lombard's* Sentences. MS Lat 265, f.47ʳ.

156. Emily Dickinson, *Of Bronze—and Blaze—* and *There's a certain Slant of light,* autograph. MS Am 1118.3, s.74, shelved with fascicle 23.

161. Ralph Waldo Emerson, autograph letter to Lydia Jackson, 2 March 1835. bMS Am 1280.226 (1773).

162. John Ashbery, *Farm Implements and Rutabagas in a Landscape,* typescript with autograph revisions. Ashbery papers: AM 6.

165. *El Diario,* Sunday supplement to *La Prensa,* 16 April 1967, Popeye in Spanish. Ashbery papers: AM 6.

168. Christopher Smart, *Jubilate Agno,* autograph. fMS Eng 719, f.1ʳ.

172. Elizabeth Bishop, *The Map,* from *The Complete Poems,* New York, 1970, with autograph marks. *87EB-70.

178. *Universi qui te expectant,* gradual for the first Sunday in Advent from a missal fragment; North Italy, 11th cent. Hofer bequest, uncatalogued.

180. Alphonse de Lamartine, *Le Premier regret,* autograph. MS Fr 107.1, s.4.

184. Henry James, *The Awkward Age,* London and New York, 1913, Sir Max Beerbohm's copy. *EC9.B3927.Z913j.

186. Herman Melville, *Billy Budd,* autograph: Billy ascends. MS Am 188 (363), f.310ʳ.

189. Ostracon, Egypt, 131 A.D. Ostraca 2.

Concordance of Shelf Marks

CATALOGUE NUMBERS	SHELF MARKS	CATALOGUE NUMBERS	SHELF MARKS
34	MS Am 188 (363)	4	fMS Lat 338
26	MS Am 1118.3	14	MS Richardson 32
8	fMS Am 1237	22	bMS Russ 13, T-3731
27	bMS Am 1280.226 (1773)	18	MS Typ 50
11	bMS Am 1704.13 (130)	2	fMS Typ 122
13	bMS Am 1883 (1336)	23	MS Typ 194
7	MS Eng 233.1	17	fMS Typ 228
20	MS Eng 258.2	3	fMS Typ 233
29	fMS Eng 719	16	MS Typ 311
21	fMS Eng 947.6	15	fMS Typ 555
10	fMS Eng 1279 (2)	1	MS Typ 592
32	MS Fr 107.1	12	*AC85.L8605.847ea
24	MS Fr 270	28 (twice)	AM 6
6	fMS Ger 171.1	33	*EC9.B3927.Z913j
3	MS Gr 17	31	Hofer bequest, uncatalogued
5	MS Keats 2.27	35	Ostraca 2
3	MS Lat 39	30	*87EB-70
9	MS Lat 246	19	*78M-48 (1)
25	MS Lat 265		

Index